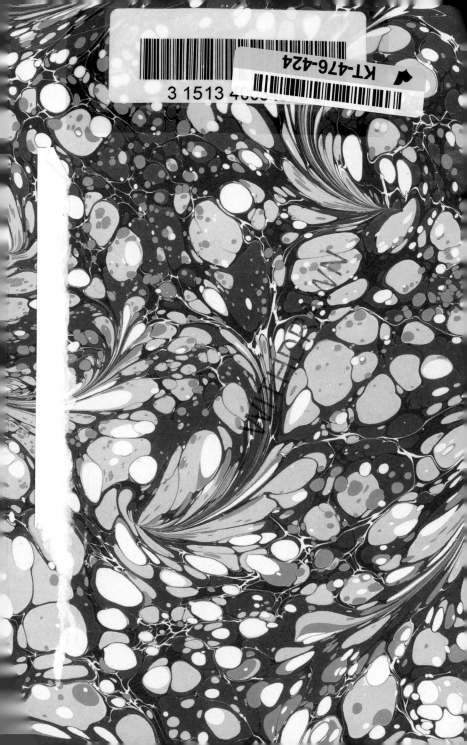

Grief Works

A gift from the

Jean and Ben Ross
Memorial Fund

Grief Works

Stories of Life, Death and Surviving

JULIA SAMUEL

PENGUIN LIFE

AN IMPRINT OF

PENGUIN BOOKS

Penguin
Random House
UK

First published 2017

005

Copyright © Julia Samuel, 2017

The moral right of the author has been asserted

Set in 11.5/13.5 pt Bembo Book MT Std
Typeset by Jouve (UK), Milton Keynes
Printed in Great Britain by Clays Ltd, St Ives plc

A CIP catalogue record for this book is available from the British Library

HARDBACK ISBN: 978–0–241–27074–5
TRADE PAPERBACK ISBN: 978–0–241–27076–9

www.greenpenguin.co.uk

MIX
Paper from
responsible sources
FSC® C018179

Penguin Random House is committed to a
sustainable future for our business, our readers
and our planet. This book is made from Forest
Stewardship Council® certified paper.

This book is dedicated to
Michael,
Natasha, Emily, Sophie and Benjamin
With all my love always

There is no love without pain; but only love can heal that pain which it causes

– Father Julio Lancelotti

Contents

Introduction

Annie, the first person I ever counselled, lived in London at the top of a high-rise block of flats, behind the Harrow Road. She was in her late sixties and had been devastated by the death of her daughter, Tracey, who'd crashed her car into a lorry on Christmas Eve. The cigarette smoke and boiling heat of Annie's room, with its three-bar electric fire, combined with her furious grief, are as alive in me today as they were twenty-five years ago. At that time I was a volunteer for a local bereavement service, and I'd had only ten evenings of training before I found myself sitting opposite Annie. I felt inadequate and frightened in the face of her loss; but I also felt a quiet hum of excitement, for I knew I had discovered the job that I wanted to do for the rest of my life.

Annie gave me an insight that has proved true for the many hundreds of people I've seen since: that we need to respect and understand the process of grief, and acknowledge its necessity. It isn't something that can be overcome by engaging in battle, as in the medical model of recovery. As humans, we naturally try to avoid suffering, but, contrary to all our instincts, to heal our grief we need to allow ourselves to feel the pain; we need to find ways to support ourselves in it, for it cannot be escaped. Annie railed against the truth of her daughter's death, blocking it out with bouts of drinking, and fighting with her family and friends who tried to pull her out of her loss. This pain was the very thing that eventually forced her to find a way of living with the reality of her beloved daughter's death – and it had a course of its own.

Death is the last great taboo; and the consequence of death, grief, is profoundly misunderstood. We seem happy to talk about sex or failure, or to expose our deepest vulnerabilities, but on death we are silent. It is so frightening, even alien, for many of us that we cannot find the words to voice it. This silence leads to an ignorance that can prevent us from responding to grief both in others and in ourselves. We prefer it when the bereaved don't show their distress, and we say how 'amazing' they are by being 'so strong'. But, despite the language we use to try to deny death – euphemisms such as 'passed over', 'lost', 'gone to a better place' – the harsh truth is that, as a society, we are ill equipped to deal with it. The lack of control and powerlessness that we are forced to contend with go against our twenty-first-century belief that medical technology can fix us; or, if it can't, that sufficient quantities of determination can.

Every day thousands of people die, expectedly and unexpectedly; 500,000 deaths a year occur in England alone. On average, every death affects at least five people, which means that millions of people will be hit by the shock of the news. They will forever remember where they were when they heard that their parent, or sibling, or friend, or child was dying or had died. It will impact on every aspect of their world for the rest of their lives and ultimately alter their relationship with themselves. How successfully they manage their grief will, in turn, come to touch all the family and friends around them.

The pain we feel is invisible, an unseen wound that is greater or smaller depending on how much we loved the person who has died. It may be that we are grieving a sudden death or an anticipated death. Either way, the sky we look up at is the same sky as before the death, but when we look in the mirror the person we see has changed. We look at a photograph of ourselves, and wonder at the innocence of that smile. Death is the great exposer: it forces hidden fault lines and submerged secrets into the open, and reveals to us how crucial those closest to us have been. But those surrounding us don't necessarily understand the complexity of what has happened or the depth of the injury we are carrying.

I have regularly seen that it is not the pain of grief that damages individuals like Annie, and even whole families, sometimes for generations, but the things they do to avoid that pain. Dealing with pain requires work on many different levels, both physical and psychological. It is not possible to do this work on our own. Love from others is key in helping us to survive the love we have lost. With their support, we can endeavour to find a way of bearing the pain and going on without the person who has died – daring to go forward to trust in life again.

In my profession there is a wealth of well-researched practical strategies as well as psychological understandings that are essential for anyone who is grieving. As a therapist I have witnessed how this knowledge can help the bereaved to avoid worse consequences through inappropriate support; research studies show that unresolved grief is at the root of 15 per cent of psychiatric referrals. The fear that surrounds death and grief is largely caused by lack of knowledge, and the aim of this book is to address this fear and to replace it with confidence. I want people to understand that grief is a process that has to be worked through – and experience has taught me that grief *is* work, extremely hard work; but, if we do the work, it can work *for* us by enabling us to heal. The natural process of grieving can be supported in such a way as to allow us to function effectively in our daily lives, and I hope that this book will come to play a useful role in providing this support.

Here you will find case studies of grief based on real people's experience. Although they have been grouped according to the relationship of the individual with the person who has died (i.e., the loss of a partner, parent, sibling or child), each is, nonetheless, unique. These stories demonstrate that we need to become more familiar with what is going on inside us; we must learn to recognize our feelings and motivations, and genuinely get to know ourselves. This is necessary if we are to adjust to the new reality brought about by loss. Grief doesn't hit us in tidy phases and stages, nor is it something that we forget and move on from; it is an individual process that has a momentum of its own, and the work involves finding ways of coping with our fear and pain, and also adjusting to this new version of ourselves, our 'new normal'. That most people can somehow find a way to bear the unbearable says much about our extraordinary capacity to evolve as we work towards the rebuilding of our lives.

Although the case studies in this book are framed by my counselling relationship with each individual, the focus is, however, on the grief rather than on the therapy; and they show that really listening to someone is just as important as talking with them – the power of a person being fully heard as they tell their story should never be underestimated. The ability to listen well is by no means the sole preserve of professional therapists; it is something we can all learn to do, and we may be surprised by how much our friends tell us and how helpful we can be when we take the time to listen to them properly.

In my sessions with clients, they explore their previous assumptions about life and their perceptions of the world. They discover words to describe what may never have been voiced before, the freedom not to have to protect me from their deepest pain, their worst fears or thoughts. They voice their worries, their preoccupations; they feel lighter and often make new connections in themselves. They explore the different versions of themselves that may be doing battle, or the whispering critical voice that overlays every action. They have the space to find out what is really going on beneath their defences, defences that may have protected them in the past but are thwarting them now. They reveal themselves more fully, and can come to terms with the parts of themselves that are, for example, like their parent – behaviour they've either hated or found themselves imitating. Having a place where they can bring the twisted feelings that have been silently tying them in knots – a place where such feelings can be unravelled and then searched for nuggets of truth – can sometimes alleviate the pain of unalloyed grief.

The 'Reflections' at the end of each section give my broader thoughts on how to approach this kind of loss, as well as practical facts and guidance about the topics that emerged in the stories. Providing readers with the statistics relating to large numbers of those who have been bereaved should dispel inaccurate negative impressions that individuals may have about their grieving that can be undermining them. It may also be useful to read sections of the book not directly relevant to your experience in order to see the universal processes that we go through when a person has died – and even be surprised to see much of ourselves in someone who is grieving an entirely different death.

Because our attitude to grief is embedded in our culture, I have included a brief outline of how our attitudes have changed since Victorian times; and certainly there are practices in the past that we could do worse than to adopt today. The chapter on friendship contains my cumulative insights into its importance, and I cannot emphasize enough how critical a role friends play in the recovery of anyone who is bereaved, though they have the potential to hinder as much as to help. The final section shows how we can help ourselves, viewed through the image of pillars of strength.

I would like this book to be a resource that can be continually revisited. I want people to understand their grief, or the grief of the people they care about. I hope it will be used by friends and family to reassure the bereaved that lives can be rebuilt, trust developed. We may no longer be innocently hopeful, and we may always have times when we feel the pain of loss, but the deeper understanding of ourselves that we have gained will, in time, feel like growth.

Understanding grief

What is grief?

Grief is the emotional reaction to a loss, in this case, to death. Mourning is the process we have to go through to adjust to the world in which the person has died. As this book illustrates, grief is an intensely personal, contradictory, chaotic and unpredictable internal process. If we are to navigate it, we need to find a way to understand and live with the central paradox: that we must find a way of living with a reality that we don't want to be true.

It forces us to face our own mortality, which we have spent an entire lifetime denying, often through the creation of order – because if we have order, we have predictability and, most importantly, control. Death shatters control; it is brutal in its ultimate power over us, and it is this fact which we find so impossible to accept.

To grieve we need to find a way of enduring the pain of the loss, not fighting or blocking it, and for that we need support – the love and support of our family and friends; and we need to understand what the process entails.

The process of grief

Everyone always talks about the process of grief, which is as much the activity that is going on below the surface as above.

The image often used to illustrate it is an iceberg: what we see above the waterline – our words, our appearance, our expressions – is only a third of the whole. And the process that is hidden below consists of a tug-of-war between the pain of loss and our instinct to survive. The process is in the movement – the back and forth – between the loss and restoration. Sadness, tears, yearning and preoccupation with the person who has died alternate with present-day tasks, functioning, having hope for the future and having a break from the grief. Over time, we adjust incrementally to the reality of the death; and, as we adjust, we become a little more emotionally available to invest ourselves fully in our present life. This process, which is both conscious and unconscious, is intense at the outset but then grows less so as we learn to better manage our grief.

The paradox of grief

The paradox of grief is that finding a way to live with the pain is what enables us to heal. Coping with grief doesn't involve immersion theory; rather, it is enduring the pain as it hits us (this often feels like a storm crashing over us), and then having a break from it through distraction, busyness and doing the things that comfort and soothe us. Every time we alternate between these two poles, we adjust to the reality that we don't want to face: that the person we love has died.

The essence of grief is that we are forced, through death, to confront a reality we inherently reject. We often use habitual behaviours to shield us from the pain of this unresolvable conflict, but these can work for us or against us.

Pain is the agent of change. This is a hard concept to understand. But we know that if everything is going according to plan and we are content, there is no impetus to change anything. If, on the other hand, we suffer from persistent feelings of discomfort, boredom, anger, anxiety or fear in our everyday lives, it usually leads us to question ourselves to find out what is wrong: is it a problem with our relationship or with our work? What is it that needs to change before we can feel content, even happy again? When someone dies, the change is imposed on us; the pain we feel is heightened, forcing us to adapt to different external and internal worlds.

It is often the behaviours we use to avoid pain that harm us the most. The behaviours that we develop early in life to protect us from emotional pain are our automatic way of coping with difficulties. For some people these default behaviours work well, while others are not so helpful. Talking to a friend when something troubles us is a positive behaviour; numbing our pain with alcohol a negative one. Our task is to differentiate between them while at the same time learning new behaviours that support our capacity to bear and express the pain.

The person who has died feels alive to us, even though we know that in actuality they have died. We envisage their body as if it were alive: we wonder if they are lonely, or cold, or frightened; we speak to them in our minds, and ask them to guide us in the big and little decisions in our life. We look for them in the street, connect to them through listening to the music they loved or by smelling their clothes. The dead person is present in us, yet, at the same time, not present physically. We may have a sense of an ongoing relationship, while knowing that nothing will ever move forward again. When this is unacknowledged or even denied, our minds may become disordered or unbalanced; but when this is understood, our overwhelming feeling will be one of relief.

Alternating 'letting go' with 'holding on' is something we need to learn to live with. Rituals such as the funeral or visiting the grave give a shape to the letting go, the acknowledgement that this person has died and is no longer physically present. People then assume they must entirely forget their loved one and subsequently suffer guilt for abandoning them; but the relationship does continue, although in a radically different form.

Death steals the future we anticipated and hoped for, but it can't take away the relationship we had. The connection to the dead is maintained internally through our memories, which are probably the most precious gift we will ever possess; they become part of us, our guides and our witnesses as we carry on with our lives.

We may want to be happy again, knowing it is right and fair, but feel guilty, because somehow it seems wrong and bad. There is often a conflict between our head and our heart; our head knows it was, for example, a terrible accident, but in our heart we feel as if we had done something wrong. There can be a pitched battle between the two, leaving us feeling debilitated and exhausted. These polar opposites need to find a place where they can sit side by side. Understanding that we need to hold both concepts inside us can be liberating.

Society approves if the bereaved person is brave and getting on with things and disapproves if they withdraw and fail to cope. Paradoxically the grief that should cause concern is one that has been cut short, by self-medicating against the pain, for example. As a society we need to learn to support a healthy grieving, and to help people to understand that each person goes at their own pace.

Our culture is imbued with the belief that we can fix just about anything and make it better; or, if we can't, that it's possible to trash what we have and to start all over again. Grief is the antithesis of this belief: it eschews avoidance and requires endurance, and forces us to accept that there are some things in this world that simply cannot be fixed.

When a partner dies

Love disturbs the even tenor of our ways, complicates our plans and upsets political machines. It is worshipped and deplored, longed for and dreaded. We take great risks when we embark upon love relationships and greater risks if we abjure them. One way and another we need to find a way of living with love.

– Colin Murray Parkes

Caitlin

When Caitlin rang my doorbell, I was curious. What would she be like, what was her story? I heard a warm, energized voice speaking on the stairs in a soft Irish accent well before I saw her; and when she came through the door I saw a tall redhead with long wavy hair, a blue-eyed smiling woman. She was in her late forties and strode purposefully towards me, then stopped to straighten a rug she had accidentally disturbed.

Because Caitlin spoke quickly — she was articulate and funny — it took me a while to see the fragility beneath her armoured self. Her story was a difficult one: David, her husband of ten years (together for nearly twenty), had just been diagnosed with terminal liver cancer. At their last hospital appointment she had pushed the medics to give her some idea of his life expectancy and was told he had between nine and eighteen months to live. David had chosen to know the bare minimum, but privately Caitlin had needed more information; the part of her that was feisty and strong said, 'I'm sailing this ship, I need to know what I'm dealing with', though she cried as she told me this. Theirs was a complicated relationship that had been affected by his addiction to alcohol, but she still loved him.

Her greatest concern was for their two young children, Kitty, nine, and Joby, six. She hadn't told them their father was dying. The overriding feeling that emanated from her was one of fear, great wafts of it: fear of the unknown, fear of survival, fear about whether she/they could cope, fear about money, fear for her children and, of course, fear about David's dying. Caitlin was all at sea. She felt naturally protective of her children, as they were very young; she had already been telling them white lies to cover up David's drinking. She was worried he would suddenly drop dead and she wouldn't have any time to prepare them. I asked her what she thought they knew. She said, 'Nothing.' I told her that was unlikely, because children are smart; they sense immediately when something is wrong, even if they don't know exactly what it is. And, in fact, she later mentioned that they had said, 'Daddy is like daddy but smaller.'

We discussed whether David would be involved in the conversations, and she was clear that he wouldn't be. We agreed that she should start by asking her children what they knew about their father's illness. I told her that over time they would need to be told the truth – not all at once but in bite-sized chunks. Her answers to their questions needed to be literal and factual; what children don't know they make up, and what they make up can be more frightening than the truth. If they were told the truth, they would trust her, and the truth would be the foundation stone of the support they would need during this incredibly difficult and frightening process.

In a later session Caitlin told me about how she had broken the news of David's impending death to her children. She explained to them that 'Daddy is very sick, and doctors can usually make people better, but Daddy is very, very sick now and this time the doctors can't make him better.' They didn't cry at first, but when she asked them what they were worried about, she cried, and then they all cried. She'd shown them it was okay to cry, and good to do it together.

They'd had lots of questions. Was he going to die? Were they going to die? Caitlin was honest and gentle with them. She said, 'Daddy will die when his body stops working; we don't know exactly when that will be, but I'll always tell you the truth.' Then they got on with their usual routine of tea and bath and stories, with extra hugs, which soothed them. It had been a heartbreaking conversation, one of many they would have over the weeks that followed, but, difficult as it was, she had managed it with great courage.

I was confident I would be able to build a relationship with Caitlin. She was like a revved-up motor, and she needed to be able to trust enough to slow down and to feel safe. 'Safe' had been the key recurring word in many of our sessions. She needed a reliable, consistent person who would listen to her with care, and not be overwhelmed by her story – someone who could give her the tools needed to structure and then manage her very real fears. She loved her husband but also hated him at the same time for everything he had put them through – his drinking she described as 'dripping poison on to our family' – and she felt that his dying would damage them irrevocably forever.

Caitlin carried her anxiety about with her in a whirlwind of agitation. She would fly into my room speaking incredibly quickly, as if the faster she spoke the more she could stave off the pain, like someone leaping between hot coals. She knew of very few ways to calm herself down when she became anxious, which only intensified the distress attached to her grief. She often spoke about her mother, whom she saw regularly and loved deeply. But what soon became clear to me was that her mother's parenting had been erratic; like David, she was an alcoholic, and this inevitably meant Caitlin couldn't trust her. Caitlin told me about experiences she'd

had around the age of ten: her mother would often be late to
collect her from school, and Caitlin would be forced to hide
behind the bus shelter, hot with shame and overcome by a
desolate feeling of loneliness that would never leave her.
These episodes revealed the roots of her sense of abandon-
ment and how the lens through which she saw the world had
been formed, her first thought in any stressful situation being
'I'll be left alone.' Shame and fear were recurring words in
our sessions. But she loved her mother and would vacillate
between deep, warm love and painful anger. My interpretation of these emotions – which she didn't agree with – was
that she had the 'magical thinking' of a child, hoping that
her affection might control her mother's drinking bouts. She
believed that if she was good, her mother would also be
good, and that if her mother was drunk, it was because Caitlin was bad. Of course Caitlin ultimately came away with a
fixed idea of her own badness.

Into that fault line a devastating tragedy struck when she
was seventeen years old. Her beloved father, who had been a
huge-hearted and successful man, became mentally ill, and
hanged himself in the woods near their family home. His
death came after a brief and unfathomably deep bout of
depression. Caitlin said it had been like 'carrying around a
bottle of cyanide' in her stomach since his death. She told me
that her father had been 'a great man' whom she'd loved. As
she was speaking, I could feel myself becoming fuzzy-headed;
it was too much to take in. I told her this, and she cried.
Something about my acknowledging how overwhelming it
all was allowed her to acknowledge it as well. The raw shock
of her father's death had been vividly with her for decades;
our time together allowed her to touch on it, but only for
brief moments at a time. Although this submerged grief,

which felt to me as if it had scorched her at a very deep level, was inevitably evoked by her approaching loss, now was not the time to deal with those wounds. It would destabilize her at a time when she would need all the resources she'd built up to work for her, in the face of David's death and its myriad implications.

Caitlin was the youngest of a large professional Irish family with many close, open and good friends. But with men she was different. She looked to men to validate her and to make her feel lovable; she believed she had to put on a show to please them, prioritizing their needs and, in the process, ignoring her own, with the result that she ended up feeling empty and used. At this point in her life, her man-obsession came in the form of Tim. Caitlin said that she loved David – he was kind to her, had chosen her above all others and was the father of her children – but his drinking had made her lose respect for him. It had fractured the fragile trust between them, and her desire for him had drained away.

Tim was a fantasy figure who, she knew in her sensitive, intelligent mind, was totally unsuitable. Tim worked in marketing and was full of charm; he had recently separated from his second wife and was in financial and emotional turmoil, having to pay for three children in two homes as well as for his own flat. Caitlin knew he was incapable of giving her what she needed, but no amount of 'knowing' influenced her behaviour. 'I'm like a heat-seeking missile, constantly waiting to hear from him, planning when I can see him, rehearsing over and over in my mind the things I'll say that will make him want me.' Her fantasy was that he would realize he was 'madly in love' with her and make passionate declarations of love. There were two dialogues running concurrently in her head: the 'I love you' one; and the one where he would declare his love and she would tell him to 'bugger off'. The reality, however, was harsh. When they did meet, he was unpredictable: sometimes charming and seductive, sexually drawing her in, and at others times quite dismissive. She would be anxious and needy, constantly hungry for his next text, checking her phone every minute, unable to concentrate until the message arrived. When it did, she would read and reread it, forensically trying to extract meanings that the actual words rarely conveyed. Disappointed, she was left hungry for another message. This pattern – in which she rejects him in the hope that he will chase her – is a common one in relationships; one person is shouting 'go away' when what they really mean is 'fight for me, come close to me, show me you want me'. It is also very commonly found between children and their parents.

Influenced by her Catholic beliefs and upbringing, Caitlin wanted a version of herself she could be proud of – but inextricable from this was her need to be desired. For Caitlin, Tim was a magnet, pulling her with insurmountable force towards him. He brought out aspects of her younger self, desperately longing for her mother's attention; Tim's inconsistency mirrored her mother's, and her sense of being a bad person, not worthy of being loved, remained in her.

Caitlin would speak looking at the floor, and then look up sideways, checking that I was still there, worried that I would be judging her. She later said that it was in these moments that she finally felt someone was seeing her for who she was, warts and all. She didn't feel she was being criticized, and this freedom from judgement enabled our relationship to grow. At the point I mentioned an assessment, to see how we were doing, she broke down. 'Oh, you're going to leave me as well are you?' she snapped, and then cried. She thought that this was my way of ending our sessions. I explained our ending wasn't something that I would impose on her; we were both in charge of it, and we would agree it together. It was important to let her know that I wasn't going to repeat the pattern established by her father and husband and suddenly disappear from her life. The emotional armour with which Caitlin had girded herself as a young child was like a coat of varnish, as impermeable as it was invisible. It prevented her from taking in and retaining positive feelings and blocked the very nurture she needed most. In fact, she drew away from real, authentic loving, although it was ostensibly what she had always been seeking. As a result of our work and the care she received, she very slowly began to believe that she was lovable.

However, Caitlin's obsession with Tim couldn't just be dismissed; but, at the same time, I was aware that it was acting as a kind of anaesthetic, numbing the pain of David's approaching death. It was also a way of relinquishing her sense of self. I needed to ensure that the Tim drama did not divert me away from her fear of being abandoned, which was the key to her continuing damaging behaviour. If she could find a way of soothing her internal agitated child, rather than hurling that poor child into his weak and insecure arms, she would be better protected. In effect, I needed to find a way to help her take care of herself. The metaphor she used to describe herself was a pint of Guinness: she showed everyone the frothy layer on top, but most of her was contained in the bubbling darkness below. We were able to look at the 'dark below' together. 'Grief has hit my confidence bang in the gut. It's like walking around with no petrol in my tank; everything is harder than usual and feels doomed to fail. I'm angry all the time and I can't see an end to it.' We discussed ways to cope, such as giving herself a manageable number of tasks during the day: doing comforting things like buying nice food and cooking for the family and eating well, all of which helped her to feel more in control.

I gathered David hadn't been able to fulfil his potential professionally; loss of confidence closely coupled with his alcoholism had thwarted his talent. Now it was impossible for him to work. He was undergoing treatment – radiotherapy to reduce his symptoms – but it wasn't going to prolong his life. He would be very tired for a few days afterwards but then recover reasonably well. Although he wasn't drinking, his pain-relieving drugs made him behave in much the same way as if he were drunk, which Caitlin found just as disturbing as his drinking.

Caitlin told me they didn't talk together about his dying; nor did he want to attend our sessions. He clearly wanted to live as long as possible for the children, and he intended to press on as if everything were going to be okay. Caitlin often spoke tearfully in a proud, reflective way of his ceaseless bravery, grace and stoicism in the face of his terrifying illness. He was a wit, and the humour that had originally attracted Caitlin was now holding them together on their journey through hell; he used to say, 'Thank God it's not you that's dying – you'd be a bloody NIGHTMARE!' One of the hardest aspects of the situation was the uncertainty, the not knowing when he would die; and also the knowledge that afterwards things wouldn't be better but worse.

Caitlin and I saw each other for eighteen months before David died. She was the sole breadwinner, and working, caring for David, parenting and managing her own inner turbulence all at the same time was incredibly stressful for her. She often felt agitated and saw no light, 'only black fear'. But she found a way of living with it. The most fragile part of Caitlin always underestimated her resilience; she was much more robust than she would allow herself to believe. On some subconscious level she knew this, and denied it because she didn't want to feel regret or guilt (her default emotions) after David's death. She had made a promise to herself to be kind to David, not to get furiously angry with him, as she had in the past. She found ways to put right the difficulties of their relationship. She bought wonderful smelling oils and rubbed them into his hands and feet; she stroked his cheek and they had close, intimate hugs with real warmth – real love.

There were times she came in broken and needed to pour out all her struggles, and there were other times when she could only cry for David and the children. She rightly felt proud of what she had so far managed to achieve. She often didn't sleep well, which made everything harder (it always does, and is common in grief), and we worked together to find ways to help her sleep better.

Occasionally she would stay out late partying, sometimes making reckless sexual choices, which led to days of despair and remorse. Often it was anger that kept her awake, many layers of anger: with David for being an alcoholic and how that had contributed to his illness; anger with herself for having chosen him as a father to her children; and anger at the situation as a whole, one that she was powerless to change. Her moods yo-yoed up and down: she had phases when she felt she could cope, and others when she felt full of fear. All this was accompanied by a nasty strain of self-loathing.

The question of whether David felt jealous of his wife because she wasn't dying was never brought up by Caitlin. It is common for such difficult feelings to be avoided by the couple in an effort to protect each other. The reality of the dying and the jealousy it can engender are understood yet also denied. Whether jealousy is voiced or not, it is nonetheless very likely to be present.

David's deterioration was erratic. There were days when he had energy and could engage with family life: play with Joby and Kitty, go out to see his friends. On other days he'd be much weaker and spend most of the time on the sofa. The children would clamber around him while he made jokes, tickled them, hugged them; they'd sit and watch their favourite TV programmes with him, curled up under the duvet. The last phase of his illness came very quickly, and, although it had been expected, it still came to Caitlin as a shock. His pain increased and he had trouble walking. They decided together with his doctor that the hospice would be the best place for him. It was a warm, safe place, where the children felt welcome and could run around. The wonderful nurses loved his jokes and took great care of him, in particular ensuring that he wasn't in any pain. One of Caitlin's most beautiful and also harrowing memories was his reading out the messages he had shakily written in books for his children.

I remember well the day he died. It was a warm spring day. I looked at my phone and there was a text saying, 'David died peacefully this morning. He was holding my hand.' I phoned and asked Caitlin if the children had seen David's dead body. She answered 'No', and I suggested that she take photographs (bizarre as this sounds), as they would be very important to both her and the children later on.

The night before the funeral Caitlin called me from the funeral parlour, her voice quiet and slow; she told me that they had all seen David looking peaceful, like alabaster. She had placed a love letter on his heart, and each child had placed a soft toy in the coffin and then kissed the casket. She sounded calm and steady, sweetly thanking me for my advice and saying that she felt a sense of 'pride and completeness'. For Caitlin there was also an unbidden and unexpected sense of relief: what they had most feared had come, and they had survived intact. I felt, in turn, a surge of pride for her, for all of them.

Often the most we can do in the face of death is to be creatively alive. Caitlin was a creator and she was a force. She focused her energy on David's funeral and, with his family, made it a tremendous tribute to his life, full of her love for him, and full of the love of his family and numerous friends. The crisis had brought the best of Caitlin to the fore – her deep capacity for love and loyalty to David and the children – and I could only admire and respect these immensely powerful qualities.

As she had loved him in life, boy oh boy she missed him in death. 'He hadn't by any means been the perfect husband, but he was MINE.' Now she was alone. In their bed she was distressed by the empty space of his absence; she would bury her sobbing face into his last-worn T-shirt to smell him. But there had been something clean and clear about his death: there were no regrets between them; they had cared deeply for each other and for their children; and his cruel illness had finally righted their wrongs with dignity.

Caitlin's pain hit her powerfully six weeks after David's death, when the numbness had begun to fade. It came in great blasts of loss, and left her blown away and exhausted. She cried. She had taken a photograph of David after he died, and she said, 'In death he looked smoother, round, beige'; it made her cry to remember. She was able to miss him because she could throw away the 'crappy bits of the past'; 'I wish I could smell that greasy neck I used to tell him off for, revolting, but smooth and comforting.'

Sometimes she would resist feeling the pain and 'act out' in harmful ways, such as non-stop partying or fighting with colleagues. Sex is a natural survival mechanism for all of us, and one that she went for. Caitlin had lost intimacy, and she was doing all she could to claw it back. At its most basic, sex is about creating life, the very opposite of death. She craved it, but she rarely had a good experience; often she felt used afterwards, because her priority was always to give to the man, and then she wasn't satisfied. She had one friend with whom sex and friendship worked better; enjoyed on the hoof between work and home, it resembled what my parents' generation referred to as *cinq à sept*. The sex was more satisfying and not at all complicated, which she liked; but always lurking in her shadows was Tim. On the edges of availability, he was full of promise that came to nothing. He had helped her with the wording of David's service sheet. She was grateful for that, but then he was unable to give her the attention she craved, hollowing out further the hole she was struggling to avoid. Yet she was still able to use the strategies that she knew from experience worked: taking the children to the park, buying and cooking nice food, listening to meditation tapes at night, reading her favourite books. She became disciplined enough to leave her phone outside her bedroom, to stop herself manically looking for Tim. Most importantly, she would regularly meet the friends who really loved her, laugh with them and cry with them.

We talked a lot about Joby, 'my boy', and Kitty, 'my girl'. They were doing well, both instinctively gravitating towards

David's brothers, who would come and play footie with them or take them for days out. They missed David's hugs, and small things could easily upset them enough to cause meltdowns. Caitlin resisted the temptation to break their basic rules of bedtime and manners, for we had discussed their need of boundaries to keep them safe and stable. At night they would light 'Daddy's candle' and often tell a funny or sweet story about him. She could see David in them: 'Joby holds himself in a way that is like his daddy, little tics and things' – what she called 'nature, nurture and Nietzsche'. She remembered that she used to tell David off for holding his knife the wrong way round, and Kitty now held her knife just as David had, but she never corrected her. She used to tell David not to pile the scrambled egg too high on the toast, and as they do it now they say cheekily, 'Daddy did it.' These were touchstones that would later enable them to find their father within themselves. Scrambled egg touchstones.

Sometimes the fierceness of Caitlin's love for her children frightened her. It reminded her of her mother: 'One minute she'd be sweetness and light, and the next she'd turn into a rage like a Hokusai wave.' She had a vivid memory of cosily eating toast with her mother in her parents' bed; the next minute her mother was on the rampage, screaming about the untidiness of the house. Caitlin remembered: 'I was sobbing, purple-faced, because I was wearing all the clothes which I'd put on to get them out of the way. She'd gone mad; the bile that came out of her mouth! I'm never going to do that.' This awareness would prevent the wave crashing out of her and turning into violence. She could breathe, or count to a hundred; she could tell her children to go to their rooms, knowing that she needed space so as not to harm them. She developed strategies that allowed her to change, to become the person she wanted to be.

We both recognized she was back on track about eighteen months after David's death, because she was coping well with everyday life: sleeping better, having times of happiness. Increasing the time between sessions was a conscious, and joint, decision, one that was made in order to see how she managed with fewer meetings. She knew there would be times when she was 'lurchy' – out of control and scared. But she also knew that her work was going well, her children were thriving at school, and she had finally detached herself romantically from Tim, though he was still a friend. She had a new man, not perfect in every way but someone whom she called 'a gentleman'. He was kind, reliable and sexy. They had a good time when they saw each other.

I liken the image of Caitlin's life that I hold in my mind to a mosaic, the sort you might see in a Roman villa: some tiles might be scuffed or cracked, and some might be really broken. Others are untouched and show a perfect picture. Caitlin's capacity to give and receive love is what unifies these fragile but precious tiles. David's dying had split parts of the mosaic but Caitlin's generosity and natural exuberance still make the image as a whole shine brightly in the darkness.

Kayleigh

Kayleigh smiled nervously. She was young, in her early thirties, too young to be a widow. Her long-term partner,
Mitchell, of Afro-Caribbean descent, had been killed while
cycling three months earlier. She kept smiling, but her small
brown eyes had the startled look of a frightened animal. I
could see beads of sweat on her brow, beneath her thick, dark
fringe, and her body was jittery. I wondered how on earth
she was able to be a parent to her two-year-old son, now a
fatherless little boy. Kayleigh's general appearance belied her
fragility: physically she was quite thickset, and often dressed
in tracksuit bottoms and a black top. I could see she was wary
of me. She had difficulty finding her words, and the few she
did manage were spoken with big gulps of air, the shock of
Mitchell's death still alive and palpable in her every breath. I
was facing a dilemma: if she was traumatized by the images
of her partner after his accident, I didn't want to push her –
there is a place in therapy for silence – but at the same time I
felt that a 'therapeutic silence', in which the therapist waits
silently for their client to speak, would be perceived by her as
punishment. We talked about how she might begin to tell
her story. I emphasized that there was no hurry, and that if
she got stuck I would help her through the session. We could
take it in turns to speak, and she would be in charge of how
much she said each time. This would provide her with control and ease her fear of the enormity of her experience, so
that it didn't overwhelm her.

Kayleigh's grief was taking a severe toll on her body. She wasn't sleeping, she felt sick most of the time, and she found it hard to eat. Finding a way to calm her and ease her physical symptoms was a priority. I started by doing a relaxation exercise with her, then asked her to talk me through her day, to enable us to work out a system that would reduce her anxiety. Although she found this difficult at first, her shakiness visibly dropped a few levels as the sessions progressed; and she was able to speak.

Still hesitant, however, she grappled to retrieve her words, as if she had lost them down a dark passage. Many times she repeated 'I can't do it on my own' and 'I'm living behind a wall of fear', followed by yowls of pain. I reflected back to her almost word for word what she had said; I wanted her to know she had been accurately heard and listened to (reflecting back is a technique I use frequently, because it allows the person to feel they have been fully understood). I could sit with her behind her wall of fear, and, while I knew I couldn't 'fix' her, I would at least be beside her. I wanted her to know that what she said was enough, that it had value, and that she should in no way attempt to belittle it. The sessions advanced slowly over the course of many months.

The day Mitchell had died had been an ordinary wet November day. They had first met at the department store where they both still worked. On the day of the accident they finished work at the same time and said goodbye outside the store. He always cycled and she always took the tube. She picked up Darel from the baby-minder and happily went home – that she had been happy when he was already dead bothered her greatly later on. She had a nice chat with her brother Pete on the telephone, but as soon as she realized

Mitchell was late she started to fret. Frightened that something was wrong, she told herself that she was being stupid, even though she had good reason to worry: he wasn't answering his phone, and he always picked up her calls when she rang. Four hours later two policemen arrived, a man and a woman. They asked Kayleigh to sit down and told her Mitchell had been killed. Although she remembered screaming and screaming, the rest was a blank. Her brother, Pete, went over to her flat immediately, pale with shock himself, and together with little Darel they made their way to the hospital.

Mitchell was lying in a room with a sheet over him. Kayleigh looked at him briefly, but 'It wasn't Mitchell any more. Too silent and still.' She saw his terrible injuries, became hysterical and had to leave. But she visited him every day in the week that followed, always with her brother. 'I couldn't bear to see him like that and I couldn't bear not to see him.'

Kayleigh had been too shocked immediately after Mitchell's death to think about all the practical arrangements that would be involved. She knew there would have to be an inquest, and that it was a legal requirement for him to have a post-mortem. She absolutely hated the thought of his being cut open; because he still felt so alive to her, she wondered if it would hurt him. We discussed whether she should see him again after the post-mortem, but she said, 'I've said goodbye to him now, I can't do it again, I might not leave this time.' Then we talked about whether Darel should see him. I told her that even very young children, if prepared properly, can see a dead body, but she felt he was too young.

The system kicked into action: witness statements had been gathered for them to go over with the police. It was agony even to think about what had happened to him, and yet the not knowing was also gnawing away at her. In the end, the momentum of events took over, and Mitchell's family insisted she go with them to meet the police. Together they heard how he had been approaching a mini roundabout and going too fast; the bike hit a sign post, which catapulted him backwards; travelling back across the roundabout, he suffered fatal injuries. Weeks later she went with her brother to the spot where Mitchell had died, and they saw the remnants of flowers and ribbons that people had kindly left to mark the death. It had been a terrible day, one that brought to life all the terrifying images of his crash, and when she recounted it to me her whole frame shook; but she managed to subdue the worst of her fantasies so that we could work on the actual facts relating to the accident.

Mitchell's family organized the funeral. For Kayleigh it passed in a blur; she recalled only that it had been 'packed': all their colleagues from work came, as well as their friends and a lot of people she didn't know. Everybody said the same thing to her: 'I'm sorry for your loss' and 'You're being so brave.' Kayleigh didn't feel brave; she felt numb. Her rational head told her Mitchell was dead, but no other part of her could believe it.

Mitchell had been the only boyfriend Kayleigh had ever had, and she'd relied on him entirely to make decisions in every aspect of her life. It was through loving him and being loved by him that she knew what she had been missing her whole life. He wanted to receive her love as much as she wanted to give it – she hadn't ever experienced that before. Mitchell knew her as she knew herself, with all her faults, and thereby brought her 'best self' to the fore. Without him, she felt she didn't have a complete self; she'd been thrown into an unknown place where she had no map, no way of navigating. Her spiralling despair left her in a state of confusion and insecurity. Stepping into her world, I found a landscape of desolation and desperation, with a great well of loneliness. I could feel the weight of it pressing down on me, and, imagining what that might be like 24/7, I came away with total respect for her ability even to get up and get dressed every day and to feed her little boy. I also understood why there were some days when she couldn't.

Kayleigh asked me if I'd noticed that she always wore black – of course I had – and she wanted me to know she wore it for Mitchell. She couldn't bring herself to dress nicely, wear any colour or put on make-up; it was her way of showing the world she was in mourning. But she felt the world hadn't noticed and could care less. Relieved that I'd noticed, I agreed that wearing black as a traditional expression of mourning was certainly something lots of people now missed being able to do. I thought she had taken on board what I'd said about mourning clothes, but instead she kept asking 'Am I stupid?' Kayleigh would always look down at her hands when she spoke, then briefly look up, as if to check that what she'd said was okay.

She couldn't make decisions. Kayleigh had tried to sort out her flat-rental payments, but she said that she 'just couldn't do it. I'm hopeless and I'm so worried about money.' She found herself drinking a lot in the evening: 'I want vodka and tonic for my dinner; I can't be bothered to cook.' When I reflected back the extent of the pain she was feeling in that moment, she withdrew from me by sitting on her hands, her default mode when the pain became too much for her. I worried about her, and I also worried about Darel's safety; knowing how difficult it was for her to ask for help and also knowing that her friends and family might not want to intrude, even though she was in great need of them, I feared she was becoming increasingly isolated. She said, 'I don't want to bother my family, though my brother's around a lot'; and, much to my relief, she told me that her mother had taken over Darel's care. Imagining how I'd feel seeing my daughter in as distraught a state as Kayleigh's, I realized how distressed her mother must be, and recognized that, by looking after Darel, she was helping her daughter in the only way she knew how. The other stabilizing element in Kayleigh's life was the job she went to three mornings a week. It didn't sound like she managed to do much there, but even the act of getting there gave her a break from her all-consuming grief. Thankfully her manager was patient with her, as she had been bereaved herself; I nodded an invisible thanks to this kind woman who was more sensitive than most would have been.

Often Kayleigh didn't want to come to see me; she couldn't see the point. When she did come, she expressed her over-whelming sadness in gales of failure and fury – 'I can't sleep without him; I always pressed my foot against his at night, and now there's only the cold space of my bed . . . without Mitchell my life has no meaning' – and yet she knew she needed to recover for Darel's sake. Kayleigh was fright-ened for Darel: the image that haunted her was that she might die and he would find her body – a legitimate worry. I could feel a kind of unexpressed fury, silent and deadly, which sat in her body, contaminating every other feeling. It brought with it a lot of fear when she felt out of control; she tried to block it but it would build up into a combustible fury, and she would find herself thumping pillows and then drinking to numb the rage. Over time she learned that she felt calmer after she cried. Once she spent two days crying at home, and then began to improve, proud that she hadn't resorted to the bottle. I was glad that she had let her tears do what they are designed to do: release the sadness that had built up in her body.

Kayleigh hated the unpredictability of her feelings, how being in pain left her feeling 'vulnerable and small . . . There's a big black deadening thing on my chest, suffocating me.' I wondered if there was an earlier emotional wound that I didn't yet know about: the defence mechanisms she seemed to have developed at a young age had left her feeling trapped and diminished, something she dealt with by shutting everything down in order to shut everything out. I wondered what environment may have triggered the building of such steely defences, but I also knew it was too soon to approach it in our sessions. However, the mechanism of clarifying herself to herself through talking to me was working.

Our relationship grew, tentatively, though she remained ambivalent about trusting me: it was still 'scary' for her. She was ashamed of revealing her raw feelings, and admitted to a fear that I would somehow harm her. She was amazed that she had made the commitment to come each week; it was unlike her. Yet it was just at the point I became confident that she was developing coping mechanisms that she went off the rails. She lost weight and said that she wanted to 'disappear'. More fragile than ever before, she felt 'alone and overwhelmed. I'm drinking every night.' Alcohol – a depressant – blocked her fear temporarily but also plunged her into a frightening cycle.

One morning I arrived at work to find her sitting on the floor in the corridor outside my room, curled up in tears. She cried throughout the session and kept saying 'I don't see any point. I want to hurt myself.' She made very little eye contact, and I could feel myself getting increasingly anxious, trying to find a way of responding to her that she could take in. After half an hour she said, 'Can I leave?' I wanted to shout absolutely not, but what I said was: 'I very much want you to stay so that we can find a way of getting you support, but of course it's your choice if you want to go.' She left.

I felt panicked. I was seriously worried she was going to take her own life. I immediately rang my supervisor and we agreed a plan: a priority would be to confirm who was taking care of Darel, and that when I saw Kayleigh the following week our focus would be on working together to keep her safe. I would ask key questions: 'Do you have suicidal thoughts?' 'How worried do we need to be about this?' 'Do you think you need medical help or to be hospitalized for your own safety?' I felt calmer once I had a structure in my head that would enable me to work constructively with her. But after I telephoned her about Darel and got no response, I became intensely worried. It was unlike her not to send some form of reply, because when she felt unable to speak she would text. I rang the next day and the same thing occurred; my anxiety mounted. I telephoned again on the Monday, and to my huge relief Kayleigh answered the telephone. I told her I'd been concerned about her and Darel's safety after our last session. She told me she had taken an overdose on the Friday, but had rung a friend who'd bundled her off to hospital, where they had pumped her stomach and let her out the next day. Her parents had been looking after Darel all week, as they'd seen how distressed she was, though they'd had no idea she might go so far as to take an overdose. I was concerned that no psychiatric appointments or assessments had been booked for her by the hospital. We agreed to meet on the Wednesday.

I was thankful I had Keith, who was my cool, super-tough, kickboxing teacher. Every Wednesday we met: I punched, kicked and elbowed him with all my force. He hit me hard; and I hit him harder. I swore out loud, and there was something about the way I swore that always made him laugh. The fear and tension I was holding in my body needed something to hit against; the satisfaction of feeling the power of my body attack was a great release, as if my man-gled insides had been rinsed clean in the shower.

Kayleigh came in grey and shrunken on Wednesday. I let her know how worried I'd been, and how sorry I was that she'd been in that much pain, and also how relieved I was that she was safe. I asked again about Darel and heard he was still with her parents, being well cared for. We talked together about what she understood of why she had taken an overdose. She said, 'I've always had that addictive gene for food, drink, drugs. It stops the hurt.' She explained that she hadn't wanted to die; the overdose had been a way to stop the pain, 'I couldn't bear it . . . I could see decades ahead without Mitchell. It's like my head is under water, and I lift it up for air, and I think this is quite nice, fresh air in my lungs, then I think of Mitchell dead and it drags me back down.' I wanted her to be confident that I would do what I could to support her, but that it would have to be a joint effort: we had to work collaboratively to keep her safe. I wanted her to know that, as much as I cared about her, I was responsible to her, but not for her. This meant I had a professional responsibility to work to support her best interests, but that I wasn't, nor could I be, responsible for the actions she took or the decisions she made in her life. I asked whether we could work up a no-suicide agreement for her, and to that end put a set of emergency numbers on her mobile that she could call if she felt suicidal. My heart was thumping, as I was still gravely worried about her. I asked her if she still had suicidal thoughts; she covered her face and replied that she was frightened she might 'slip into it'. I told her I was frightened for her and asked, 'What else do we need to do to protect you and Darel?' She agreed to see her GP, whom I rang while she was with me. She decided to join Darel at her parents' while she was in crisis. She needed to let her mum parent her; at such times she became young and childlike, and there wasn't enough adult in her to look after herself. She promised she would contact me if she felt suicidal again, and I would get back to her as soon as I could. I explained that it may not be immediately, but she could be certain that I would respond. On leaving, we had a hug and she whispered, 'Hold my hand'; I promised her that I would.

I learned later that she went to see her GP that day; he prescribed some medication and asked her to come in to see him every week for a month; he also made an appointment to see me, so that we could discuss our joint care of her.

Kayleigh had a volatile few weeks while she waited for the medication to take effect. She oscillated between letting herself be okay and not okay, with good days and bad days. The letting herself be okay was an important step, because up to then she hadn't given herself permission to have a break from her anguish, believing it was a betrayal of her love for Mitchell. I also learned more about her relationship with her parents: they loved her yet were unable to talk to her; as a result she didn't feel in any way 'known' by them. They were obviously good people and had more than shown their commitment to her and Darel since Mitchell's death; and, in fact, Kayleigh would never have coped without them. It wasn't that they withheld their love from her; rather, they couldn't articulate their emotions in words and showed their love by doing things rather than by saying them. For a highly sensitive person like Kayleigh, it hadn't been quite enough. Kayleigh realized for the first time that it was not having her love received by her dad in particular – not having it overtly appreciated or enjoyed by him – that had left her feeling brittle. Her brother Pete was her lifesaver: she could be open and expressive with him.

Kayleigh's turbulence had become contagious: I felt shaken up, and it was harder and harder to remain emotionally steady. I came up with the idea of a small object, one that she could hold in her pocket, that would represent everything that neither of us could ever fully do – a concrete object invested with abstract therapeutic content. She liked the idea. I gave her a special stone of mine, a quartz, shiny and hand sized. Kayleigh took it and rolled it around in her hand, stroked it. We agreed she should keep it in her pocket. And much later she told me she would regularly take it out and twirl it in her hands, feeling its earthy ancient origins, as well as the connection to our sessions. In therapy-speak it's called a 'transitional object' – and it worked for her.

She started going to AA meetings, got a sponsor and began to see some value in the philosophy of 'letting go and letting God' – learning to surrender our individual will in order to recover. Though Kayleigh was far too shy to speak a word, only her name, listening to people in the group helped her to listen to herself. We talked about her crisis, how close to death she had been and how this had scared us both. We wondered if the warning signs could be identified much earlier: how might she protect herself? She said, 'I felt the build-up for days, a turmoil in all of me.' I asked, 'Was there a point much earlier when you could have alerted me? Could you be aware of that for the future?' And she agreed to let me know.

We came to understand that there was a narrative to Kayleigh's turmoil and it was sending her 'a bit mad'. In her heart Mitchell was still alive and she'd been abandoned by him, although she knew perfectly well in her head that he was dead. The rage because he'd left her overtook everything else in her life. On some level she felt that if she got angry enough, fought hard enough, shouted loud enough, she would get him back. But when she started to feel a bit better these thoughts tipped her into despair, because she realized anew that he wasn't coming back, and it was almost as if the loss were being repeated over and over again. Her image of life without him was one of 'total blackness', and at such times she withdrew from food, company, work, caring for her son – all the activities associated with a fully functioning woman.

I realized Kayleigh was one of those people who was born highly sensitive – it was like walking around with a layer of skin missing. This, combined with her parents' lack of emotional openness, left her vulnerable and exposed when facing any of life's difficulties. Mitchell had, in a sense, acted as the missing layer of protective skin that she'd needed; and now that he was gone, she felt more helpless than before. What most people would experience as an irritating mishap – like leaving a credit card behind when shopping – Kayleigh would experience as a disaster, and she would fall into a cycle of self-recrimination and shame from which it would take days to recover.

Our work together went slowly. It was hard for her to allow herself to trust in life again – she would sometimes pretend she didn't care any more and put on a feisty 'fuck life' attitude – but it wasn't what she truly felt. She worried that if she let herself stop hurting she would lose the image of Mitchell that was inside her. She read his texts over and over, kissed his photograph to express how much she missed him. We both felt relieved when we arrived at a key understanding about how to accommodate her loss, how she could find ways of living with all the complexities and contradictions of her grief. She realized that she didn't have to get entirely better or be blissfully happy; she was allowed to be angry and sad, but she could still give herself permission to have a nice time with Darel, who was thriving. She was free to move between anger and happiness, like jumping in and out of puddles.

Months later she was calmer, staying sober, going to work and developing 'good habits'. The therapeutic prescription we worked out together consisted of two runs, two meditation sessions and the writing of one journal entry every week. Over time her anxious depression was so reduced by the combination of running, meditating and journal-writing that she was able to forgo her medication altogether (the research on this combination is strong enough for it to be a NICE guideline). A policewoman friend (one of the very few friends she ever mentioned) had told her of the acronym JFDI – (Just Fucking Do It), which made her laugh and gave her a kind of kick up the arse; she had it as a screen saver on her phone.

It was at this time that I heard about Mr Wooley, her maths teacher, who was the missing piece of the jigsaw in Kayleigh's childhood. I was exploring with her the root of the 'I'm stupid' mantra when she reverted to the age of nine right in front of me and tentatively told the story. She burned with shame as she recalled him. During most of her lessons Mr Wooley would tell her to come to the front of the classroom and then ask her a question. However easy the question, she wouldn't be able to answer it, not because she wasn't clever enough but because being exposed in that bullying way completely overwhelmed her. 'I'd stand there dumbstruck. He would wait. It felt like ages, then he'd shout and send me back to my desk totally scorched. It happened all the time.' This would have had an impact on anyone, but particularly on someone as sensitive as Kayleigh, who was ill equipped to deal with it. Kayleigh's mother had complained, but nothing had been done about it. As the consequences of Mr Wooley's bullying sank in, I became furious. Kayleigh's humiliation lived on in her daily life: every interaction held the potential for her to feel as stupid as the nine-year-old in Mr Wooley's classroom. She believed she had 'I'm stupid' branded on her forehead, and she had to overcome that fear before she could say a single word to anyone. Our mutual hate for Mr Wooley, now renamed 'Mr Bastard', became an important point of connection between us.

By this point we were at the end of our second year of working together, and Kayleigh was facing the next phase of life in some confusion. She knew she couldn't hold back time, but continued to feel bad for engaging in ordinary life. She wanted somehow to stretch out her arms and bring together the past and the present in a single embrace.

Looking up, she said, as if to Mitchell, 'Will you forgive me if I go on?' We talked about her knowing and trusting that she could access Mitchell at any time – he was inside her. She'd worked out that she didn't have to stop loving him now that he was dead; but she had yet to accept completely that he was gone. The reality of his death still hit her unexpectedly at times. Breathing a big sigh, she whispered, 'I had to fill out a next of kin form the other day. I didn't know who to put . . . I'm not the "other" person in anybody's life.' I noticed that she had begun to wear a few colours, not bright, but no longer black. This was an aspect of her new reality, one that was slowly advancing her towards a different future – not the one she had planned, but one in which she could still have a life.

Kayleigh said she wanted order and tidiness in her feelings, to have them as well organized as her sock drawer. But life was messy and hard and unpredictable, and she hated the lack of control. She also grieved for the version of herself that she'd been with Mitchell. For when he became part of her life and loved her, it had changed her: she had felt 'bigger inside, and happy, so, so happy, ah, I will never be happy like that again'. We acknowledged she would never be the same again, but she might successfully move on to another, different self.

Kayleigh surprised me one day by saying she wanted to talk about what to do with Mitchell's ashes. They had been in an urn beside her bed for two years. His parents wanted to scatter them in the park where he had played football. As it was a place where she'd spent a lot of time with him, that was fine with her. There was a part of her that never wanted to let them go, and a part that felt it was the right thing to do. Our talk took the now very familiar pattern of push and pull. A few weeks later she announced she had made the decision; she would do it. The family made the date and asked his closest friends. We talked about how to tell Darel. She knew by now that she needed to tell him the truth, that he was always curious and that if she brought up the subject, she could then follow his lead, letting him ask what he wanted to know and not forcing on him what he didn't want to know. She'd said to him, 'As you know, when daddy died his body didn't work any more; he couldn't feel anything, his heart wasn't working, and we put his body in a special metal box that gets very hot, until the heat burns away his body, and we are left with the ashes, which are small pieces of bone. We've kept those ashes, and now we are going to scatter them in a very special place.' It sounded a bit brutal, but Darel, like most children, wasn't as squeamish about death as an adult. He asked lots of questions – how hot was it, why was the place special – and they finished their talk with Kayleigh telling him funny stories about his dad. The ceremony was simple: his father scattered the ashes; Kayleigh couldn't bring herself to. There'd been silence, and then they all sang a Gospel hymn, crying, smiling, singing. It had been the right decision.

Kayleigh was doing well in her job at the department store, but now she was in a different role, and it was awakening a part of her that was not tied to Mitchell. She was going out occasionally, but, despite the pressure to date other men, she wasn't ready for that. Her AA meetings had become a significant part of her life: she'd started to speak at them, and they were connecting her to new people, building her confidence. I could tell from the way she said 'Hello' these days that she felt differently: it was as if she were stepping into the hello with a great big smile.

The pain still hit her, but she now possessed the tools to reach internally and soothe herself. She said, 'I couldn't get up in the morning if I couldn't see his face, but these days when I focus I can see his smile, and that sees me through.' She was such a loving, lovable woman that I didn't like the idea of her being on her own: 'I want to see you being loved again.' She smiled at me, not the nervous smile of our first meeting, but quite a twinkly one, and told me that she remained madly in love with Mitchell; she didn't want to be 'unfaithful'. I heard her vehement 'no', and privately thought that this was a part of her life that might stay on pause forever. She might never again press play, but I hoped that she would. Her joy was Darel, four years old now, chatty and full of life.

There seemed to be less and less for us to talk about: her life was busier and she was happier. Kayleigh most certainly would not have said she was happy, but she had more energy, she was able to take pride in herself for having survived what she feared would kill her. Recently, with a work colleague, she had laughed in a way that she hadn't for years, 'really cried laughing'. The bullied little girl in her was no longer so frightened, and she didn't need to hold my hand any more.

Stephen

Stephen was a tall man with a large stomach, a 62-year-old eminent Professor of Biology. He found it hard to walk up the stairs to my room, and was red faced and breathing heavily when he arrived. He was wearing a beautifully cut tweed jacket and immaculate suede shoes, showing his sense of style.

This wasn't a man who wanted to see a therapist or even really believed therapy could help him. His family had told him: 'You need help.' His sister was worried that he was either working obsessively or bingeing on food and drink – a destructive cycle that he was using to anaesthetize the shock and pain of his wife's recent death. She had rung me, asking if I would see him, and I told her he needed to refer himself. He made an appointment for an assessment session, which is when he told me his story.

Stephen's wife, Jenni, had died suddenly and traumatically in a car crash six months previously. She had gone to the supermarket, and on the way home her car had skidded on ice and crashed into a wall. Had the accident occurred a hundred feet before or after that spot, she may have survived. An everyday, random act of death in life. Her osteoporosis had dealt the fatal blow, when her fragile bones were broken by the impact.

He had been at work when the hospital rang him to say his wife had had an accident. When he arrived there, he was led to a small dank room and told that Jenni had died. Then he was taken to the room where her body lay, but he couldn't bring himself to go close to her; he only made it to the doorway.

I shuddered at the cruelty of the 'What ifs': that a simple domestic chore could put an end to someone's life. Stephen spoke quietly, without looking at me and breathing heavily between sentences. He spoke in the third person, like an observer looking at someone he knew. I wondered if he was this detached in every aspect of his life. He seemed to be the kind of man who had 'All I want is a quiet life' tattooed on his forehead.

I could imagine his horror when he told me: 'Ringing to tell the boys was the worst thing I've ever had to do, I can still hear Andy's scream. It was like an animal's.' His sons had returned home for a couple of weeks after the funeral, but, once they'd gone, he'd found himself getting home from work and, on most nights, turning to a bottle of Grey Goose. 'At work I feel like I'm enveloped in a fog.' Work may have been acting as a distraction, and on the weekends at home, without the fog to mask the horror, he binged on food and booze. He looked down at the carpet as he told me of this pattern, and I wondered if he feared that I was judging him and didn't want to see this in my face. I sensed the loneliness and fear beneath his behaviour, and said that numbing must have felt like a better option than hurting. He nodded, and seemed to be taking in at least some of what I was saying.

I felt emotionally enormous as I sat opposite him, as if my capacity to feel and express myself might overwhelm him. I was also a little intimidated by his academic cleverness; because I was aware that not being clever was my own particular hang-up, I'd have to be careful not to cut myself off from him. That sense of intimidation stayed with me, though, and the distance between us didn't seem to diminish: I found myself working hard, asking lots of questions, which was always a sign for me that something wasn't working well.

Over the first few sessions I was curious to know what kind of relationship he'd had with Jenni. What had she been like? What did he miss about her? By asking, I hoped to help him find a way of relating to her through memories. I learned she had been very attractive. They had met in their mid-twenties and dated for many years, during which time she had wanted to marry him, but he hadn't been sure. He realized as he was speaking, as if for the first time, that this had been a fault line that ran through their entire relationship: she'd resented his time-wasting — he'd taken 'too long' to marry her, and then 'too long' to decide to have children.

When I found myself as a woman empathizing with his wife, I pulled myself back to be onside with Stephen. He had clearly been ambivalent, but this had come from his desire to do things 'logically and be secure'. He'd wanted to be earning enough money to be comfortably off when he married. But they'd had problems conceiving their second son, and she blamed him for that too.

In some ways he was relieved to be living without Jenni, for when he got home he didn't have to talk to her. She'd regularly criticized him about his weight gain over the years and had withdrawn from him physically in the last decade; he had always felt that he wasn't 'enough' for her, and that she was disappointed and bored by him. He felt guilty about that, but what he really missed was the four of them together as a family. She organized their family life and was at its centre: holidays, birthdays, weekends. As he remembered those days, I could feel his emotions bubbling intensely through his system, despite all his efforts to quash them. I said quietly how painful that must be. But he wasn't having any of it: he hrumphed and quickly changed the subject. As I saw him clench his fist tightly, I imagined him as a six-year-old, digging his nails into his palm. I couldn't push him at that point, because it would only cause him to re-double his defences, but I clocked it. The more vulnerable he felt, the more the 'Intimidating Professor' emerged.

Stephen had two sons; George, eighteen, at university, and Andy, twenty-four, working in technology and living with friends. I asked him how they were doing: 'The boys have been good, amazing actually.' They sometimes came home at the weekend, and when they did the three of them would go to watch their team play football, eat together and talk about everything – everything, that is, except their mother. Their family culture was to avoid anything difficult, to secrete it away under a very thick carpet. Stephen told me their family's catchphrase was 'Least said, soonest mended'. I asked Stephen what he imagined would happen if they talked about Jenni, if they were to peek under the carpet. He reddened, a tear appeared in his eye, and he whispered, 'Once we start being sad, we won't stop.' He showed a little of his vulnerable self, which enabled us both to understand a bit more about why he'd needed to block the pain. I could feel myself warming towards him and I came to realize that he was a man of his time: many men of his generation don't have a vocabulary for their feelings and subsequently find the idea of them hard to grasp; some don't even know when they are sad. I suggested that they walk and talk together as a family. It isn't as intense as sitting and talking, there is less eye contact, and something about the movement of walking side by side seems to bring about a kind of emotional release. I suggested he might start by saying, 'I remember when Mum . . .' He agreed it was a helpful, practical suggestion, and he could imagine himself doing it as they walked to the pub. In that brief moment of connection, he seemed to have found a new awareness of himself in relation to others. He later told me that it had worked for them as a family, and he was confident about using it again.

At the beginning of each session it took quite a while for Stephen to get his breath back, having climbed the stairs, and then a bit more time to be present. Well, 'present-ish' – the bubbling up of difficult feelings that he swiftly dispatched was a familiar pattern. I still had little idea of what lay behind this coping mechanism; I might have known his story but I still didn't know what his internal world was like; I could only guess at how sad, confused, angry, powerless and empty he felt. His ambivalence towards his wife was mirrored in his ambivalence towards our sessions, in that he couldn't come regularly because his diary needed to be flexible. I'm more relaxed than many therapists about being flexible, but with him I wondered out loud if it was a way of keeping one foot in the room with me and one foot outside the door. He wasn't having any of it: 'No, no, it's just practical diary arrangements. Don't read anything else into it.'

I wanted to know if he was still in the cycle of working very hard, and then drinking and eating a lot at weekends, but I didn't want to shame him, nor be like a mother to his six-year-old self, checking up on him. My guess was that he was probably stuck in the same pattern. In order to narrow the distance between us, I needed to find some mutual experiences, and recognized that Stephen was similar to me in an earlier period of my life when I had been quite shut down and stuck in stiff-upper-lip mode. It had been useful, even essential at times, to adopt this behaviour; the mistake had been to apply it universally in all situations – it was, for example, necessary to switch to a different emotional state for intimate relationships to evolve. I asked Stephen what coping mechanisms he'd used as a child when dealing with difficulties. He told me he was from the North, although he didn't have a trace of a Northern accent; he was from a working-class background, and his mother, of Irish descent and a practising Catholic, had been angry and domineering. His Geordie father was a builder, a very good one, anxious, quiet and loving, but an alcoholic. This is the textbook upbringing of men who armour themselves against feeling, particularly with women. And the more I understood this, the more I was able to empathize with him and to appreciate his brilliance and his vulnerability, without being put off by his protective shields.

Stephen was the product of a generation of parents who had lived through the Second World War, and their chief tenet for raising children was 'Spare the rod spoil the child.' His liberation came during his school years, when he discovered the power of his brain; he had few friends, but flew through the work, and did extremely well in his exams. Learning excited him, and still remained his greatest source of pleasure. He could spend days researching papers, following an idea to its logical conclusion. He didn't particularly like teaching, but occasionally was pleasantly surprised by a clever student. Watching him as he spoke about his subject, I realized what I had entirely missed: that this was where his emotional self resided. He loved his subject; his heart was in the life of his intellectual mind.

Stephen didn't know how to access his emotional self, nor did he want to. I could see in his eyes the very thought of it sent huge alarm bells ringing. When I asked him to close his eyes, breathe and focus on an image in his body, he saw nothing; he absolutely would not go there. And I felt like an idiot for even suggesting it. He could no more understand this than I could understand his field of expertise, biology.

His great release was following and watching football. He'd played a lot as a child and been pretty good. That skill had gone now, but going to games was his weekly form of therapy. Stephen invested a passion in football that he wouldn't dream of bringing to other domains. When he spoke about his team – pink-cheeked and vibrant when describing a particular game – I could see more of him than at any other time. It was the big connector with his two sons, and it gave them a touching sense of belonging and intimacy.

There was a moment in one session when he said, 'I've been offered a lot of money to go to work in America, but the project doesn't interest me, and the money means nothing. I want to buy time, and that isn't an option.' I told him I thought it was a meaningful metaphor, and he smiled at me with soulful eyes. The death of Jenni had definitely shattered his illusion that death was something that only happened to other people. He was now highly sensitive to his own mortality and had finally woken up to the value of his own life. 'I'm going to make sure I live every moment of my day,' he said, and then quoted Goethe: 'I'm going to plunge boldly into the thick of life.'

I had seen Stephen intermittently for about ten sessions when he told me, much to my astonishment, that he had started to date someone: a South American woman he'd met through a dating website. I was surprised he'd dated online; this wasn't what I'd come to expect from him. I knew the research shows men tend to want to get on with their lives and replace a wife who's died, while women tend to grieve for longer, but I'm always shocked anew when confronted by how different men and women are in their reactions. Stephen had by no means finished mourning his wife of twenty-seven years: it was less than a year since her death. But here he was, at the beginning of a new relationship. Quietly excited by it, he seemed more energized, and rather impressed with himself.

I realized I was giving in to my own prejudices, and had become a bit jaundiced by hearing so many times the same story: men replace and women grieve. But, as I sat looking at him, I was pleased for him. I realized that he had been alone for a long time, for many years before his wife had died, in fact. Stephen hadn't had close physical contact with her for over a decade, and the contact they did have sounded like the perfunctory and mechanical gestures of habit. Whether this new woman would be long term or not wasn't important; she was kindling new life into him, physically and emotionally, and he was now hopeful in a way he'd never been before. There is an intimacy that only sex can create, where rational thought is suspended and animal instincts take over. Through this woman, Stephen could connect to a younger version of himself and hopefully feel liberated. He was now full of possibility. I have often seen how transformative a loving relationship can be: people who have seemed encased in their brittle armour can shine brightly in the newness of being loved.

I never found out what happened to Stephen, because he didn't return. I wonder about him sometimes and recall that tall, rotund, rather brilliant man, who was lit up far more by ideas than by people.

Reflections

Most of us want to find a partner with whom we can build a meaningful life and, as a couple, experience life's joys and difficulties. Loving is always risky, and requires trust in oneself and the other for it to be sustained. Yet, when couples commit – whether it be through marriage, cohabitation or a civil partnership – death is rarely something that they envisage, certainly not until old age.

Few events are as painful as the death of a partner. It is the death of the dream of the imagined future, as well as the couple's current life together. It is the end of a mutual set of circumstances: companionship, status and often financial security may all be affected by unwanted change. Many people define themselves in relation to their partners, and subsequently when that partner dies they fear they will fall apart. Their grief is emotional and physical, severely disrupting the stability of their world. And one of the most painful aspects of losing a partner is having to parent alone.

Caitlin, Kayleigh and Stephen all experienced the death of their partner, but that is where their similarities ended. Each of their responses was entirely individual. Their reactions were shaped by a combination of many factors: not only did their genetic make-up, personality type and the events surrounding the death play a part, but also the story of what had happened to them in their lives, and the belief systems and expectations that came about as a result. Their relationship with their partner influenced the extent of their loss, and the course their grief would take, though the support available to them would also be influential in how well they would manage after the death.

The difference in numbers and attitudes between men and women

In my practice I have seen many more women than men whose partners have died. This does not mirror exactly the actual statistics. In 2014 there were 3.5 million widows and widowers in England and Wales, about 7 per cent of the population. Of these, 48 per cent were male and 52 per cent female. Women tend to seek social support following a bereavement, while men rely more on their own resources to cope.

It is important to point out that counselling is by no means the only form of support. Talking to friends, writing a journal, painting – whatever the route, the important thing is to find a way of expressing the grief.

The difference in attitudes to grief depending on age

The generation born before the 1960s don't tend to seek therapy when a partner dies, as they were brought up to be self-reliant and to view mental illness of any kind as a weakness.

When the death conforms to a general idea of life expectancy, interestingly, the men over eighty seem to suffer more from the loss and take longer to recover than women of a similar age. My guess is that research in the next ten years will show that men who are in their twenties to forties now will be much more likely to seek counselling when they are older – something I am already seeing clinically, as the number of younger men coming to me has increased.

The difference in grief when the death is after a long life or a life cut short

Statistically, the majority of partners' deaths are people who have lived a long life. Their surviving partner is likely to be very sad, but they recognize it isn't a tragedy, as it has fallen within the normal life span. And there can be relief when someone who has been ill for a long time finally dies, particularly when they have been in pain and their suffering is at an end. Relief may also come from the partner no longer having to assume the role of carer and all the limits on individual freedom that that entails.

When the partner who dies is younger, the grief can be more intense: the surviving partner is mourning the future they expected to have together as well as the death. If it is a sudden death, the level of distress is magnified further. Even when the couple are much older, sudden death can bring about an intensity of loss that is the same.

Physical impact of grief

It is an uncomfortable truth that the bereaved suffer higher rates of heart disease than the general population. A bereaved person is six times more likely to suffer heart disease than the national average, which gives credence to the concept of being 'broken-hearted'. Some recent research revealed that surviving partners were 66 per cent more likely to die within the first three months to the first few years after their partner's death. This is supported by new developments in our current understanding of cellular chemistry and physiology, which show that, when living cells are removed from someone who has been bereaved, they function less effectively than those removed from a person who is not grieving.

Bereaved men

In my experience it is very common for men in their mid-fifties and older to be reluctant to seek support, and they are doing themselves no favours. The research shows that in not acknowledging their hurt, anger and confusion, men may have higher rates of both mental and physical illness, and become more depressed later in their bereavement. Men also have higher mortality rates in the first two years following a bereavement than women. A recent mental health report notes the difficulties faced by older men when accessing psychological support and recommends different methods for addressing this problem.

As mentioned in Stephen's story, men tend to start new relationships within a year of their partner's death. When that doesn't happen, widowers who were bereaved for three years or more were found to have more bitterness than before their bereavement.

Importance of social support

Social connection and emotional support are beneficial to the well-being of both men and women. Women's tendency to be open and express themselves is a significant healing element, and they tend to have a greater network of friends, which gives them a psychological advantage. Men are not getting the support they need through their friends, because they are not reaching out to them.

Financially, men earn substantially more than women, and therefore women tend to be under greater financial strain at times of bereavement than men. They may have to move house, causing their children's school life and friendships to be disrupted; or they may have to find a job, which can be very difficult as a single parent because of the problems associated with childcare.

Drugs and alcohol

It is very common for those who are bereaved to increase their consumption of alcohol and drugs in order to anaesthetize the pain of grief. We might know how bad a habit is, but we do it anyway. Maybe we haven't fully taken on board the fact alcohol itself is a depressant; nor that when we are bereaved we're particularly vulnerable to drug addiction as our usual defence mechanisms aren't working as well as normal. Drugs and/or alcohol taken to medicate depression only exacerbate it. Those who experience anxiety and depression are twice as likely to be heavy or problem drinkers. A third of the people who are depressed in the UK also have a drug and/or alcohol addiction, and often unresolved loss is at the root of this habit.

The line between a heavy drinker and an addict is a difficult one to draw, but their respective attitudes towards the drink and/or drugs are what usually differentiate the two. An addict's central relationship is with their drug of choice, and they *use* the alcohol/drug because they believe they are unable to function without it. It controls them. A heavy drinker may binge or regularly drink too much, and could become dependent, but still believe they have control. Addiction often runs in families, and there can be a genetic predisposition, while some believe it is a personality type; but the most likely factor in its transmission down the generations is conditioning: children learn from their parents that drinking or taking drugs is an acceptable way to deal with difficulty.

Whatever the reason for their abuse, drugs and alcohol increase the risk of bad outcomes for the bereaved, and, as a consequence, their children, sometimes even many generations of their children. Addiction can prevent people from accepting the reality of their situation – and it is this absolute determination not to surrender to reality that prevents people from moving beyond their grief and living the life they've been given to the full.

Sex and relationships

Caitlin's and Stephen's need for sex was a healthy biological response to death, and is, ostensibly, an impulse to generate new life. Grieving people often try to connect to their erotic side, in an effort to push back the feeling of deadness. Our sex drive is the playful, creative part of ourselves that seeks out vitality and unpredictability. It may also be a source of comfort for people who have been left feeling alone and cut off from others; it is very common for people to want to hold someone close when the fragility of their world threatens to overwhelm them.

At the one end of the spectrum of comfort sex is reckless behaviour. People might engage in this as a way to stop having any feelings at all; or, because life now feels dangerous anyway, they are tempted to put that danger to the test. At the other end is shutting down from sex altogether. I've worked with many people like this. They may physically be exhausted; or they may feel guilty for having any sort of pleasure at all. Some people even feel the person who has died is watching them, leaving them unable to forge a relationship with someone new.

For those who do move on, the greatest complication that lies ahead relates to their children. A new relationship inevitably impacts on the children, whether they are young or older, and a successful outcome for everyone will depend on how the transition is managed. I have often seen adolescent and even adult children struggle to accept a new person in their surviving parent's life; one twenty-year-old bereaved daughter summed up the conflicts that occur when she said: 'I want Daddy to be happy, and I like Sarah, but I feel like he's being unfaithful to Mummy. I HATE her being in Mummy's bed, Mummy's bedroom, and want to scream when she's cooking in the kitchen.' And she would show her disapproval by going to her bedroom and not coming out until after her father's new girlfriend had left. A good deal of sensitivity is required by the parent in these circumstances, as well as a lot of patience and persistence: neither giving in nor blowing up when the child makes a demand that the new partner be sacrificed to the memory of the dead parent. You could try something along the lines of: 'I'm in a relationship with Gillian and you don't have the power to stop that – but I do understand how much this upsets you. Let's think about what might help: say, having special time together on our own, and also things we might want to do with Gillian . . .'

Death ends a life, but it does not end a relationship and survivors often struggle to resolve what seems like an unresolvable contradiction. We need to have a better understanding of our capacity, as human beings, to have multiple relationships, to hold both past and present loves within ourselves at once. The resolution of grief is not a return to life as it was before, for there is no going back. It is more, as one bereaved wife called it, a new sort of normal. The process cannot be hurried by friends and family, who may want to 'fix' a widow or widower by arranging a new relationship for them. However well-meaning this is, it frequently ends in disaster, because recovery and adjustment can take much longer than most people realize.

Equally, friends can be judgemental and critical if they believe a friend has got over the death of their partner too quickly and is dating someone new before an 'acceptable' amount of time has passed. Taking the time to listen to these friends explain their point of view is a better option than withdrawing from them in anger. There is no right or wrong in grief: we need to accept whatever form it takes, both in ourselves and in others, and to find the strength to live with that acceptance.

When a parent dies

The life of the dead is placed in the memory of the living

— Marcus Tullius Cicero

Brigitte

I spoke to Brigitte at length on the telephone before we met. She was a 52-year-old barrister whose mother had died suddenly from a heart attack. She said angrily that everyone kept telling her she needed to 'support herself' when she didn't even have a clue what that meant. I acknowledged how annoying it is to be told you need support, but added that some people can benefit from a tap on the shoulder from a friend, who might see them more clearly than they see themselves. That lengthy telephone call was also about control, mine as well as hers. She wanted to know how I worked. What model of therapy did I use when working with clients? Would it help her? How did I 'know' I could help her (I didn't)? And finding a date that suited both of us was a struggle. My control issues reared their head when Brigitte kept asking for a late-evening appointment, but I don't work in the evenings. I thought to myself: What part of 'I don't work evenings' isn't clear? Her questions irritated me, because I believed she was pushing me to see where my boundaries lay. I imagined she was also wrestling with the idea of whether she should give herself permission to seek help: she probably didn't want to be one of those people who need therapy. It was after six months of intermittent calls that we finally met up.

Brigitte didn't look at all as I'd imagined her. She was smaller, and she was immaculately dressed, with long brown hair perfectly coiffed and polished nails. I couldn't help but wonder how she managed to do all this grooming when she worked so hard, and also had to care for a child. She was nervous, but sat bolt upright; only the tapping of her fingers revealed her anxiety. I was pleased to finally meet her and to have an opportunity of seeing more of who she was. I felt great respect for her courage in asking for help when it was counter to her normal way of coping, and this demonstrated to me how much pain she must have been in. With the intention of giving her clarity, which might help to allay her uncertainty, I told her once more how I worked: my fees, the contracted number of sessions, the reviews, my note-taking, confidentiality and the only reason why I'd break confidentiality – if she was in danger of harming herself or someone else, I would be obliged to contact her GP.

She watched me vigilantly with hooded eyes; it would take time for her to trust me. I asked her to tell me about herself. She was German born, the only daughter of an engineer and his wife who had worked all over the world. She had been educated and based in the UK since she was sixteen. Her parents had retired to the UK. She had a very slight accent and chose her words carefully. She worried about her father, and loved her husband, Tom, and her child, a teenage girl whom she'd named after her mother, Zelma.

Brigitte had been at work, fortunately not in court, when her father rang to tell her that her mother had collapsed and they needed to go to the hospital immediately. It was four hours away. She told me about the panic of the journey by train, not knowing if her mother was alive or dead; running into the hospital and being directed through brightly lit hospital corridors, getting lost, and finally stepping into a bare, clinical room and seeing her mother. She had died. 'It looked like Mama, and yet she was gone. It wasn't her. I touched her but she was cold. She'd died two hours earlier.' I noticed that she shivered and realized that the coldness of the death was still in her body. She spoke on autopilot: there was no connection between her head and her heart. It was as if she were telling me a story that had happened to somebody else.

There had to be a coroner's post-mortem because it was a sudden death, and the thought of this upset her. But afterwards her mother's body was still intact, and Brigitte was glad that she'd seen her mother again before the burial. 'I sat with her. Not for very long. I kissed her lightly on her forehead, I talked to her.' Brigitte had put her mother's favourite rose in the coffin, dressed her in her best dress and put socks on her feet, because 'She always had cold feet.' The family had arranged for the mother's body to be brought home before the funeral: 'We wanted her to see her garden again.' They chose a closed wicker coffin, and all the family came to say goodbye. Brigitte couldn't really remember the funeral: it had passed in a blur. She wished she had recorded it. Everyone kept saying to her 'You're doing so well' and 'You're so brave.' She didn't feel brave; she felt outside of herself, watching a surreal film from which she wanted to wake up, only to find her mother back by her side.

Over many months I discovered how exceptionally close Brigitte had been to her mother. They had spoken every day, sometimes several times a day. Her mother texted her every morning and every evening. It brought an image of breastfeeding into my mind that I didn't voice for fear it would shame her; but it gave me a useful way of symbolizing how close their bond was. Her mother was the person whom she had worked hard for, whom she wanted to achieve for. Whenever good things happened to Brigitte, it was her mother she always told first. I could see that she was struggling to find the words with which to express herself; part of her seemed to be trying to push the words down. She tentatively tried out the word 'I', and then cried out 'I miss her', as if saying the words and facing their truth might break her; but, as her words and tears flowed, she found that the breaking she'd feared was a kind of opening – a release.

A little later a childlike rebellious tone came into her voice when she said, 'It's my mother who should be comforting me now,' and glanced at me. I knew I was no substitute. Nobody could be. I knew how frightening it is to feel so needy, and therefore how important it is that we learn the best way to comfort ourselves.

In one session Brigitte told me that she'd 'primitively yowled' the day before, which had scared her, but it sounded to me like she had finally started the process of grieving. She was frightened that she would miss her mum this much for the rest of her life. Because her mother's approval had been behind everything that she did, she could no longer find meaning or value in anything that she accomplished. I heard repeatedly that it was her mother's shining pride, her mother's look and loving hug, that had motivated her to succeed. She wasn't sure what she really believed in, for herself, any more.

Brigitte couldn't settle. She would take on work she absolutely knew she didn't have the time to fit in. We looked at what drove her to send herself a curve ball like that, to punish herself in effect. The answer had to do with control. When she wasn't working, she was out of control: constantly pining, constantly searching for her mother. She was frightened she might lose the ability to conjure her mother in her mind, that she might forget her. She missed her presence acutely: she replayed her mother's voice messages and longed to climb into the phone and find her. Rage about the death, silent rage, was locked inside, and she had no idea how to free herself from it. Brigitte couldn't go to the places where she'd gone together with her mother; she couldn't even bring herself to pass by Starbucks, Zara, their favourite local restaurant. Diversionary routes were devised to avoid them. Some music, such as opera, comforted her, but other music would tip her into desolation. When she did manage to sleep, she woke in tears. She had to force herself out of bed, because facing the day felt daunting; only running took the edge off the pain, so she ran every morning.

Brigitte felt there was a schism between the self she had been when her mother was alive and this new self who didn't have a mother. The Brigitte who had previously existed had died along with her mother. Her husband, Tom, kept telling her he would look after her, but he was no replacement for her mother. He was becoming frustrated with her; he wanted the old Brigitte back. But Brigitte was certain her old self was never going to come back, and her new self shouted repeatedly at her husband. She acted as if her loss entitled her to behave however she wished because she was suffering, and this entitlement eclipsed any needs her husband might have. This, in turn, left him outraged and unresponsive to her. And so they continued, caught in an ever recurring cycle of pain. Brigitte was also impatient with her daughter, Zelma, who both resented and missed her mother. Zelma told Brigitte she was being 'pathetic', which had really hurt. Brigitte started to drive her daughter to school to try to keep their relationship on track, but Zelma wouldn't speak to her, and Brigitte would, once again, end up shouting at her.

Many weeks into our therapy Brigitte described herself as 'having fallen from grace through grief'; it hadn't made her a better person but rather brought out the 'monster' in her. It was important for me to help Brigitte integrate these different versions of herself; for, although she felt her old self had died, that wasn't how it seemed to me: I thought the death of her mother had simply brought out aspects of her personality that she had never experienced before, and certainly didn't welcome. It was as if the different configurations of herself changed, chameleon-like, according to the environment or the company in which she found herself. There was the desolate child; the formidable barrister; the loving mother and wife; and the scratchy, impatient, shouty mother and wife.

Then she finally dug down deep enough to bring out her adolescent self, the 'fat girl on the sofa'. It was through this discovery that our relationship began to grow. I'd often commented that she would regularly denigrate herself, and it was such an integral part of her that she didn't even realize she was doing it. I called it her 'shitty committee', and it was relentless in its criticism of her. As we explored further, we came to know the young Brigitte. She'd been unpopular at school, bullied for being fat, and her only protection was to work hard and do well at exams. She felt ashamed of that version of herself, although it had served her well then and was still serving her well today. When, one day, she showed me a photograph of herself as a teenager, I felt deeply touched and tender towards her. She was unrecognizable from the woman she was today: an over-bright smile, lank hair, specs and fat. 'The fat girl on the sofa' became a shorthand phrase we could use when she was attacking herself. It was painful to witness how she kicked and hated 'the fat girl on the sofa'. We acknowledged she would never speak to a friend, or even a stranger, with the viciousness with which she spoke to herself; it surfaced as a continuous, low-level muttering, and was deeply corrosive and undermining. My aim was to plant a seed of awareness in her, so she could recognize that she was a woman of value and worthy of both respect and love.

Brigitte loved her husband Tom very much, and historically his love for her had been the source of her growing confidence in herself, diminishing the powerful presence of her adolescent self. He had been physically attracted to her, loved her body, relished just looking at it as well as touching it and making love to it. That connection had been the mainstay of their relationship. But since her mother's death she hadn't wanted to have sex with him. For the first months he'd respected that, but now his frustration had grown into anger. This was because he loved her – hate isn't the opposite of love; indifference is – but she was too self-absorbed to see it. Her response was to withdraw from him further. In return, he lectured her, telling her how lucky she was to have him and their daughter, their lives together, how her mother wouldn't want her to be acting like this. He only succeeded in alienating her further, leaving her feeling more misunderstood than ever. And she felt her mother was all around her, watching her, which made having sex impossible for her.

After we spoke more about it, I reflected back to her that I could see both the clenched jaw of her anger with Tom, as well as the very young child who just wanted to be held, comforted by her mum. The pain of grief was what was keeping her mother close, and she was by no means ready to relinquish the only connection she had to her. We spoke together about how she might keep hold of both these aspects of herself simultaneously. She didn't have to push Tom away in order to be close to her mother; she could allow herself to move between the two relationships.

The all-consuming nature of work distracted her, but it also exhausted her: 'The unrelenting demands of work and my home are difficult, and when Zelma has an adolescent tantrum, I want to have one too!' She was fed up with being the one who always coped, who could always be relied on; the idea of having a breakdown felt quite attractive. I asked her about her ability to say 'no'. If she had a proper 'no' that she believed and trusted in, it could protect her from doing what she didn't want to do, or what she didn't have enough time to do; this would transform her 'yes' into a positive, energetic one. Brigitte understood the concept of boundaries and the advantages of clear and decisive 'yeses' and 'noes', but she couldn't, at this point, implement them in her life. I could see that saying 'yes', being capable and reliable, was a key part of her identity, and she wouldn't be able to adapt it to better suit her needs until she was more robust.

Brigitte's capacity to be giving and loving at this time was extremely poor. She disliked her feelings of resentment and anger towards Zelma, but, instead of dealing with them, she projected them on to Zelma herself. 'My daughter is making me angry . . . it's her fault.' When I challenged her gently, suggesting the projection, she shouted me down. She felt I was criticizing her and using impenetrable 'therapy-speak' to do so. Fair enough. I told her it was important for our relationship that she could be cross with me, and that we could then talk about it and repair any rupture. I was reminded that good disagreements can be central to progress and, counter-intuitively, positively creative in their outcome.

The post-mortem results showed that Brigitte's mother

had had atrophied arteries and that her death was inevitable. This put an end to Brigitte's circular 'What ifs?' She returned to the hospital where her mother had died to thank the surgeons and nurses for their care; she walked through the corridors, holding her father's hand for the first time since the death. They visited the grave together, and cried together. Other good things happened to her which cheered her: on the tube one day she'd been crying soft tears, and a total stranger, a young man, had gently given her a tissue. A simple act of kindness, which had stayed with her, buoyed her.

Brigitte still felt devastated by her mother's death, but she was aware that her family and friends believed she should be getting over it by now, that the pain should gradually be growing less and less with time. They didn't want to talk to her about her mother any more. They expected her to be 'okay', to be back on track, happy and going out, which she certainly couldn't do. As a result she withdrew from them and suffered a terrible, cold loneliness that swept through her in waves and left her tired in every cell of her body. She often cried as she told me about her mother. They had both loved clothes and had spent a great deal of time shopping, browsing and trying things on together. Although her mother had been adventurous and, because of her husband's work, lived in many countries, she had chiefly devoted herself to the traditional role of wife and mother. She had wanted something different for Brigitte, however, and had imbued in her a sense of how important it was to be independent, something she could achieve through work, career and using her brain to its full potential.

Brigitte got through a joyless Christmas, the happy memories of past Christmases forcing her to confront her new loss. And then there was the build-up to the actual anniversary of the death; this for Brigitte was terrible. The evocative smells, the weather, counting down the days – Brigitte felt herself being propelled back in time and made to relive every moment of her mother's death. Her anxiety developed into panic attacks that debilitated her further and she had to take time off work. In the end the actual anniversary of the death wasn't as bad as she had feared: she spent the day with her father, and they'd gone to the cemetery and kept vigil together, not really talking or moving, just sitting, remembering and giving time to her mother.

Brigitte's grief had impacted on another relationship in her life, and this was causing her low-level but continuous distress. Her closest colleague at work, a barrister with whom she shared all the stresses and successes of being a working mother in a very demanding job, had been 'shit' at acknowledging her loss. 'Danielle briefly said something perfunctory like "I'm sorry for your loss" when Mama died, but since then not a word. She hasn't asked me how I am, nor has she mentioned my mother's name. Now I can barely look at her. We used to be close – we'd pop into each other's offices all the time – now we don't even speak. I miss her, but I'm furious with her.' I asked Brigitte what was she prepared to do to repair the rift and the answer was 'Nothing'. Her anger was exacerbated because she felt 'I shouldn't even be thinking about her – I don't want to give her my headspace – but every time I go into work it bothers me.' Brigitte stonewalled any ideas of conciliation, though clearly she really missed her friend. But she didn't have the energy in her to fight for this friendship at that moment. I hoped that when she began to feel better she would make some effort to sort it out, but I also knew that many friendships had foundered because someone wouldn't, couldn't or didn't know how to acknowledge grief.

At the start of one session we laughed when I commented on how smart Brigitte looked and she had replied, 'The worse I feel, the better I dress.' And the laughter brought with it a basic truth: that sometimes we need to have active habits just to help us get up and out the door. Brigitte's confidence in her ability to work effectively was fragile, although in reality her success in court hadn't diminished.

At night she often cried frustrated, angry tears in the dark, driven almost mad by the stress of juggling the roles of mother, wife and barrister. She said, 'I need a wife, a bloody good housewife at that.' I nodded vehemently in agreement: yes, she did, she bloody well did. There is an epidemic of busyness in our world today, and Brigitte displayed a full-on version of it. Her Smartphone, which was hermetically sealed to her hand, perfectly embodied the false idea that busyness is potency. She did her daily shop on it, bought tickets to America, scheduled appointments and spoke to people all over the world. Yet, by constantly checking it, she switched off her feelings and also the emerging messages of discomfort in her body, all of which was information that she needed to be listening to. It gave her a misleading sense of efficacy, as if she would be able to achieve anything if she could just keep up with everything the screen threw at her. Devoting all her attention to it meant that the part of her that was needed to weather powerlessness, impotence and uncertainty became atrophied. I suggested that she should do a relaxation exercise with a meditation app. She looked at me as if I were speaking Greek and said, 'I don't have time for it!'

If all this wasn't enough, Brigitte was also worried about her father, and exhausted herself with frequent visits to him. She hated that she was powerless to help him, and seeing his sadness and grief intensified her own. But the unexpected benefit was that she felt closer to him. He had always been reserved and detached, and that hadn't changed; but spending time together on their own, doing simple things like cooking and shopping, enabled them to forge a companionship that she found soothing.

Over time some improvement occurred in her relationship with Zelma. Brigitte recognized that she had been in so much pain that she hadn't been able to see that her daughter was grieving the death of her grandmother too. Brigitte had seen her crying at the funeral, but, with little emotional energy to spare, she had neglected to talk to her daughter about how she may have been feeling. Strangely, Brigitte recognized that she felt a bit jealous that Zelma still had a mother, while hers was gone. When she listened to how much her daughter had loved her grandmother, she felt closer to her, and eventually they found ways of sharing this love: they went to her house together and carefully chose their favourite plates, took them home, washed them and put them on the shelves in their kitchen. Despite the teenage angst and the grieving, they discovered they could still have fun together, doing the things Brigitte had done with her own mother.

It is hard to pinpoint the moment when grief subsides and life emerges: sometimes the transition comes quietly over time; sometimes it can feel like a dramatic shift. For Brigitte, in the months that followed, she found herself actively choosing to do positive things, which showed me she was ready to invest in life again. And when Brigitte missed three sessions in a row, due to work and other commitments, I realized she was really functioning better, able to hold her mother's love warmly within her, talking to her, asking her questions, while still actively engaging with the world without. Towards the end of one session we did a lovely visualization in which she could go to a safe place inside herself, be mothered and also feel calm. It enabled her to harness the mother in herself, rather than the grief-crazed child.

After having had a good summer, she came in with a new hairstyle and the news that she was feeling much closer to Tom.

And I felt that we had now done all that Brigitte had needed to do. She had developed an inner core of emotional strength and possessed concrete ideas about how to support herself. We were both at ease about the ending of our relationship. The safe space we had created in the therapy room enabled Brigitte to work through and understand her feelings; now she could create this safe place for herself when her mother's loss ebbed and flowed, as we both knew it would.

Max

Max was twenty-nine years old, but seemed much younger. Although American born, he had been living in the UK for the last twelve years. He'd come over when his father had moved here with his third wife. Max was tall and handsome, with an athletic build, chiselled features and sharp blue eyes. He slouched as if he wanted to make himself smaller, and yet fizzed with energy, having run up the stairs to my room. He had shaved half of his head, and I could see a tattoo crawling up the side of his neck; on the other side of his head, his golden-red hair hung loose.

I realized I was old when I found myself wanting to tidy him up and to give him a good 'clean cut'. He brought the mother in me to the fore, but I needed to remain his therapist. He was a musician who deejayed to pay the bills and occasionally got gigs playing guitar.

It was the break-up with his girlfriend, Mina, that had brought Max to me. It sounded like a horribly destructive relationship. I had no doubt he'd played his part in its demise; but, as I sat listening, I was shocked by the level of dysfunction. I wondered why on earth he had stayed with her. It had started three years previously and been full of love and excitement. But after the first dazzling months were over, it had become toxic and manipulative. Max would make a bid for Mina's affection and she would freeze him out. Then, when he least expected it, she'd seduce him, but refuse to kiss him, wanting hard, rough sex. He felt that she was controlling him through sex. He was constantly trying to work out how to get her to be as loving as she had been at the beginning. He rehearsed conversations with her in his mind over and over, and would get glimmers of hope that would hook him back in, followed immediately by harsh rejection.

One day Max had sneaked a look at her phone and discovered she was paying to have sex with strangers. He logged into her webcam account and asked for the same service, telling me, 'I got off on it.' He never told her that he knew about this. He began to check her emails obsessively in an addictive cycle from which he couldn't free himself. When I asked him if the relationship felt abusive to him, the question didn't seem to make sense to him. He looked directly at me quite innocently, as if to say, 'What do you mean? It's fun.' Even as he was telling me that she had dumped him for another man, he was still fantasizing about how to get her back. He wanted to have a baby with her. He knew that, on one level, she only did him harm, but, on another, was deluding himself that if he could only win her back, all his problems would be over. I was upfront with him and didn't mince my words: the relationship was one of self-harm and addiction. His actions fit the behaviour pattern of an addict: nothing was ever enough; carrying on knowing full well it was bad for him, but unable to stop; thinking that if he could only find the magic words to seduce her, all would be well. He nodded thoughtfully as he left, but I knew he was plotting how to get her back before the door had closed behind him.

The roots of Max's behaviour became clear when I heard about the death of his mother. They had been living in Colombia; he'd been four and a half, his sisters six and nine. Burglars had raided their house and his father chased them out. Their mother had followed and, as she bent down to pick up a dropped object, the burglars had turned and shot her straight through the heart. Max had no memory of this; in fact, he had no real memories of his mother at all. He told me he felt an intense jealousy of his siblings – it was unfair they could remember her and he could not. 'I'd do anything . . . I just want to have lunch with her. One lunch. That's all, a lunch. Have a pint . . . but, um, I don't know what she'd like to drink or eat. Maybe she'd like wine.' It was heartbreakingly poignant that he wanted something as small as that, the sort of thing most grown sons take for granted. For Max, it would have been like the world's riches.

Life after this tragic event was turbulent and fragmented. Their father married again the following year, bringing a stepdaughter into the family. He divorced a few years later, and their family no longer had contact with their stepmother. His third marriage was to an English woman, and she held the purse strings. They'd had two children, half-brothers whom Max loved and hated in equal measure. He absolutely loathed his stepmother. Neither he nor his elder sisters had been made welcome in her home. When she turned his bedroom into a guest room, it had been the final straw in a litany of insults.

Max's father loved him but was chaotic and inconsistent. He sounded like the kind of charismatic man whom people are fond of because of his charm, but whose weakness causes real damage to those around him. Although the death of Max's mother was unusually violent, his father's behaviour afterwards was all too usual: embarking on new marriages, constantly moving from place to place and maintaining a distance from his son. This lack of security had fomented Max's addictive yearning for someone to love; and Max had chosen the one person who was least likely to give him what he craved.

I asked Max what he wanted from his work with me. He didn't really know, 'Maybe to feel better?' He wanted me to tell him what he needed; it felt as if he thought I could provide him with a guidebook for living. I realized his 'not knowing' was similar to the kind of shame I feel when I get lost in my car because I can't read the map, a shame at my incompetence. I could feel myself being drawn to sit him down, get bossy and tell him how to 'pull his life together'. For a start that would mean no longer sending long desperate emails to his ex-girlfriend – he was to have no contact with her whatsoever. It really seemed to me like he didn't know how to care for himself, with no knowledge of what was right or wrong, and no foundations for decision-making. He seemed intent on exclusively seeking pleasure and he would scoot away from anything uncomfortable, laughingly saying, 'That feels horrible.' It soon became clear that what I actually needed to offer was the support for Max to feel safe and the therapy that would allow him to develop his own resources.

A few weeks later, he came in saying, 'Wouldn't it be awful if I got killed on my way in to see you?' He'd cycled without a helmet, weaving madly in and out of cars, and very nearly had an accident. He recognized that he was constantly taking risks with himself: 'I'm a chancer. I'm a total chancer.' And he relayed to me a catalogue of serious car accidents and near-misses that sounded alarmingly dangerous.

With a mixture of relief and fear, I told Max that I was both worried and annoyed. I wondered if he was testing himself in some way, but his only response was to laugh and say, 'I'm an idiot.' Then he said, 'I need someone to watch over me.' Catching his deeper meaning, neither of us said anything for a moment, and then he said he could sense his mother within him and still felt the sadness of losing her sharply. I wondered to myself whether it was okay if I were the substitute version of her for a while.

The best way of helping Max seemed to be finding out what was going on underneath his busy mind and obsessive behaviours. I suggested we do a visualization. Max closed his eyes and saw himself 'in a grey limbo, very alone, despairing'. When I asked him what he might need to be safe there, he said he couldn't imagine a real, happy place. A few moments later, tears running down his cheeks, he made a first step towards creating a 'safe place' by imagining a stage-set meadow with a stream and a bridge. I asked him to breathe, to stay with his feelings – they seemed to move through his body, peaked and softened. He told me he saw an image of his mother, surprisingly real, chatting to her friends. He couldn't get close, but he whispered 'Hey' to her. I was deeply touched by that 'hey'; its poignancy stayed in my mind for a long time afterwards. It encapsulated his life's longing and her absence in a single syllable.

Max was always on time and always got the date right, interestingly responsible for someone who was so disorganized. He would bound up the stairs, full of energy, and wrap himself around the chair, sliding about, laughing, seductive and playful. We realized quite early on that every action Max took was motivated by instant gratification, but the result was often long-term failure. I was reminded of a quotation by Annie Dillard – 'How we spend our days is, of course, how we spend our lives' – and asked Max, 'How do you spend your day?' Typically he would awaken late and faff about: 'I'm a big faffer. I faff all day long basically. I feel faffy inside.' Before he knew it, it would be night-time and, having accomplished nothing, he could only hope that tomorrow would be more productive than today had been. Any offer of fun would illicit an instant 'yes'. Some nights he deejayed, but his dream was to be a musician and he wasn't composing.

Max's feelings would erupt in fragments. He would say, 'I could start crying right now because I realize everything I tell myself to do, I don't do; there's a huge gap, and I don't know what the fuck to do about it. Now I feel horrendous', he'd laugh and then pull up his jersey over his face, as if he were trying to hide from me. I asked him, 'If you weren't laughing, what would you be doing?' He froze. 'Crying.' It had gradually become clear how hard he had worked all his life to stop feeling sad, and to stop his father from feeling sad.

Max was still emailing Mina. We spoke about how difficult it was for him to believe the relationship had ended. I quietly said, 'Accepting the reality, as opposed to the dream, may be the hardest part of grieving in this case,' and we linked that to his mother, whose death he had also been unable to accept.

As Max spoke, he understood that pain was his only conduit to his mother, and that when he wasn't feeling it, it was as if he had abandoned her. He told me tearfully it was bad enough that his mother had been killed; she didn't deserve to be abandoned by him as well. And he also understood, at a deeper level, that from the time of her death he had taken on the role of making everyone happy by being funny and chirpy. Being the family fixer had been such hard work for so long that it had cost him the connection to his own identity in the process.

The following week Max was full of joy. 'Last week, after

we talked about not being able to do things and abandoning Mom, I went home and I wrote pages, and it was a real shift, it was really, really odd for days afterwards. I suddenly started to feel that "not feeling good enough" isn't where I am now, and, actually, why the hell would I be worse at doing something than somebody else? It's made me feel very "can do".' The session had released his energy and he felt fantastic.

Despite that shift of understanding, over the next weeks he felt overwhelmed by a huge anxiety that swamped every other feeling; he wasn't sleeping, and for the first time was worried about money and about the future; he had an image of being alone, struggling with no money for the rest of his life. He had supper at a friend's home – there was a fire in the fireplace, kids eating a roast-chicken dinner – and it seemed both ordinary and special at the same time. He texted me a few days later: 'It's all about love.' He realized that was what he wanted: a family, a proper life. But now it felt inconceivable that he could build such a life.

Max's tension grew and grew, because everything that he did was guaranteed not to get him what he wanted. He was neither getting nor giving love, and it was nowhere in sight. He could not stop contacting Mina, and he was sleeping with people he didn't like. Most of his days were unconstructive: he got nothing done, and he could barely live off the small amount he got from gigs. Music was his best soother; he had a playlist of particular songs that could reconnect and restore him to himself. When he could get himself to write music, or even to listen to it, he felt calmer. But sometimes music had the opposite effect: 'You know what it's like when you start to love something so much you start to hate it?' Some structure to his days helped to steady the inner turbulence ignited by the reawakening of the loss of his mother, and that was where our work centred.

I asked Max to bring in photographs of her. He brought me a very glamorous image of his mother standing under a tree and stroked it with his thumb as he spoke about her. He was trying to find her inside himself, but he could find only the space where she was missing – 'the empty mother-shaped space in my heart'. He came to realize all his behaviours had been attempts to fill that space: 'I'll chuck anything at it: sex, drugs, fun, parties, I just want to fill the fucking thing up.' With all these things swirling around in that inner vortex inside him, it was no wonder he struggled to focus. And, true to form, just as he was describing how huge the loss was, he laughed, made a dismissive comment and managed to scurry away from himself. I told him I'd noticed him doing this. But it wasn't up to me to try to pull him back. This protective pattern was twenty-five years in the making, and it was not my place to rip it away prematurely, though I hoped that was the direction in which we were heading.

From the beginning Max had said he was a good researcher. He went on a Sherlock Holmes mission to try to get as much information as possible about his mother. He had a frustrating conversation about her with his father, who couldn't really fill in any of the gaps, although he did remind Max that the man who'd killed his mother had never been caught, which sent Max spinning out of control for a few days. All this was only too familiar to Max: he loved his dad and knew he wasn't a bad man, but he couldn't help but feel angry at his passivity and detachment. I wanted to give his dad a good sharp shove.

Although he was jealous of his sisters' memories, talking to them about their mother helped him to gain a better sense of what she'd been like. They told him the stories they remembered: going on picnics, singing an 'I love you' song to each of them every night. When they went out shopping or walking together, they remembered him safely tucked up in a carrier on her back. As he gathered more memories, he'd be joyous, thrilled by the discovery of more and more pieces of the jigsaw. But then he would fail to follow up leads to his mother's friends and family. He couldn't finish a task. Max never stopped looking and searching, but he couldn't derive the satisfaction of completion from what he found; he was hooked on the hunt.

The pain of grieving his mother began to emerge slowly and became very intense for him. He described a 'cataclysmic few days, I've never felt anything like it before, lower than I've ever been in my life. I couldn't see any light in my life again, totally bleak. I felt frantic and dead.' There was a kind of liberation in allowing himself to feel this low, grinding right down to the bottom. But he did find himself doing something he didn't usually do: speaking to his friends. Normally he was a closed book – he neither sought confidences nor received them – but, to his surprise, his friends couldn't have been more helpful. Then he went through phases of being on the verge of tears and actually in tears, which he hated, but then came to like, as they offered him a kind of release.

He told me: 'It's so familiar, the discomfort and running, and always feeling separate, and out of the loop and running, that's my go-to resting state. Which is shit.' I wondered if we could find a safe place inside him, where he wouldn't need anyone else. Our best route to achieving this with Max was through visualization. He described an image of his heart 'battered and pulped'; then, to the surprise of us both, he said he could visualize it healing, regrowing, becoming 'plump and pink again'. 'It's very small, not the heart of a 29-year-old, it's very young.' I wondered if it was perhaps the heart of the four-year-old he'd been when his mother died. He wanted to keep it safe, let it grow. But the nub of his problem was that he needed another person for it to grow with; it couldn't grow alone. He couldn't visualize who that could be; there was no one there. I offered myself, but it didn't work: he could feel himself resist lots of people who came to mind. He couldn't trust anyone, so he had to create someone inside of himself. Then he discovered he could find his mum in a 'spirity way' and that worked. Because she had already gone, she couldn't leave him again. This was an image he was going to work with on his own, and it was incredibly powerful for him.

In the weeks that followed, Max gained in strength, and he finally came to see how much Mina was damaging him. 'I had a little epiphany cycling, which often happens when I cycle. I create consciously and unconsciously situations where I'll get hurt. She hurts me, and hurt takes me straight to that Mom place.' It was as if someone had flicked a switch in him, and he was able to stop seeing her. It took time for him to reconfigure the space his lack of 'seeking what I can't find' left in him. He felt released, and he wanted to find a new girlfriend, but decided he would give himself time – a first in itself.

Max started to focus his energy on his work. He had a new determination: less 'faff' and more resolve. We came up with a plan: he'd work during five fifty-minute slots each day, with ten-minute breaks for treats in between, and a bigger treat at the end of the day. The treats varied from having a delicious coffee and doing the crossword, to watching sport and downloading a new track. That the fifty minutes were an echo of the therapeutic hour was clocked by us both. The plan worked: he worked regularly and felt steadier, all without losing his lightness of touch, the sunniness that made him so likable.

We knew that, for now, our work was done, and the ending of the sessions had a bitter-sweetness to it — a sadness yet also a pride in what had been accomplished. Max's parting words said it all: 'What I couldn't do was to find something to fill the mom-sized hole. Relationships, women, drugs, playing — nothing could fill the hole, because they weren't, and would never, be what I wanted them to be. Now, rather than continually kicking around looking for something, I've got hold of Mom, and I've put her in me; she sort of feels like she's in there. I sometimes say: "Okay, Mom," time to help now, and I do use the fact that she's in there. I don't feel I'm looking for her at all any more . . . I feel much more sort of valid as a human being and less like I have to make an effort — that I'm all right just as me.'

He was more than all right just as him.

Cheryl

Cheryl had no pleasure in life – neither in her marriage nor in her work. Her mother had died two years previously of heart disease, but she hadn't joined the dots between how she was feeling and her mother's death. I asked her what she hoped to gain by coming to see me. 'I want to feel better,' she said. 'I feel like I'm living in a grey capsule.' I was aware of our similarities and our differences as she sat opposite me: a black, 55-year-old, well-spoken, well-dressed woman. Would I be able to reach across and connect to her? What lay beneath her greyness? She described this greyness as 'a non-reflective hard mirror, or like a tumour. It's where all the bad in me lives. I can't stand it. I want to get rid of it.'

I asked her what in particular had brought her to see me now. Part of the difficulty was that she found herself being angry in her job. As a senior sister on a paediatric ward she needed to be patient, and she could feel that her temper was becoming harder to keep in check. The day before she rang me, she'd had a dreadful experience with a child called Teddy, who'd screamed 'NO' repeatedly while she'd tried to give him an injection. She'd wanted to pick him up and shake him, and had only just managed to get herself out of the ward in time. It was the signal to herself that she needed to change something, to do something different. When she'd spoken to her husband, Jason, he'd suggested she see a counsellor.

Cheryl's vulnerability was concealed by a brittleness that

could trigger a short, sharp attack. I tried to imagine what it had been like living in that grey capsule for so long and saw how hard it would be for anyone to get through to her. It's one of nature's design flaws, and feels cruel, that often when we are in pain, we give off messages that say 'back off', or we get angry and reject those around us, which just produces the opposite response to what we actually want, and most profoundly need: to be loved.

I asked Cheryl to tell me more about her grey capsule. 'I don't know, I wake up and feel so black. I have to force myself out of bed, the day looms so long in front of me. I have to just talk myself into each bit, tell myself to get dressed, to wash, to eat breakfast, because if I looked too far ahead I wouldn't get out of bed. Look [she showed me a list], I have to write it down, "Get up . . . get dressed . . ." The only thing that gets me to work is learning poetry. I got the idea from a magazine, and I sit and learn a few verses every morning on the tube. It's the only way I can distract myself enough to get to work.' It was obvious how bleak her days were. But she had also shown me that she had an instinctive fight to keep going, and a capacity for discipline that would serve her well. The poetry reminded me of a Nietzsche quote: 'Art takes an ice pick to the heart.' I needed to find out more about the grey capsule. But, first, I needed to know who else was in her life.

Cheryl told me about the people she cared about, those closest to her who helped her get through its twists and turns. She had her husband, Jason, and her best friend, Donna. She hadn't repeated her mother's mistake of choosing a violent and unpredictable man; Cheryl hadn't seen her father since she was six years old, when the family had fled from him. It was a conscious and smart decision; Cheryl was an emotionally intelligent woman, who'd made good choices for herself. Jason's personality type was the opposite of her father's: he was quiet and kind and very level-headed; he didn't offer excitement, but she'd seen how 'exciting' could go wrong, and his presence was a centring one. Jason was genuinely interested in Cheryl: when he asked her about her day, he actually wanted to hear what she had to say. He shared in their domestic chores, and was a much better cook than she was, she told me with a sweet smile, 'humming as he made the supper'. She loved him for his stability. 'He's the best hugger in the world. I'm not really the hugging type, but he takes hold of me with such force that he gives me strength.'

Cheryl had met her best friend, Donna, at school. She was very unlike Cheryl: bubbly, chatty, an extrovert. They laughed together and met most weekends. Having only brothers for siblings, Cheryl thought of Donna as the sister she'd never had. Their friendship was built on memories of painting their nails, aged four, giggling about their first kiss as teenagers, going into adulthood, marrying. Donna could tease her, and tell her truths no one else could. Donna had loved Cheryl's mum too: she'd been a big part of her life. She had cried at Cheryl's mother's funeral, and became emotional when Cheryl talked about her. But after her mother's death, there was a lot Cheryl hadn't talked about – not because she wouldn't but because she hadn't known how.

I learned from Cheryl that her relationship with her mother had been a dutiful one. 'We were a kind of show family that looked good from the outside, but with only occasional proper loving on the inside.' Since their abusive father had left when Cheryl was six, she had had no contact with him whatsoever, and possessed almost no memories of his presence. Her mother was a churchgoer, ambitious for her three children, urging them to work hard at school. 'She died quite sad. She was "old school", and had that proud air about her all her life, but she died with stuff on her chest. When she was on your side, it was love, fighting love. It's easy to forget now, but my mum had this view when she got to England, at eighteen, that it was the "Mother Country". She had great respect for it, but when she got here there was a lot of prejudice. She was so young when she married "the beast", as she called him, but she wouldn't talk about her problems; she'd say, "I don't like people in my business," and she'd just get on with things.'

Cheryl was quietly angry most of the time, and she rarely looked me in the eye. I told her about the dual messages I was receiving from her – 'Take care of me' and 'Back right off' – and about my sense that she was pushing and pulling with me, and then she shut right down. In as understanding a voice as I could manage, I let her know that talking about our relationship might be scary, that I wouldn't push her to do it; at the same time, if she were honest with me, I wouldn't attack her. She looked up at me, and just for a moment we connected: the first foundation stone of our relationship. But over the weeks that followed she never really moved beyond this pattern, talking at length about her work but not much else. I was aware that I was seeing a 'show Cheryl' who mirrored the 'show family' she'd told me about previously. Occasionally, however, there were revelations of what lay beneath her protective mask.

Gradually, I gained glimpses into her family history. When they had run away from her father, her elder brother had gone into care for six months, because the accommodation her mum had found wasn't large enough for all of them.

But her mother had worked hard in a biscuit factory and, after she'd saved enough money to move, her brother joined them. It had been a tough environment for her mum – who had suffered herself in childhood because she had not been brought up by her own mother. I was beginning to gain an insight into the causes of her mother's toughness, which had been a necessary survival mechanism. In our sessions together we recognized that Cheryl loved and respected the mother she'd had, but also grieved the mother she would have preferred: a more loving, sensitive one.

Cheryl had fought with her brothers over their mother's funeral. They had chosen their own readings and rejected hers, which, at the time, had felt like 'the be all and end all, but it's okay now'. Despite the conflict, 'We're okay, we get on well enough.' Their mum had told them, 'I want to go into fire, nobody's going to dig up my bones,' and they had honoured her wishes.

Sometimes Cheryl would break out of her capsule with nuggets of vitality, particularly when she talked about her fourteen-year-old son, Jackson. Then she would smile into my eyes, and I could feel my chest expanding with her love for him. Like most mothers, she'd found it very difficult to witness his sadness about his grandmother; it had felt 'intolerable' to her. She had instinctively felt the need to shut down his sadness, to tell him 'to be okay', just as her mother had told her. We acknowledged that this maternal instinct to soothe is often 'hard wired' into mothers, yet its negative underbelly is the suppression of difficult feelings in their children.

Cheryl was obsessed by the events that took place from the time of her mother's first heart attack to her death. When she said, 'I feel I should have done more,' her words came

with great sighs from deep within her chest. She had a tight-
ness in her throat 'like a block of stone'. As layer upon layer
of anxiety about her failings was peeled back, a burning fury
emerged to attack her. She went over every treatment and
appointment in forensic detail, particularly those she had
missed. As a nurse, she'd felt she should know more, but,
as a paediatric nurse, she actually knew very little about
coronary disease in adults. And she had never spoken to her
mother about dying, for fear 'it would bring bad karma',
superstitiously believing that mentioning the 'dead' word
would waken from their sleep the Bad Gods, who would
then visit death on her mother. They had talked about future
holidays, Christmas plans, never once even mentioning the
possibility that her mother might die.

Cheryl would increasingly say things that showed a growing awareness of her new reality. I was beginning to see more
of her, and beginning to see the strength that had been sup-
pressed by her silent fury. Unable to visualize Cheryl's
mother or to picture them together, I asked her to bring in
photographs or anything that would give me a clearer image.
She arrived laden with a whole backpack of family material:
sweet photographs of her and her siblings as children, her
mother's favourite brooch and her mother's scarf. It lay innocently on her lap, while she told me family stories of holidays
in Jamaica with her powerful grandmother. I could feel her
pride in her mother growing as she described the life from
which she'd come, the opportunities her mother had worked
so hard to give her. Her eyes glistened as she spoke.

Unconsciously she picked up the scarf and smelled it: she
was completely overwhelmed. Tears poured down her face.
She buried her face in the scarf, repeatedly smelling it and
crying and wiping her tears in a rhythmic movement every

few minutes. Like a Proustian madeleine cake, the smell of her mother's perfume had thrown her back in time to the days when she sat in her mother's lap, singing songs, burying her head in her chest. Our first sense is the smell of our mother, before we can focus and see her clearly; and some believe it is the last sense we have before we die.

From this point our work unfolded more easily and remarkably quickly. Altogether, I saw her for only six sessions, but they were enough: it was as if she had been waiting to be unlocked. She had rediscovered the mother who had loved her as best she could. 'I thought if I blocked her love it would block the pain . . . it's stopped me living . . . The dark side I'm well acquainted with, whereas this, feeling happy, is like a new friend. It's as if I'm breathing oxygen for the first time in ages, pure oxygen that isn't contaminated with something else. I'm finding the me I'd lost for ages.'

Cheryl was much more extraordinary than either of us had at first realized. When she laughed the sun came out, a deep, shiny, vibrant laugh. She connected to herself both as a child and as a mother. I hugged her and, as we both cried, I felt as if I were also crying for all the daughters who had tried to do their best and somehow failed.

Reflections

Usually the first faces our eyes lock on to when we're born are those of our parents. The first hands to hold us are theirs. Every relationship we have is, in some way, related to the foundations that began with our parents. During our childhood they create the environment that shapes us and fires up our natural predisposition towards good or ill. Their psychological make-up, their beliefs, their attitudes, their behaviours, their presence and their absence – we soak up all of this like a sponge.

When a parent dies, we are inevitably affected by it, and the intensity of what we feel will depend on the relationship we experienced. As with Brigitte, we may feel that the person who loved us most in the world has died, leaving us utterly devastated. Or we may be relieved that it is the end of a relationship that has always been disappointing or hurtful. We may have complex feelings of love and hate, relief and guilt. Undoubtedly it puts us in touch with our own mortality, because we are the next in line to die.

The people about whom I've written are widely different from one another, which demonstrates that people's responses to death will be as varied as their personalities. I chose Cheryl and Brigitte because their stories will, I hope, be easily recognizable to grieving adult children; and because their examples may reassure people that what they are going through is not, in fact, abnormal, but only the natural and universal experience of grieving.

I chose Max because I was fascinated by how extraordinarily powerful the influence of his dead mother was in him, even though he had known her only as a small child. His story illustrates how much attention we must pay to bereaved children, to ensure they don't suffer for the rest of their lives. Many adults mistakenly believe protection is better than truth for a child – the reverse is true.

Both Brigitte and Cheryl had secure family lives that they could rely on, although they took a bit of a knocking through their bereavements, and I believe this was the most important factor in their recovery. Most people deeply desire to be in a relationship, to have meaning in their lives and to have a certain amount of autonomy – desires that were pretty well met for Cheryl and Brigitte. Their families were the extra ballast that they needed to endure the pain of their grief.

Max's rackety upbringing meant he didn't know how to be in an 'ordinary' loving relationship, nor did he have an internal place of safety to retreat to outside of our sessions. His jobs, his habits, his associations – everything lacked consistency, and in the consequent chaos it was much harder for him to withstand his pain. His attempts to find his mother within himself may sound too much like something that happens only in therapy, but the creative use of dreams and magical thinking has long permeated our culture as well as all the cultures of the world. Paul McCartney, who was fourteen when his mother, Mary, died, was inspired to write 'Let It Be' after he saw her in a dream (the lyrics addressed to 'Mother Mary' are a literal, rather than a biblical, reference).

When Brigitte put socks on her mother's feet, fearing they would be cold, she demonstrated what most people feel after someone they love has died – which is that they are in some way still alive. Although the bereaved know this isn't actually the case, they nonetheless act as if it were – for example, Brigitte chose her mother's favourite cake for the wake, knowing full well her mother wouldn't be there to eat it. Pathologists, coroners and doctors need to be more aware of the sensitivities of the bereaved in this regard and temper their words and actions accordingly.

Grieving by adult children

Contemporary research shows that the grief adult children commonly experience includes withdrawal from friends, losing interest in previously enjoyable activities, expressing anger or feelings of guilt, and sleep disturbances. Reactions such as crying, missing their parent and being preoccupied with thoughts of them can continue for long periods of time following the death, and these are completely normal.

Anticipatory death

Research shows the 'type' of death has an impact on the grief reaction that an adult child experiences. For some, enduring long periods of time in anticipation of the death, without having the opportunity to address the emotions or issues that arise in connection with their parent, can heighten their anxiety.

For others, an anticipated death may be seen as a more natural and less stigmatized way of dying, potentially making the grieving process slightly easier. Also, anticipating the death of a parent can give adult children time to prepare themselves, enabling them to draw on their psychological resources. Coping can be less painful when the crucial chance to say goodbye is not denied.

Sudden death

Sudden death can lead adult children to feel the death is unfair and magnify the sense of powerlessness that is part of most people's grief. Research shows that those who are suffering in this way may believe they aren't coping well, while what they are experiencing is perfectly normal.

The difference between mothers and fathers dying

Some very interesting research showed that adult children may have a better relationship with their mothers than with their fathers, as a result of shared views, greater emotional closeness and the greater stability the mother provides. This would suggest, then, that the loss of a mother would have a more profound effect on the adult daughter than the death of a father.

However, research has found that the death of a father may have an increased impact on sons, with studies demonstrating increased depressive symptoms and decreased psychological well-being in sons compared with daughters. Although the study found both sons and daughters reported lower psychological well-being, daughters were also found to engage in behaviours such as binge drinking and have lower self-esteem.

The sense I make of this research is that the parent we identify most closely with will have the greater impact on our feelings of loss. I wonder about the report of daughters' binge drinking – whether they are beginning to take on some of the more typical 'male' behaviours.

Both mother and father dying within five years of each other

In the case of both parents dying within a five-year period, research has shown this to have a similar effect on both sons and daughters. Each gender reported lower self-esteem and lower psychological well-being. Daughters exhibited greater depressive symptoms, and sons reported decreased overall health. It is common sense that grieving the death of two parents in a relatively short time would intensify the feelings of loss: a new death will always summon up the previous one, regardless of how effectively that first loss was grieved.

Death of a parent and existing relationships

We all know that when we are suffering, it is the people closest to us who are forced to suffer with us. Research evidences this: there are more numerous incidences of spousal abuse, drunkenness and extramarital affairs, as well as sibling conflict, following the death of a parent.

Saying goodbye

Brigitte and Max never had the opportunity to say goodbye to their parent, and Cheryl was unable to fully make use of the time she'd had with her mother. I don't believe in the concept

of 'closure' – the idea that there can be a complete and finite
end when someone dies – because I don't think we are as
mechanical as that idea implies; but having had the opportunity to say everything that we need to say to our parent is a
vital comfort before and after their death. Taking photographs
together, recording their voice, creating positive memories –
all these things become terribly precious after they've died. In
my experience, clients who sometimes feel guilty because
they recover quite quickly following a death usually did most
of their grieving while their parent was dying.

Anger

Anger is one of the well-recognized responses to death. It was
clearly felt by Brigitte, and bubbled just beneath the surface in
Max and Cheryl. My understanding of anger is that it is a
primitive expression of hurt, like 'Ouch, you're hurting me,
STOP hurting me.' The key question is how best to express it
without causing harm to oneself or to those around us.

Research shows that repressing anger can lead to depression. But, while venting it can feel satisfying and empowering,
this only leads to greater anger; it doesn't provide a release.
Anger in grief isn't the same as 'stuck in traffic anger' or 'you
can't say that to me' anger. It can be very pervasive and get
in the way of everything else, to the detriment of positive
feelings. According to research, men tend to vent anger,
which can lead to violence, and women tend to suppress it,
which can lead to depression.

When I work with clients who are angry, I help them to
manage it by suggesting they take constructive action on
what provokes the anger whenever possible – which means

assertively explaining what you are angry about, not raging. Or, if you can't voice it, writing down your feelings in a journal, to stop the debilitating feeling that the anger is running you, rather than the other way round.

When no constructive action is possible, anger can be healthily discharged from the body in three ways:

- First, exercise. I often suggest competitive sport if someone is opting for this route, because that can be more satisfying than other forms of sport in releasing pent-up anger. But others often choose to run or cycle, and they find it helps.
- Second, laughter. This is a tough one to bring off when you're grieving, but it is restorative. Laughter is incompatible with anger: it stops the ruminating that fuels the rage.
- Third, calming techniques such as meditation and breathing exercises.

A package of techniques can work well if practised regularly. The following takes about an hour to complete:

- ten minutes writing in a journal about everything that's swirling around inside you
- twenty minutes running
- ten minutes meditating
- twenty minutes watching or reading something funny

Family systems

I've often seen whole family systems shaken up when someone dies. Brigitte's husband and daughter, for example, wanted things to remain the same, but with the death of a significant family member that isn't possible. Family myths and roles can often be called into question and existing family struggles intensified.

Family systems that are 'closed' don't have open, honest communication within them. There is less trust and taboo subjects can't be tackled for fear of reprisal. Max's family was clearly a closed system, and these can lead to more difficulties after a death than an 'open system'.

In an 'open' system, there is trust and therefore better communication. Each member of the family can ask questions without fear of a fight or being criticized – for instance, financial matters can be discussed, as can the circumstances of a death or how they feel about it. Secrets aren't hidden around every corner, and the transition to the new reality that invariably follows a death can be weathered without the whole system fragmenting or imploding.

Supporting bereaved children

This section broadly outlines the needs of a child whose parent has died, but the principles can be applied to all deaths, whether it be a grandparent, sibling or friend.

As our understanding of children's mental health has grown, so has our concern for responding effectively to bereaved children. The common response is 'Children are amazing; they bounce back', and we now know that they can be resilient. However, they are like adults in that their resilience cannot grow without support.

The child's age and developmental stage determine the context for their understanding of death and dying. To very young children, death is an abstract concept and they don't understand it to be permanent, while primary schoolchildren do grasp the irreversibility of it, and teenagers often find it complicates the struggles of adolescence that they're already grappling with.

Telling the truth

All the parents I have worked with, understandably, want to protect their children from suffering. It seems intuitively wrong to tell them the truth, whether it's information that their parent is dying or, for example, details relating to the funeral. It feels too sad and scary, but research shows that children experience that protection as an exclusion.

As a result, when those children grow up, they may well be carrying around resentment towards their surviving parent.

The message that I want to present consistently throughout this book is that *children need to be given as much information as adults, and it should be conveyed in age-appropriate and concrete language*. What they don't know, they tend to make up, and what they make up can be much worse than the truth, for their imaginations can be haunting and limitless. The truth, however difficult it may be, is better than a lie, and will mean that the child can trust their parent. It is important to remember that children absorb information from their environment: they may hear conversations or, worse, half hear them, and they will be alert to the distress in the adults around them. Having concrete knowledge that explains what they're observing, being able to understand the how and the why, is central to their well-being.

Research has shown that mothers are often able to give loving, attuned attention to their child following the death of their partner, and we should be aware that surviving fathers may need extra support.

Young children

I've found very young children in particular are often shielded from the ongoing events surrounding a death; I'm usually told: 'What they don't know, they won't miss.' Both my experience and published research refute this. Children of a very young age are likely to pick up on the distress in the body of their surviving parent, and be disturbed by it. In the wake of a death, very young children may be deprived of a single, consistent carer and shunted from pillar to post by different ones, which is also disturbing for them. Children divested of such memories experience their absence as a damaging block when they reach adulthood. Unless a full, rich image of the dead parent's identity is created, the child will suffer from such a void; the surviving parent needs to build up a picture of the dead parent through stories and mementos, to act as a valuable resource that the child can revisit for the rest of their life.

Explaining that someone has died

Giving children bad news is extremely difficult, and parents may feel 'bad' doing it, but it's important not to conflate the feeling with the facts. Ask another family member or close friend to be there to support you, should you sometimes struggle to find the words. Find a quiet room and be physically close to the child. It is helpful to signal that you are going to tell them bad news by saying, 'I have sad news to tell you . . .' Then say the news as simply and as directly as possible: 'Daddy died this morning . . .' With young children, explain what 'died' means: 'When somebody dies, their body stops working. Their heart does not work any more and they cannot move, their body will be quiet and still. A dead body cannot feel any pain.' It may be that you'll need to tell the full story gradually, over time – for example, a child may be told that their father has died, but the circumstances of the death could come later. Follow the child's lead: if they do want to know more, give them the truth, but be careful not to overload them with information all at once. Check the child's understanding, and allow them time to take it all in. Let them ask questions; and, if they should ask the same question repeatedly, it is best to repeat the same answer – as with adults, it isn't necessarily that they haven't understood (although it can be), but rather that it takes time to assimilate the idea of death, and repetition is sometimes required.

Seeing the body

Many of us are understandably frightened of seeing the dead body of someone we love, and we may strongly feel that this will also be true of children. Yet we need a memory upon which we can focus that enables us to know, in a way that is irrefutable, that the person has died and is not returning. Seeing the dead body can be a way to help a child face that reality, and to begin to make sense of what has happened. There are no rules, except that a child shouldn't be forced to do something they don't want to do. Raise the subject openly, answer questions honestly and emphasize that the child can change their mind at any point. The parent should see the body first, so that they can judge whether it is appropriate for their child to see it; they can then prepare their child as to what their mother or father looks like, what the room is like, who will be there and what is likely to happen. Taking some flowers or cards to leave with the dead parent can be comforting and lets the child feel they've contributed with their own special gift. With gentle support and lots of comfort at the time and afterwards, it is likely to be a significant step in their understanding of the death. It is important to show, rather than tell, the child what might be appropriate in the circumstances – for example, by first touching or kissing the body, you can demonstrate to the child that this is something that they too can do.

Going to the funeral

We may assume that children know what a funeral is and what it is for, but, unless children have been to one previously, they are unlikely to have any real idea about what will occur. Even if very young children go to the funeral and have no memory of it when they're older, they may still be glad to know that they were included; I've never known a child regret having gone. When talking about the funeral to children, first explain its purpose and what is likely to happen. This will be determined by culture and religion but a simple way to describe it that applies universally is: 'When someone dies, we have a special ceremony called a funeral. Because Daddy has died, we're going to have one just for him. Our family and friends will be with us and we'll remember Daddy's life. His body will be in a special box called a coffin – remember, he is dead and he doesn't feel anything any more. At the funeral we will . . . [say what will happen]. At the end of the funeral we'll take his body to the graveyard, where a very deep hole will be dug and Daddy's coffin will be placed inside. This is called a grave. This will have Daddy's name on it, so everyone knows where he is buried.'

What you say about cremation needs to be handled sensitively and will depend on the age of the child, for they may be upset by the idea of their parent's body being burned. It is important to reinforce the fact that dead people can't feel anything. One way of saying it is: 'Daddy's body will be turned into soft powdery ashes at the crematorium. The ashes are then put into a pot called an urn. We are going to put the urn . . .'

Many families have found it helpful to go to the church or cemetery the day before the service to give the child a sense of what it will be like and to help them imagine it, so that they won't be overwhelmed on the actual day. And an audio or video recording of the funeral might prove a valuable resource for the child when they're older.

Children protecting adults

Just as we want to protect children, so they too can be protective of us, not wanting to show that they're distressed. When they switch, often quite quickly, from sadness to joyous play, they may be doing so to conceal their unhappiness. It is helpful for the parent to set apart a special time, such as after tea, when they can check what's really going on inside their child.

Regular routines

The uncertainty that accompanies a parent's death can be very upsetting for children, and our wish to comfort them by allowing behaviours we wouldn't usually accept is completely understandable. The line between comfort and discipline is a hard one to draw, but as a general guide it is best to stick to regular routines, as well as normal discipline, as much as possible. With familiar boundaries and structures in place, the child is more likely to feel safe and secure.

Survival instincts

Research has shown that the children of dying parents have an instinctive drive to survive, and so move towards the living parent and away from their dying one. Their overriding question is 'Who's going to look after me?' They may blurt out questions that may seem a bit callous, as if they care only about themselves and not about the parent who's dying, such as 'If Mummy can't take me to school, who *is* going to take me?' This is their survival mechanism kicking in and is a natural, reflexive response to their situation. It is helpful to actively encourage children to stay close to their sick parent, encouraging them to do small but considerate things like rubbing cream on their hands, or reading stories together, or creating a playlist of favourite songs. This not only enhances the child's self-esteem, but also provides them with a memory of being close to their dying parent, with the result that they are protected from feelings of guilt for having retreated too soon.

Children and adolescents grieving

Caring for a child can be very difficult when the parent is suffering themselves. But the quality of the parenting is the key to the child adapting healthily to their parent's death. According to the research, when a child's environment allows them to express their emotions about the death openly to their caregiver, they suffer fewer depressive and maladaptive grief symptoms. And the sooner the child is given the appropriate support, the better they will be able to adjust; conversely, the later the support, the higher the risk of detrimental effects.

Learning to grieve by observing the adults around them

Children learn to grieve by observing the adults around them. If they see their parent expressing their sadness and then getting on with their tasks, they will know it's possible for them to do that too; equally, if they never see their parent being upset, they are likely to mirror that behaviour, or become confused about their own feelings of sadness and whether they can show these overtly. Adults often feel emotionally young when they are grieving and want to be looked after themselves; finding their own support is essential to their successful parenting of their children.

An image that is used for bereaved adults is that their grief is like wading through a river: unremitting, and each step is hard work. The metaphor commonly used for children's grief is that it is like jumping in and out of puddles. When they are sad they jump in the puddle, and cry, or become withdrawn, or get very cross. Then, once they've been comforted, they jump out of the puddle and happily return to their games.

We must observe children's behaviour to see when they need our support, as their ability to express how they feel in words may be limited (although sometimes astonishingly clear). They may not only be tearful or angry but also regress, sleep badly or lose their appetite. They need to be reassured they are loved and that they will be looked after; and that there is nothing wrong with their responses, no matter what they are – from being upset to being happily at play.

Young adults

Stephen's children were young adults when their mother died, and it is important to note that, however old we are, we can feel very young when our parent dies. It is as important to give young adults support as it is young children, but often their needs are not acknowledged.

Grief over time

Children are likely to grieve for their parent through different phases of life, as their understanding of the concept of death changes with their advancing cognitive development. Significant birthdays or life events will reconnect them to their dead parent, and they will need to rework their loss each time. It is not, as some people perceive it, that the grieving hasn't been done, but rather that grieving is a lifelong process that has different implications for us at different times of our life.

The concepts of death with which younger children struggle

To fully understand the concept of death – that it is permanent, irreversible and universal – a child needs to be about eight years old. Although all children need death explained to them in accurate, age-appropriate language using clear terms, with younger children you can do this and they still won't grasp its permanence. As they grow up, they will begin to understand death differently, and you will need to revise your explanation accordingly.

Most children of late primary school age or approaching their early teens are thought to have the cognitive ability to fully understand the finality of death. This does mean that they also fully understand the enormity of their loss, and therefore they will need good support to help them cope.

Delayed/no reaction to the death of a parent

Some children who experience the death of a parent demonstrate very little upset. Research suggests their expression of grief is actually only delayed, and that they will have a grief-reaction at a later date, with studies showing this can occur as much as two years after the bereavement. In order to protect children against suffering in the way Max did, a parent can (if not too debilitated by their own loss) help to elicit their child's expression of grief in a number of ways, including reading appropriate story books together, or creating memory books and photograph albums; there are also activity packs and books that can be bought from organizations like Child Bereavement UK. If this proves to be too difficult, or doesn't seem to be working, referring the child to the school counsellor or seeking help from a bereavement support organization is advised. Children who intentionally suppress thoughts and feelings related to the death have been found to be at increased risk of developing psychiatric symptoms, so it is important to intervene for the child's own benefit.

When a sibling dies

Unable are the Loved to die
For Love is Immortality

— Emily Dickinson

Ruth

The day Ruth first walked into my room is a vivid memory. Medium height, slim, brown wavy hair, casually dressed, she sat down confidently and with her brown eyes looked at me directly. She wanted to know how I worked, how long each session would last and, most importantly, would I be able to help her. I'm smiling as I remember her, because I found this approach stimulating rather than daunting. There was something refreshingly honest about being faced with a woman who wanted to know if it was worth her time in coming to see me; it set the power dynamic straight away. This wasn't a woman who was going to be grateful for anything she got; Ruth was going to make sure she got what she wanted.

I was very quickly given a huge amount of information. Ruth was forty-six years old, and Jewish. She was coming to see me because her half-brother, Daniel, had died in a car accident three months previously; and she had experienced many pregnancy losses, each one leaving its mark on her. Although her half-brother's death had led her to me, it wasn't where most of her pain lay. Her relationship with him had been ambivalent. He was the secret illegitimate child of her father, and his existence had been made known to the family only a year before her father's death. The central piece of work we had to address first was Ruth's relationship with her father, who had died more than a decade ago, but her grief for him was still untouched and raw – he had left a tangled web of good and bad in her that she needed to unravel.

Towards the end of one early session, I noticed her mood change. As we were discussing the number of sessions available, she began to look frightened; her voice dropped and her words slowed. I saw an expression of vulnerability that hadn't appeared before. In a soft voice I commented that something seemed to be disturbing her, and she was able to tell me that she was worried about 'dropping into a hole' while having to pretend that everything was fine. The idea of the hole was horribly familiar to me, as was the pretence of being fine, and I could tell it scared the hell out of her. I wanted to convey compassionate curiosity to her without pushing too hard. She associated the hole with a specific image: herself as a small child sitting curled up on a rock, shivering. It felt like it was at the bottom of a deep well. She waited for someone to come and find her – but no one came. I knew I would have to sit with her at the bottom of that cold and lonely well. I let her know that I could see her there and asked her what she needed from me: did she want me to stay with her or to lead her out? She was shivering, and her head was right down, tucked into her chest; she couldn't speak for a while. I understood her frozen position and her silence – wanting to find the words, but somehow being unable to force them out. I reassured her there was no hurry: there would be time in this session, or in future sessions, for her response. Her life had been one in which she was continuously pressurized into responding and made to jump by others. Just as we were coming to the end of our time, she whispered, 'Stay with me,' and I said that I would.

Interestingly, in the weeks that followed she couldn't

revisit that wordless hole; she preferred to maintain the articulate version of herself. I gradually learned more of her story. Her father had been a property developer. As a child during the Second World War he had been imprisoned for two years in a concentration camp. He was the only survivor in his family, and had arrived in England at the end of the war. It became clear as Ruth talked that she held in her body some of his traumatic experiences. This transgenerational trauma meant she had no ability to control her anxiety and aggression. She became frightened very easily, felt disaster was never far away. This trauma played out in her life in many ways, but the most damaging was the way she recklessly courted danger, needing to feel the intensity, and also somehow to prove she deserved to be alive. She was unable to trust in life.

Ruth told me that her life had been sustained by four pillars – Zionism, feminism, socialism and Judaism – but that now all four had 'crumbled'. I could feel the passion and commitment she brought to such beliefs, and how Ruth had developed them in order to keep herself intact. She was acutely aware of the desolation that had followed in their wake. I was already familiar with these four pillars, and, while I was aware that they provide a strong intellectual structure and a sense of identity, I also knew from experience that abstract constructs don't necessarily help anyone work through their feelings, which accounted for the loneliness of the cold well in which she often found herself trapped.

Over the weeks that followed, I heard Ruth reel off a series of complex and sometimes disastrous experiences from her past. She had lost her virginity at fifteen, and been raped twice at seventeen. 'I sleep-walked through my thirties dating unavailable men, and then my dad died, and when I looked around all my friends were having babies.' Then followed her half-brother's accidental death. How had she ended up here and how might she change her situation? Every decision was paved with a torturous 'Shall I?', to which Ruth could find no answer.

She would announce a headline for each session when she arrived. One morning she walked in and said, 'It's all about control.' Control was something Ruth wanted very badly, yet eczema defied her attempts to eradicate it. The Jewish mythological figure Lilith, known as the 'night hag', was very powerful in her; 'erupting' when she felt controlled. This archetype had played out in every aspect of Ruth's life, and she was only now beginning to see how it had influenced her: she'd had no trouble finding jobs, friends, boyfriends, but then felt controlled by them, and turned destructively against them. The loss of these relationships had left 'burned-out craters' within her. This sadness was new to me, as previously I'd heard more of the angry narrator, and this softer, less certain side of her drew my tenderness. As she explored these destructive patterns, she began to make sense of them. She recognized that she had been 'over-attached' to her father. But the pressure of constantly having to be a good obedient daughter had brought out the rebel in her.

It was beginning to be clear how thoroughly Ruth had attacked herself. She had deprived herself of all the things she actually wanted – a home, husband and children – and it was as if she had pulled those four pillars down around her head. She would speak of the 'attackers' and the 'psychos in my head' and then laugh. She recognized the polarities in herself – 'all success or all failure, then sliding into gloom' –

and that she was addicted to psychological self-harm. In an attempt to find the underlying, probably unconscious motivation for this, I asked her, 'What's the payoff for you?' Uncharacteristically, Ruth took some time to think about this, and realized it had afforded her a sort of maladaptive protection since she had been very young, 'I had to keep them good, so I had to be bad.' She had turned the way she thought her parents viewed her into how she viewed herself. For example, when her parents shouted at her for breaking a glass, a simple childish accident, she wouldn't feel that the breaking of the glass had been bad, but that she was a bad little girl. Over the weeks and months, Ruth allowed herself to be human, neither wicked nor heroic; vulnerable, yes, flawed, yes, but also a powerful woman who had lifted herself out of a very black well.

The therapy seemed to be working effectively in Ruth's case. I was actively seeking to establish trust, and consciously accepting and valuing whatever Ruth brought into the room. When I was gentle with her, she opened up and let out the pain of her losses, sometimes in great noisy bursts of emotion, at others in swallowed sobs. She told me that in experiencing the pain there was 'a richness that's better than numbness' and said, 'I'm coming alive at last.'

All of this took time. There were periods full of bleakness, when she told terrible, unbearable stories of the Holocaust that haunted me between sessions. I ran and kickboxed them out of my system; I wrote in my journal, and used Mindfulness techniques when I couldn't switch off her story in my head. The headline of one of her sessions was: 'Do you have shoulders broad enough to carry abortion, miscarriage and the Holocaust all at the same time?' I felt my jaw tightening and had to consciously stop clenching my teeth. But I found that I could sit with her and hear how her father's experience of death in a concentration camp had seeped into her like poison, 'murdering the possibility of new life . . . my babies'.

We came to understand that early in her life Ruth had tried to block out the terror and fear that had been transferred to her from her father, in effect numbing herself, but this had cut her off from the parts of herself that informed her of what she needed emotionally, and blocked her ability to have intimate relationships, which had left her feeling dead inside. As she grew into adolescence, she was hungry to feel anything in preference to the nothingness, but the dangerous, reckless choices she made led her to suffer dreadful consequences as a result.

Israeli Research gave me a great deal of information about the secondary transmission of trauma that children of survivors experience: mental health difficulties, increased vulnerability to illness and digestive problems are often common problems. Ruth had taken on her father's survivors' guilt: the abiding sense of shame for being alive when millions of others had perished. The trauma in him was very much alive, despite the decades that had passed, and it was also responsible for his inability to moderate either his anxiety or his anger. For example, her father had jumped up as if he had been shot whenever a door slammed; he was constantly on the alert for an expected threat. Ruth felt her father had placed her in a double bind: on the one hand, he would insist that she go out into the world and succeed, to honour all those he'd loved who had perished; but on the other, he wanted her to stay home, stay close and not leave him.

In one important session she finally began to accept that

she wasn't entirely to blame for her actions and saw, perhaps for the first time, that she could feel compassion for herself and for her father. She was astounded as she realized she didn't have to continue to punish herself or to court danger at every turn.

At her next session, Ruth couldn't believe how differently she felt: lighter, like a weight had been lifted off her chest. She wondered whether she should trust this feeling, but came to the conclusion that she could: she really did feel better. 'My voices have quietened. They whisper now and again, but not loudly.' I asked about these voices in her head and heard she was now able to put them at the back of her mind, so that they no longer interfered when she went about her day.

Over time Ruth's feelings became less intense. She was still dealing with the central themes – her brother's death, her lost pregnancies, her relationship with her father – but now there was movement on these issues. She was able to express more anger with her father, and to be clearer about her own needs. After her father's death she had agreed to manage his rental-property business, but as a career it held no interest for her. After many long discussions with her mother, some of which ended in tantrums on Ruth's part, they agreed to sell the properties. For Ruth this represented a seismic shift: externally it created space and distance between her and her father, and internally it allowed her to trust her judgement and to act upon it. Once this huge problem was no longer hanging over her, she was freed to talk more deeply about the death of her brother, Daniel – about the pain and waste of so much potential, and the fact there would always be things she'd never know.

When Ruth thought about Daniel, her main feeling was

one of desperate sadness. She cried for the future that he would never have, and for the relationship that she would never have with him. She hadn't known him all that well, having only met him a few times, and had no real sense of who he was or what he'd been like. She wondered whether to make contact with his mother, but, as usual for her, coming to any decision was never a straightforward process. She went back and forth, back and forth: would it be disloyal to her mother to meet her father's lover? Finally, she said, 'Daniel didn't do anything wrong; he was a victim from the minute he was born. I want to see his mother for his sake – he's *my* brother.'

After the meeting with Daniel's mother took place, Ruth felt worse, though she was in possession of more facts. Daniel had spent his whole life wishing to be recognized by his father – which never happened. He'd been a clever, sensitive young boy, but his self-esteem was severely impaired by the existence of his 'hidden father', resulting in his being an outsider at school and in most social situations. He grew into a loner. Daniel and his mother had attended Ruth's father's funeral, but sat at the back, completely unacknowledged and unrecognized. Daniel's death in a car crash mirrored his birth: out of the blue, unwanted, an accident.

In the end, Ruth and I agreed that her father's story was complicated, so far as the allotting of blame went; she couldn't simply rail against him when there were so many mitigating circumstances – after all, he too had been a victim. Given what had happened to him, he had done his best to live his life. But he had passed on some of the damage to his children, both legitimate and illegitimate.

At her last session with me, Ruth said, 'Therapy is like

using a magnifying glass: exhausting sometimes, but I've seen all sorts of things I would never have seen otherwise. Although I could do this forever, because it's such a fantastic aid, maybe I should just get out of therapy and let myself live in the world.'

Mussie

When Mussie walked into my room I felt daunted, not frightened that he would hurt me, but frightened I might hurt him, because he was exactly the kind of man I instinctively draw away from, when I'm free to choose. He was dressed in designer clothes, wore a large expensive watch and spoke loudly with a very masculine swagger. Money was at the centre of his value system: how much money he had, how big his flat was, how flash a car he drove. When he paid me, he counted out the fee note by note, which for me had the flavour of being paid like a prostitute.

Large set and of medium height, Mussie was in his mid-twenties. His Iranian father was divorced from his English mother. He smiled a lot, which conflicted with the sadness in his eyes. He had come to me because his younger brother, Hashim, had taken his own life four months previously, having shot himself while visiting their mother on her birthday weekend. It had come completely out of the blue. Hashim, who was three years younger than Mussie, was in his last year of university, and Mussie believed that Hashim had become paranoid as a result of smoking weed, probably skunk, at secondary school and university. Mussie said his brother hadn't taken his life because things were going badly, but because of his addiction to the drugs, which had 'made him mentally ill'.

Hashim had arrived at their mother's house in a terrible state, seeing paranoid images and convinced people were chasing him. Their mother was extremely worried, and the next day had the foresight to take him to A & E for a psychiatric assessment. He was seen by a psychiatrist, who prescribed medication and made a referral for the following week. That evening, as his mother was making supper, Hashim found the key to the gun cupboard (her father had been a keen shot and left the hunting rifle for his grandsons' use), took out the gun and shot himself in their garage.

Beneath the swagger, Mussie was numb with shock. He was seeing terrible images of the shooting, although he hadn't witnessed it. He couldn't begin to understand how his brother had done it; there'd been no warning. Mussie repeatedly went over in his mind the last telephone conversation they'd had: he had been driving his car, a bit distracted, and had said he would ring Hashim back. Four hours later Hashim was dead. Each time he thought about that last call, he wanted a different ending, one in which he persuaded his brother to calm down and stop his suicidal thoughts. Mussie was locked in time, he couldn't look forward: he felt that one shot had shattered his life just as much as it had his brother's. His mother, who was highly anxious anyway, was barely functioning; after hearing the gunshot and finding her son dead, she had been diagnosed with post-traumatic stress disorder. Mussie told me his father, who had become a more devout Muslim in recent years, was ashamed and could only express raging fury.

I was aware that when Hashim killed himself, Mussie felt he had lost not only his brother, but, in a sense, his parents too. His mother had told him, 'I had him in my stomach. You can't compare my loss to yours.' His parents' grief was seen by them to be of a higher order than his, which meant he didn't feel it was legitimate to have his own feelings. He had now taken on the role of acting as a parent to his mother, who spent her days lying in a darkened room. His reactions to her withdrawal were many and contradictory: resentful, protective, loving and furious. His friends would ask him how his mother was, but nobody asked him how he was feeling, which alienated him further.

There was a gap in the connection between us, and I needed to find a way to bridge it. Suicide is disturbing work. In the recent past suicide was deemed to be a sin by the organized religions of the world, and the Christian Churches and Judaism have only recently changed their view; it is still prohibited in Islam. People who had taken their own life were not buried in consecrated ground, and the surviving family were outcasts in society, repudiated and shamed. I was clear that I didn't feel judgemental in that way, I felt intensely sad, compassionate and just so sorry that such a devastating thing had happened. I knew from experience this was going to be a long haul. Survivors of suicide can be filled with a toxic mix of feelings: overwhelming guilt, murderous rage, despair, helplessness, hopelessness, fury, shame, regret, and all the 'What if's' that their imagination can dream up.

Strangely, it was Mussie who initiated the building of the bridge between us by calling me 'Jules' when he arrived for his fourth session. Very few people call me Jules, but those who do are among my best friends, so this might have irritated me, but in adapting my name it was as if he had taken possession of it for himself. Something about the genuineness of this was enough to get me past my judgements and allow me to warm to him; from this point, I began to see Mussie as he was on the inside.

It was hard to be critical of Mussie, or of anyone for that

matter, once I understood what motivated, hurt and pre-occupied him. Similarly, once he realized he could trust me, that he didn't have to perform for me, the armour that had rather put me on my back foot in the beginning fell away. I saw him as an intelligent, sensitive and wounded young man, who, I soon learned, had great resources of creativity and growth that enabled him to reinvest in life again.

Hurt seemed to sit on Mussie like a giant boulder on his chest, cutting off all feelings or connections. I could see him clenching his jaw, unconsciously biting against the pain. I asked him to tell me more about the hurt, to close his eyes and breathe into it. The pain, he said, was sharp in his chest; he saw only black, nothing but black space, then it shifted and there were spikes of red, transforming into molten lava, spreading through him. I used a softer voice to reach across to him and asked him what the lava would say if it were able to speak. Mussie said, 'It's spewing venom and rage.' He breathed a little more deeply, and tears ran down his face. The molten lava that he saw became a boiling cauldron of fury. Mussie then moved on to an image of himself standing on the top of a mountain and screaming, 'I'm roaring with rage; I'm a supernova.'

Physics isn't my strong point, so I looked up supernova later and found it to be 'the explosion of a giant star, possibly caused by gravitational collapse, during which the star's luminosity increases by as much as 20 magnitudes and most of the star's mass is blown away at very high velocity, some-times leaving behind an extremely dense core'. That certainly gave me a clear picture of Mussie's all-consuming internal devastation: it was as huge and seemingly inescapable as a black hole. I wondered how his friends and family perceived him: did they see him as numb or as someone about to explode? Would that mean they would withdraw even further from him?

I realized I didn't have a handle on what Hashim was like, or on what their relationship had been like. I did know that 'Hash was shy and thoughtful, a deep thinker.' Mussie showed me a photograph, the two of them standing with their arms round each other. I could see that they looked like brothers, but Hashim was smaller, rounder and staring at the ground. Mussie had been the typical older brother, dominant and bossy. Hashim was his father's favourite child; he had been much more biddable, Hashim was 'the clever one', while Mussie was a sociable extrovert. He now harboured terrible feelings of guilt and unworthiness for being the brother who was left alive. These played out with his father in particular, for whom, he felt, he could never be good enough: 'I'm not Hash, and I never will be.' I was aware of how loss shines a light on all existing relationships, often showing up their cracks and crevices.

Hashim had made many friends in his short life. Mussie told me: 'When my brother died, having his friends come over was such a lovely thing. They came round, had tea, helped around the house – it was as if they brought part of him with them. It was the only time my mother would come out of her room.' Sometimes they would go up to Hashim's room and play his music, hang out. Mussie loved that – it was a way of being close to him that didn't push him through the wall of his pain. He found some things annoying: 'When people were emotional around me, I'd end up reassuring them, which disturbed me. Sometimes everyone was crying, and I'd be thinking, "I don't even know these people." I didn't cry myself; I was too shocked. I found the whole thing destabilizing.' I had heard similar things many times before.

Having friends come around – staying close, being helpful but not too heavy, not weeping and wailing – is enormously comforting. What people often find difficult, is having friends round who cry so much that they end up having to cheer them up.

Over the weeks, a clearer picture emerged. Their father had left their mother when Mussie was a child, following many years of violent arguments and chaos. When he was twelve, 'Hash got a cough. It was a room-clearing cough. It was so bad he couldn't go to school, he just lay on the sofa, totally light and noise intolerant, losing weight. His whole condition ruled the house.' Mussie had found this both infuriating and very upsetting. Their mother had desperately taken Hashim from specialist to specialist, but no one could help; until, six months later, a consultant told them, brutally, that there wasn't anything physically wrong with him and that his symptoms were psychosomatic. Their father dismissed this as 'psychobabble' and felt they should all pray more. Their mother managed to find a good child psychotherapist, and over the next six months Hashim's symptoms diminished. He went back to school. Mussie's understanding was that Hashim had experienced separation anxiety following their father's departure; the 'special love' his father had for Hashim had been the centre of his internal world, and it had splintered when he'd left. Hashim had never spoken about it, fearing he would lose his mother if he told her how much he missed his father.

Mussie was trying to get on with his life; he was determined his brother's death wasn't going to define him. He worked in the City as a trainee dealing assistant. He didn't like his boss, a woman who, he felt, didn't respect him enough, and would send him on annoying personal errands.

The work was desultory, but he had to acknowledge that in some ways it didn't ask too much of him: 'It's all I can manage.' It provided the benefit of structure and enabled him to get away from himself, even if only for an hour at a time. Frequently, and completely unpredictably, he would be hit by a wave of what felt like terror, 'sometimes three times a day, sometimes not for a few days', and he felt as if he were going mad. I reassured him that this was normal in traumatic death, although it is experienced as madness. He learned to breathe through it, but it left him worn out and constantly anxious.

Our sessions were fascinating and demanding. Mussie would begin by talking about how much he missed his brother, the waste of his life, the destruction it had caused to so many people. Seeing the damage done to his parents was what upset him the most. His mother was preoccupied with asking questions that would never have a clear answer – critically examining herself and forensically interrogating anyone who'd known Hashim about his drug-taking, wishing Hashim had at least left a note to explain things to her. Mussie grieved for the mother she had been; and, although he didn't want to blame Hashim for damaging her, inevitably he did. The intensity of our sessions would sometimes make my head hurt. Once I said, 'It feels like steel nails are pushing into my skull. I wonder if that's what it's like being in your head all the time? Intense and painful, bloody agony with no respite.' Mussie's eyes locked on to mine: the relief he felt that I had had a physical sense of what he was living with every minute of the day, even if just for a few minutes, meant so much to him. That I could move into his world enough to physically experience it was key to supporting him and building trust.

Drinking too much, and battling not to, Mussie was locked in a cycle of self-recrimination and self-hate. In attempting to hold himself together, he couldn't ask for re-assurance or comfort; such neediness felt shameful. Weakness can be particularly difficult for men; it can feel like a dirty word. It related back to the conflicted relationship Mussie had with his father, who had now transferred all his expect-ations to his remaining son. It was unspoken but still vividly clear: 'He wants me to fulfil all the hopes he had of Hash. Whatever I do, I can't be Hash.' Mussie had a difficult time whenever he saw his father, and ended up feeling brutalized afterwards. 'He wants me to be more religious. I had an awful nightmare that I killed him and sold his body for money. I don't need you to interpret that – I guess I know what it means.'

We had a break over the summer, which was a bad one for Mussie: he was lonely and angry, incredibly angry, fighting with his friends, shopkeepers, everyone and anyone – telling himself they had let him down, disappointed him. He knew it was really his grief for Hashim, but that was too painful to let himself know.

I encouraged Mussie to express his rage through images. I asked him to describe different versions of supernova, which had become our recognized shorthand for his Technicolor internal fury, and this seemed to work for him. We saw him burn and roar and explode. We watched as he burned his old self as rubbish and conjured a new self from the ashes, rising like a phoenix. In one of the most powerful sessions he saw himself as a roaring fire. When I realized I didn't know what followed on from the fire, I asked him, and he cried shuddering tears, then described a desolate image for me: 'Grey all around. Nothing but ash.' I wanted to give him a hug but didn't: I sensed it would be too invasive for him. But I was able to tell him I felt close to him, that I could see how young he was and how much he needed to be held and loved. Those words seemed enough: he settled and breathed more lightly.

When Mussie was better able to function in daily life, his relationships with others became central in our work. He loved his mother, but dreaded seeing her because she needed so much from him. His fury yoked him to his father, and he wanted to be free of him. Some days he would come bouncing in, much happier, like a little boy full of life; but then the bitterness and rage he felt towards his father would be so strong that it seeped into my body and blurred my thoughts. I told him this and, again, something about my experiencing it with him eased him. He became reconciled to the idea that he would always have these strong ambivalent feelings about his parents, but that they needn't rule him. We had one very painful session in which he faced his 'shameful self', which brought on tears, and then turned to his 'better self', the self that loved and accepted him – which brought on even more tears. There was a tug-of-war between the two, holding on and letting go; but at the end he said, 'My brain's relaxed.'

Over time, Mussie's images changed, became softer. In his mind he saw Hashim, but he didn't hold on to him for long: 'If I get a memory of him, I don't binge on it. I let it come into my head and then disappear, that works for me. It floats in and it floats out.' Mussie came to one session wearing Hashim's watch and he would stroke the face of it as he remembered him – bike rides they'd had, fighting over their Gameboy, ragging together, competing on Nintendo. He missed Hashim deeply, but he wouldn't let himself think about him all the time; it was 'too painful. I need to give myself permission to have good days.'

Mussie was feeling re-energized and building his confidence through work, which was slowly improving. He bought a puppy, which excited him, and he began to learn from the dog how his behaviour had an impact, seeing the importance of consistency and boundaries. 'It's brought more life into my life.'

On one visit to his father, Mussie arrived to find him holding Hashim's birth and death certificates in his hands. Mussie told his father: 'The important one is his birth certificate, 'cause he was here, he was alive. He did a lot of good stuff and, until the last few months, had an unsullied life. There is nothing to mourn and many good things to remember.'

He started to forget to come to our appointments, and we discussed whether it was time to end. He told me he didn't 'do endings', but we agreed a date nonetheless. We did have an ending, and he was grateful. He told me he could trust me – 'I can see it in your eyes' – and he left without paying.

Faziah

My relationship with Faziah was a 21st-century one: she found my contact details on the internet and we Skyped every week. I never met her in person, but I saw her living room, occasionally her children – two teenage sons and a daughter, particularly when one son had to sort out her technical issues – and for half a session I saw her husband. I actually saw more of her world than would have been possible had she come to my consulting room.

Faziah was a 45-year-old Pakistani-born GP living in Birmingham. Her elder sister, Aaliah, had been diagnosed with motor neurone disease six months previously. Faziah was devastated. Her sister was the person she was closest to in her life. Born into a large family, they were only eighteen months apart in age and almost felt like twins; they shared all the minutiae of their lives with each other. Leaving her sister to come and live in the UK two years previously, in the hope of a better future for her children, had been the hardest decision of Faziah's life, not only because she loved her sister so much, but because it went against the cultural norm of living together in an extended family. Because the specialist medical care in Pakistan was out of Aaliah's reach, she was looked after by her family. All they had been told was that Aaliah had a life expectancy of four years, and Faziah felt impotent as a consequence.

The first weeks that we met she railed against the diagnosis, and cried and cried. Faziah couldn't bear her powerlessness:

she wanted to fix Aaliah. As a GP, diagnosing-and-fixing was her 'go to' position; it was unbearable for her to have no protocols up her sleeve. A pattern emerged where we would start the Skype with a question from me, such as 'How are you doing?', and the reply 'I'm fine' invariably came from her. Then, as soon as she mentioned Aaliah's name, her sadness would flow. Towards the end of a session she would want a 'prescription' − what could I give her that would help? The answer I often gave her was exercise. I know I'm being repetitive in talking about exercise, but it really is the best medicine that I can recommend: get outside, get your heart rate up, breathe in the air, you will nearly always feel better afterwards. I also suggested that she do things that comforted her, whether it was watching a box set or having a massage. The important thing was to choose activities that consciously soothed her. I'd also regularly remind her, despite her sense of her impotence, that she was doing more than she was willing to admit to help her sister; showing her how much she loved her − an intimate love, knowing the same world from infancy to adulthood, side by side − was a vital support.

Faziah's husband was a good man and very traditional. He could talk about practical things and suggest solutions, but he had no grasp of how important it was to listen to her. It soon became apparent that his tolerance for the subject of Aaliah was wearing thin; he would talk about something else or leave the room when Faziah started to speak about her. They fought about it, but for him to sit and listen to her was asking more of him than he could manage. I thought most people would have been angered by their husband and would probably have withdrawn from the relationship; I'm sure I would have. In Faziah's case, she accepted his limitations and worked around them, grateful that I could fulfil this role for her.

Aaliah had three daughters, who were under fourteen, but I heard very little about them, and she had a seventeen-year-old son, Hamzah, whom she and her husband were very worried about. Her family as a whole were not good communicators, their family rule being 'Be okay'. Faziah told me Hamzah was clearly furious that his mother had this devastating condition, and guilt-ridden for being furious with her, knowing logically that it wasn't her fault. He felt fearful about her dying, but he also wanted to get on with his life, like any ordinary teenager. This was a complex pool of feelings that at some level would need to be aired. Instead he kept a tight lid on his emotions and spent his time glued to his electronic screens, trying to shut out the situation as best he could.

When I suggested that Faziah should talk to Aaliah about sensitive subjects such as what her fears might be, she was understandably reluctant to do this; she would accuse me of giving her 'that look', which was a kind of 'just do it' face. When Faziah did finally ask her sister about her concerns, Aaliah told her that her biggest worry was her children, and her son in particular; she felt guilty that she was failing them as a mother. Her whole purpose in the time that remained to her was to be as good a mother as she could be, for as long as she could; her mother-love was a very real life force in the face of death. And Aaliah was frightened for herself too: frightened of suffocating, frightened of the devastating deterioration that lay ahead of her. Faziah knew instinctively how scared Aaliah was, but hearing her say it was like discovering it anew, and it upset her deeply.

Whenever I had a session with Faziah, I cried with her. Her sister's slow living death, about which no one could do anything at all, was, to me, as bad as it gets. Aaliah would progressively lose the ability to move her body, her head, her neck; she would no longer be able to speak or to communicate in any way – all while being fully mentally aware and knowing she would eventually die through the inability to breathe. When I imagined what Faziah, or any other member of her family, was going through, I felt horrified and heartbroken. Our connection sustained us both: it was heartfelt, and strengthened by a shared black humour. Faziah said that our laughing 'kicked the badness away'. The feisty banter we developed helped her to bear the sense of powerlessness that could so easily have overwhelmed her, and brought about a sense of calm in her by the end of each session.

Faziah went to see Aaliah three times a year, and these visits were fraught with difficulties. She had to leave her husband, her children and her job. It was expensive and exhausting, but also vital, because when she was there she could focus entirely on her sister. They could reconnect to their shared memories, and to their shared sibling shortcuts of understanding; she could be the sister she wanted to be. And Faziah's black, irreverent humour, the impact of which she saw in Aaliah's eyes and facial expressions, could dispel their present-day fears, even if only for a short time.

The visits allowed the many different guilts that Faziah was battling to surface. 'They spring up like octopus tentacles. I unravel one, and another comes to taunt me, wraps itself around me and squeezes tight.' We carefully unpicked two guilts together: one was her sense that she should go back to Pakistan to live with Aaliah, which she knew wasn't right for her husband and children, but was what Aaliah wanted. Faziah wanted me to understand this from her perspective: by remaining in the UK, she was breaking away from an embedded tradition of family duty, of living together as a family, and she felt a little piece of herself had broken in the process. The other guilt was that she was alive and well, could enjoy everyday life, envisage a future and play with her children, while Aaliah was confined to her wheelchair, barely able to speak. In a late session Faziah faced the 'go back to Pakistan' guilt, after she had told Aaliah that she was going to remain in England. 'It's an impossible no-win decision, but I've made it. At least I've been straight with Aaliah, and with myself.' While I could see the guilt hadn't been extinguished, it did at least seem that the terrible 'Shall I/Shan't I' wrestling was over.

After the first year of weekly sessions, Faziah's need for such regular meetings lessened. She had developed a clear understanding of what was happening inside her, and of how to support herself, so eventually we Skyped every two months. At the start of our session Faziah would give me a steely look, which told me she didn't want to cry or to feel anything at all. She was saddened that she was 'getting used to' her grief. I gently let her know that, as human beings, those of us who want to survive have to adapt, and this often means shifting our perspective; having the capacity to adapt to new realities is probably one of the most important ways of being healthy. Most of the time I said little; I listened. I reflected back what I'd heard and what Faziah seemed to be feeling.

Through the second year of our time together, Faziah's sadness shifted from an overwhelming flood of tears to an exhausting leaky tap that dripped into everything she did. She felt a slow, pervasive sadness that appeared to be mirroring her sister's illness. I allowed space for those feelings but also forcefully urged her to do things that were fun and life-affirming. My argument – and we were both quite feisty – was that this was a long game: she needed to look after herself properly, to rest and restore herself, if she were to see it through. She believed her regular prayers were enough in this regard, but, as much as her faith was a central pillar of support for her, I knew she needed to engage in all aspects of life, to enjoy her roles as wife, mother and doctor. Being a grieving sister should not have been all that defined her.

I asked Faziah about the people in her community and how they showed their support for her. She had one friend who would ask about her sister, but on the whole she felt their attitude was to 'Believe in the will of Allah, be strong and pray.' They questioned the wisdom of her constantly wrestling with her powerlessness and sadness, asking, 'Is it actually doing you any good?' All this genuinely didn't annoy her because she believed in being patient with 'God's plan' for her: 'I'm grateful for all He has given me; I'm grateful for my life.' This attitude at her core was invaluable in centring her.

As Aaliah grew progressively worse, Faziah's anger burst through over the diminishing connection with her sister. 'I'm losing her inch by inch.' In tears she described how she could imagine what Aaliah was actually feeling and thinking every day as she sat in her chair, no longer able to move her legs, control her head, use her hands, or do anything at all for herself. I cried with Faziah about the awfulness of her sister's situation. By this time, we had a closeness and a connection that worked, both heartbreaking and warm.

We talked more about Aaliah's actual dying and I asked, 'Is there anything you need to say to your sister? Make sure you don't have any regrets.' Fortunately, Faziah had already had the important conversations with her sister, and Aaliah had written an email – it had taken her weeks to do – in which she laid out her wishes for her funeral and for her family's future life.

My fourth year with Faziah revolved around the total exhaustion of everyone concerned and the interminable not knowing when Aaliah would die. With the exhaustion came the inevitable guilt-laden thoughts: 'When is this going to be over?' and 'I'm not sure I can do this for much longer.' It was an excruciating emotional cul-de-sac. Faziah's thoughts were muddy and dark; they stuck to her, colouring all her other feelings. Distressed though she was, I could see that her belief that the will of God is the ultimate power was unshaken, and I found I was envious of the solace her faith gave her.

By the fifth year, Aaliah's condition was agonizing. She couldn't interact with anyone; she was unable to move and was fed intravenously; and, throughout it all, her cognitive awareness and intelligence remained unimpaired. Chronic exhaustion had worn down the patience of her husband and their four children, and their tension often erupted into huge fights. Faziah's daily Skype calls to her had to be reduced to every two or three days.

Faziah texted me to say that she was going to Pakistan, because Aaliah was deteriorating. A few days later she texted me again: pneumonia had taken hold of her sister's lungs and she had died peacefully in her sleep. That she had 'slipped away' made a big difference to them all. Faziah had been haunted by harrowing images of Aaliah suffocating to death, but, in the end, she had been spared that.

Although I'd never physically set eyes on Faziah, I felt the heaviness of her grief for a while. My job can be very odd:

here I was, grieving for a woman I'd never known, who probably hadn't known of my existence. Yet it felt like a real loss. Aaliah had been in my mind for five years – I'd imagined her suffering, her fear, her desolation – and now she was gone.

When Faziah returned from Pakistan, she increased the frequency of her sessions for a while. Her grief was raw, and she cried all over again for the death of Aaliah, for the loss of her physical presence. Her faith soothed her, because she believed Aaliah was in paradise, and that she no longer suffered; but she nonetheless veered between intense sadness, numbness, working robotically and feeling disconnected from her children and husband. In time, however, she found herself breathing more lightly when she awoke each morning and reluctantly recognized that the weight of worry and not knowing had been lifted from her.

Her faith was her most stalwart ally. She followed the Barelvi tradition, and performed all the rituals her religion possessed to speed Aaliah on her journey to the next world: praying in ceremonial gatherings on particular days, reciting the Quran, and offering food to neighbours and the poor in the community. I could see that believing Aaliah was in a 'better place', with a concrete physicality, gave her both strength and comfort.

Over time the intensity of her sadness softened and she felt calmer. She said proudly, 'I think of Aaliah every day. I see her face in my mind. I'm not afraid any more that I will forget her. She is part of me. I believe there will come a time when we'll be reunited under more favourable circumstances, without as much suffering and pain.'

Reflections

Each of these case studies is a complex psychological portrait of people contending with a difficult death. I was drawn to write about them because I'd had particularly powerful relationships with these clients – relationships that stayed alive in me long after our work had finished.

The ideal sibling relationship gives you your 'team': the people who are on your side, through thick and thin, for the rest of your life. The expression 'an only child' contains within it the sense of one not being quite enough. The power of the sibling bond can overcome years of non-communication; brothers and sisters are forever connected through shared genetics, history, secrets, memories and language.

While few adult siblings have severed their ties completely, approximately one third describe their relationship as rivalrous or distant. But this, of course, would not make the death of their brother or sister less difficult; it would simply add a layer of complexity – the loss of the opportunity to repair what was broken and regret for the actions of the past tend to bring with them their own attendant pain.

The largest group of sibling deaths is in the older population, and these generations usually don't seek counselling. Although 80 per cent of the population have a sibling, we as a society give it less acknowledgement than it deserves as a key relationship in our lives. There isn't, for instance, a sibling support group in the way there is for widows or bereaved parents. Contemporary research is beginning to show that siblings have a much greater influence on the development of our personality than has been assumed up to now – which means that their deaths will have a concomitant impact and affect us profoundly.

My experience with clients is that the greater the emotional depth in the relationship, the greater chance the therapy has of doing some good. When clients trust the relationship, it frees them to trust themselves, and connect to the core of what is troubling them. As they reveal hidden, usually shame-based aspects of themselves to me, they are also revealing them to themselves – which, paradoxically, allows them to become more accepting of them. My belief is that the potential for depth is co-created by both partners in the therapeutic relationship: I can only go so far if someone won't open up to me. I would argue that this is true of the closest friendships too, in that when we are open and honest with each other, without judging, the richer the friendship becomes.

Suicide

Mussie's grieving process was intensified by the fact that his brother had taken his own life. It meant grieving was for him, as it is for others, more complex and prolonged, although the actual tasks and experiences are similar. The guilt that usually accompanies grief is often felt like a physical wound. There were many unanswered and unanswerable questions circling round in Mussie's head – 'Why?', 'What if?', 'If only . . .' – and these impinged on all his other mental activity, leaving him less able to function in his everyday life.

Guilt and shame commonly come along with questions such as 'What if?' The stigma in suicide can lead to a sense of extreme isolation for the person who is bereaved, because friends and colleagues don't know how to approach them, and so may not say anything at all. The survivor of a suicide also risks being branded as a 'bad brother' or a 'bad mother' – that they must have done something, or not done enough, and this had contributed to the person's suicide.

The shock from a suicide can last a very long time, and often people aren't fully aware of this. The story of the death revolves round and round in a bereaved person's head and always defies their attempts to give a different, happier ending.

One of the ways I help those bereaved by suicide is to have them think of it as a 'heart attack of the brain'. We can all understand that physically anyone, whatever their age or fitness, can have a heart attack. Some physical illnesses can be prevented; others cannot. The person who took their own life was not functioning normally: they weren't thinking rationally and their mind attacked them – had a 'heart attack', with the devastating consequence of taking their own life. For me, it helps to remove the blame and shame attached to 'choosing' to take one's own life. There may be circumstances in which that's true, but the majority of people who are of sound mind don't choose to do that.

I've seen how some people actively make the decision not to let a suicide's death define them, and they usually have the psychological strength to manage that. I have worked with others who remain murderously furious with the person who died by suicide, which only serves to keep the pain alive and unresolved inside them. People talk about 'finding a way of living with' the grief from suicide; as a bereaved mother said to me, 'You never "get over it", you "get on with it", and you never "move on" but you "move forward". You start to absorb the intense pain that such a loss brings in its wake and you begin, very, very slowly to accept.'

Family systems in suicide

Within a family, each member will grieve in a different way, which can radically disturb the family structure. In some cases this system will never revert to its original form, and it will remain off kilter; in others, it can be repaired. However, the absence of the person who has died is always felt, whether acknowledged or hidden.

Communication can be one of the most difficult aspects of grief, within families as well as within their wider social friendship group. The grieving process can be hindered by (often unspoken) feelings of blame, insufficient information and understanding about suicide, and others not knowing what to say or how to help. Family members are left isolated, pondering questions such as: 'If you loved me, how could you do this to me and leave me with this mess?' In addition, the loss of whatever the future might have held has a more powerful impact when a death is by suicide, as a decision was made by the person they love to have no future at all.

Risk of suicide

Bereavement is a risk factor for suicide. It is useful for us all to know that when someone says they are suicidal they are not 'attention seeking' and should be taken seriously. A previous suicide attempt is the single biggest risk factor for suicide. It is estimated that up to 50 per cent of people who take their own lives have previously attempted to harm themselves.

Suicide statistics

Around 4,400 people end their own lives in England each year. That's one death every two hours, and at least ten times that number attempt suicide.

Approximately 75 per cent of suicides are men, and in almost all cultures the suicide rate rises with age. The highest rates of suicide in the UK are among people aged over seventy-five, and it remains a common cause of death in men under the age of thirty-five.

People with a diagnosed mental health condition are at particular risk. About 90 per cent of suicide victims suffer from a psychiatric disorder at the time of their death.

Those at the highest risk of suicide are people suffering from alcoholism, clinical depression or schizophrenia. Up to 20 per cent of people who have made a suicide attempt try again within a year, and as a group they are a hundred times more likely to go on to kill themselves than those who have never attempted suicide.

For young people, bullying, family turmoil, mental health problems, unemployment and a family history of suicide can play a part in increasing the risk. Among the young, 80 per cent of suicides are male, and one in three young people is drunk at the time of death.

For older people, poverty, poor-quality housing, social isolation, depression and physical health problems are factors that can increase the risk. Over 1,000 men aged over fifty end their lives every year in England and Wales.

Traumatic grief

Traumatic grief is one that comes from a sudden and unexpected death such as Hashim's, which may be through suicide, murder, accident or war. It is grief that is too overwhelming to take in. The shock of the event, if it is witnessed or even imagined, is so intense that people have flashbacks, which can be triggered by one or more of their senses: sight, sound, smell, touch, hearing. The person grieving might alternate bursts of extreme emotion with states in which they are totally shut down.

It can be helpful to have a full narrative for what has happened, connecting the words with the acute feelings, and this can be done by writing a journal or talking to a close friend. Trauma is held in the body, so it's important to breathe deeply as the event and the feelings it's created come together in words. Go at a pace you can manage, and stop when it feels like too much. Allow another person to comfort you. Exercise that raises the heart rate, followed by a calming meditation, can help to reduce any feelings of panic. Doing actively comforting things is also helpful.

In circumstances where it is necessary to maintain control, such as being at work, it can be useful to have an exercise that blocks the distressing images.

- Think of a television screen.
- Visualize the distressing image on that screen.
- Take three breaths.

- Change the channel.
- Put a positive image on the screen.
- Take three breaths.
- Turn off the television and move your attention on to something else.

This exercise can be used for any repetitive habit that is bothering you. The more it is used, the more effective it becomes.

It is normal to have flashbacks for up to six weeks following a traumatic event, but if they continue after that it may be post-traumatic stress disorder, and it is advisable to seek professional help from someone such as your GP.

Secondary transmission of trauma

Ruth, and those like her – the children of people suffering untreated post-traumatic stress disorder – often have not been told the complete story of the traumatic event, and so don't have memories upon which they can focus their grief, but their lives are pervaded by loss all the same, haunted by the ghosts of people who haven't been mourned. Children can carry around these losses both physically and psychologically, but they don't understand that these are a sort of wound; they just know they always feel 'heavy' or 'sad'.

I worked with one client whose parent had been the one actually to suffer the traumatic event, and she said, 'I carry so many scars. But I don't know what the wounds are. That is harder than having been wounded.' From birth, these children develop ways of thinking and specific habits to help them block out the fear and terror.

If many families were to look at their histories, they would have a sense that there were secrets that hadn't been told, their toxicity trickling down the generations. For me, the fundamental message to take from this is that the truth, however difficult, is better than a lie or any sort of cover-up. We can't deal with what we don't know, so we can fully process an event only once we understand the 'what', the 'how' and the 'why' of it.

The capacity to manage transmitted trauma is based on an interweaving of many different strands – social environment, including prohibitions and taboos; the communication within the family system itself; the genetic predisposition of each child – so the more we understand what those strands are, the more likely it is we can help ourselves.

Faith/spirituality

Religion and culture played an influential role in the lives of Ruth and Faziah, as it does with many people, shaping their sense of themselves, their views of the world and their attitude to death.

Early on in the therapy, I ask the client where they believe the person who has died is now. Many are uncertain, but some have ideas informed by a clear spiritual faith. Others may have had faith previously, but, following such a devastating event, they are now wrestling with a God with whom they are angry, whom they find it hard to believe in or trust. This in itself can be very disruptive to the grieving process.

It is true across all religions that family, friends and colleagues coming together to bear witness and grieve together enable the grief to be shared. Having familiar religious practices and observances to follow helps to contain feelings that are chaotic and unfamiliar.

Most religions expostulate on what happens to the soul of the person who has died. Different rituals and ceremonies are performed that lead the soul to God, or Heaven, or the 'light'. The stronger their belief, the more important the rituals and ceremonies are to the bereaved families that take part in them.

For people who believe in God, faith can give meaning to the death, and religious people often imagine that the person who has died is guiding them in this world. The idea that they will one day be reunited is a key source of solace. Praying for, and to, the dead loved one is a familiar way of connecting to them, and, again, can provide great comfort.

Those who have faith say their religion or spirituality was helpful, or even essential, to getting them through their grief, although there isn't solid empirical evidence for this. My observation is faith has a positive impact on those who hold on to their religious and spiritual beliefs through their grieving.

Believing life has some meaning is a significant factor in happiness, and provides protection in adversity. People who can find meaning by keeping a sense of the presence of the person who has died inside themselves, often feeling them in their spiritual being, are better able to continue living, even without their loved one's physical presence.

When the bereaved don't have faith in any organized religion, they may nonetheless have a spiritual side that will try to reach an understanding of where the person they love has gone. Interestingly, when people don't believe in God per se, when things go wrong they still turn to God for help; it does seem to be a human instinct to turn to some higher power than ourselves.

I have met many families that want to believe there will be a reunion with the person who has died in a 'better place'. For those that do believe, it is sometimes the one thing that makes their present life bearable. In my experience this is particularly true for parents whose children have died.

A living loss

Faziah's five-year process of watching her sister die was unimaginably hard for her. It was a living loss, yet the most significant thread that runs through it is the power of love. Family and friends very naturally want to be able to do something in the face of adversity, and yet, with a degenerative disease that has no cure, there is nothing that can make it better. It is crucial not to underestimate the power of love, however; I've known many families who feel that the love they give isn't enough but who become inspired when they realize it is the single most important thing in the life of the person who's dying.

A common difficulty that can emerge in families in which one sibling is dying and the other sibling is healthy is the unspoken jealousy and envy the dying sibling directs at their family members who are well and have a future. These feelings can be hard to acknowledge, and so are often expressed through anger, sadness or withdrawal. If a member of the family can find a way of encouraging this to be said openly, there can be a great sense of relief for everyone, and fewer haunting questions for the surviving family members.

Anyone who is worn out by being a carer for many years may be veering between two unwelcome thoughts: 'I can't do this any more; I want it to be over' and 'I'm terrified of her/him dying'. Both thoughts have truth and power, but when competing with each other they can make someone feel quite mad. The 'I want it over' thought can not only instil feelings of guilt, but also switch on a version of 'magical thinking' – that by even having the thought they might be hastening the dying person's end. The 'I'm terrified of her/him dying', on the other hand, is a boiling cauldron of dark materials that need to be voiced in order to prevent the carer becoming ill or depressed, which is all too common in these situations.

When a child dies

We find a place for what we lose. Although we know that after such loss the acute stage of mourning will subside, we also know that we shall remain inconsolable and will never find a substitute. No matter what may fill the gap, even if it be filled completely, it nevertheless remains something else.

– Sigmund Freud

Henry and Mimi

I met Henry and Mimi very soon after the devastating still-birth of their baby boy, Aiden. Their anguish was tangible. Every word was painfully expressed, as if they were continually stepping on broken glass, and their breathing was sudden and short with shock. I looked at them – an attractive American couple – and I imagined the joy of discovering she was pregnant and the hopes they'd shared throughout their pregnancy, the scans and tests all positive.

They were grieving the physical presence of Aiden. They longed to hold, smell and touch him. They were also grieving for their future life with their son; they had assumed they would watch him grow through his milestones into adulthood, and they'd had every right to expect that. The gaping hole between their dream and this stark reality was palpable. I was aware of a pain in my chest, and my tummy tightening; but I trusted that a way would be found to help them live again.

Mimi was still recovering from a caesarean, and was sore, pinched white and dazed; she had milk in her breasts, which felt like an outrage. Her eyes were dark pools of sadness with no life behind them. Henry told most of their story.

They'd been together eight years, married five, lived for three of them in the UK. He worked for a global internet company, and she was a doctor. They had decided she would finish her training before starting a family, but it hadn't been straightforward and it had taken her two years to get pregnant. I could see how they had come together as a couple: they had similar values in that they both wanted to make a difference and were both ambitious. He was a tall fit man. She was neat and blonde, with beautiful blue eyes. They leaned towards each other when they spoke, reached for each other's hands and listened to each other intently. They cried individually, and they cried when they saw each other cry. It was touching to witness and gave me hope for their future.

Death doesn't happen in a vacuum, and soon after Aiden's death they faced a difficult decision: whether Mimi's parents should come over from the US. Henry's parents had simply got on a plane; they hadn't even asked whether it was right to come or not. With her parents it was more complicated: they hadn't approved of Henry marrying their daughter because he was black. Coming from an old Boston family, they had not hoped for a mixed-race marriage for their daughter. There hadn't been big explosive rows, but rather a kind of deadly silent disapproval; and the ever widening gap between Mimi and her parents had been the main reason why they had moved to the UK. I could see how torn she felt. The loss had ripped away her adult confidence, making her feel small and childlike, and she needed her mother to soothe her. At the same time, she didn't want to be disloyal to Henry, who was visibly and understandably furious at her parents' prejudice.

I thought Mimi needed her mother to come, and that if her parents were asked to stay away a further rift would ensue, which would be hard to repair. However, I didn't say this to them, not wanting to interfere, but they eventually came to the same conclusion and her parents arrived. They stayed a week, which was long enough for Mimi to feel closer to them, and not too long for their habitual conflicts to arise.

The funeral was devastating. Mimi said, 'Buying flowers for it is the only celebration of Aiden's little life we'll ever do. It's his fifth birthday party, his eighteenth, his twenty-first, his wedding.' The tiny little white coffin was carried by Henry, tears streaming down his face. The hospital chaplain had conducted the service; Henry and Mimi had both read poems and prayers. It had been a very short service, with only their families present, and every minute was weighted with sadness, a death on the cusp of new life.

I could feel the heaviness in my body as they described it, and I looked at a photograph of Aiden, perfectly formed, and wrapped up tightly he looked as though he were sleeping, a beautiful baby boy. I was glad they had taken photographs, as they would be crucial in the future, and I was relieved that they had spent time with him, held him the whole night, creating very precious memories that would remain with them forever. I asked myself how a beautiful healthy-looking baby could die and become nothing more than a memory. It made absolutely no sense and it never would.

As Mimi began to recover physically, the mental agony took over. She wanted answers. Why had Aiden died? She'd had a healthy pregnancy, ticked every box, done everything right – why, why, why? Her being a doctor exacerbated it: she pored over her case notes, waited anxiously for post-mortem results, researched medical papers. She wondered about the cheese she had eaten, the flight she had taken to the US. Was she being punished for a sin she hadn't known she'd committed? Some sort of answer would return a modicum of control to her. The not knowing made her feel powerless, which was alien territory for her – and she did not like it one bit.

Mimi's success in life up to this point hadn't in any way

prepared her for this. She had believed that if you worked hard enough at something, threw all your time and energy into it, you got results. Even when things had gone wrong for her, she'd picked herself up, worked hard again and managed to get through. This belief ill prepared her for grieving.

Ten days after Aiden's death Henry had gone back to work. Although his firm boasted of its 'caring for staff' culture, his boss wanted him to work on a big project, so he'd felt pressurized to return. He looked completely exhausted. I asked him how he was getting on. 'I worry about Mimi all the time at work. I can't concentrate, my memory's shit . . . Everything seems utterly pointless . . . It hurts every day when I remember what's happened, when I think of Aiden's little face.' Occasionally his work distracted him and, when it did, it was a relief.

Mimi talked about the responsibility she felt because Aiden had died in her body. The psychological impact of this is almost impossible to understand if it's not something you've experienced yourself. She'd carried a live healthy baby in her body for nine months, seen the scans of him moving around, sucking his thumb, heard his quickening heartbeat, listened to the recording of the scan on her phone with pulsing joy and expectation. She'd had a sense of potency as she grew the baby in her womb, and then the extreme opposite as she gave birth to death. She was tortured by the knowledge he'd died in her body during labour, and by her total impotence in the situation. There was a battle between her head and her heart: she knew in her head that she hadn't done anything wrong, but her heart felt differently. She felt that her body had failed, and that in some way she was being punished.

I noticed her glance at Henry, looking for anger or blame in his eyes. She found neither there. I acknowledged to him that witnessing his wife's suffering – the fear he'd felt when they'd rushed her in for a caesarean, and then seeing his life-less baby appear – was no less traumatic an experience than his wife's. He said, 'I keep thinking of one image, waiting outside the delivery room, and not knowing if anyone was going to come out – Mimi or the baby. Doctor after doctor was rushing in, and I was outside, terrified. It's the image that makes me cry more quickly than any of the others. I can still feel that fear in my body.'

We all felt like we were wading through mud – it was draining, heavy work for us – but, as abnormal as it felt, I knew it was normal. I recognized that how they were in grief reflected how they were in life, open and willing to seek connection. I could step into their world easily and, once there, they welcomed me. It warmed me to be allowed on the inside of such an intensely private process.

Henry's exhaustion from being back at work was causing tension between them. While Henry was patient with his colleagues, with Mimi he was grumpy and snappy – Mimi subsequently wanted the 'work Henry at home'. They seemed unable to give or receive each other's love – the one thing that would stabilize them. They decided to go to Paris for the weekend, and being away restored their sense of well-being, giving them new energy, although both knew the pressure would return with them on the plane. Weirdly, we had a Skype session from a Parisian car park, and it was good to see them smiling for the first time.

Henry wanted to be distracted, have adventures, do new things together, as they had in the past. I felt he was fright-ened that if they didn't push forward, they would fall into a chasm and never get out; but this was not what Mimi wanted. She preferred to stay at home, buy a puppy, read, and do adult colouring books – no way was she going to move or to try anything new and dangerous. She needed to shrink her sphere of life in order to manage the levels of fear that were circling round her. She always spoke articulately; she was clever and full of potential; but I could see that the dreams wrecked by Aiden's death stopped her from hoping for more than just getting through the day. Fortunately Henry had endurance and stamina; he lived patiently with the situation and never once suggested the knee-jerk reaction of a quick fix.

A few weeks later Mimi contracted a virus and became very ill. She took weeks to recover, which hit her capacity to heal emotionally. Once again, it seemed that she couldn't trust in her body, that it had let her down, and the knowledge shook her. It keyed into her fear and anger at her own mortality. Mimi said, 'I'm like a piece of a jigsaw and I don't fit anywhere, not emotionally, physically, anything. I don't know where I fit socially, I don't know what I feel like doing, I don't know what I'm interested in. And there's a lost feeling on top of it, which is the grieving, and the hopelessness, and then the all-encompassing sadness.' The only place where she would have fitted was with Aiden. There was a visceral emptiness that she felt in her arms where he should have been lying.

Discussing their differences to one another was helpful. They knew how to fight well, a key aspect of successful partnerships. They could be angry without throwing blame back and forth, and they knew how to make up following a fight. The strength of their relationship sustained them. I noticed at the end of a particularly bleak exchange how they would gently tease each other, a tiny shaft of light.

They talked together about Aiden. They'd never know who he was, what kind of personality he would have had, if he'd have been like one of them. They'd never hear his voice, and they could only imagine what he would have looked like as an older baby, a toddler, a little boy. Although this was painful, in some way thinking about him gave them a place where they could direct their complicated feelings.

Many weeks passed during which Mimi felt low. 'I didn't want to eat, I didn't want to get up, I didn't want to get dressed. Yeah, I just felt terrible, but at least I showered and did my hair.' Friends asked them out a lot, and in the past she would have loved to have gone, but now socializing felt horribly alien to them. She no longer felt safe in unfamiliar environments, and couldn't predict how she would respond if someone said something that reminded her of Aiden. Mimi wished she could control how she felt: she wanted to flick a switch that would make her feel better. She said, 'I'm so fed up with myself that I could divorce myself right now.' That is the difficult truth about grief: it's impervious to control. It does things in its own time, and that's usually much longer than anyone wants.

Mimi wanted to know how she was doing in comparison with other people. Most people do want to know 'Am I doing worse/better than everyone else?' They assume they are doing worse because of the depth of their pain. I used a metaphor with her that she found helpful: Aiden's death was like an earthquake that impacted differently on every building in the quake zone. Rebuilding was also different in each individual case, so she couldn't compare herself with anyone else.

Mimi had a powerful image for herself: she was like a 'start-up', a new business at its inception, with no systems in place or database upon which it can rely. She felt she had been catapulted into a new version of herself that she didn't know, didn't like and didn't want. The pain didn't pass through her like anger or other feelings; it squatted and wouldn't move on. She began to see she had to let it take its own course, and that the work for her would be to allow this grieving, unsure version of herself to live alongside the Mimi that was so ambitious and effective, and confident. That part of her was silent and battered for now, but she needed to trust it wasn't lost. She recognized that she was 'in limbo' – a perfect metaphor. Not really on earth, and not in heaven or hell, but in an amorphous no man's land where she had to find whole new ways to adapt in order to survive.

Henry seemed to be functioning better, but the sadness had hit him deep in his core too. At times it seemed to be harder to bear than before, because the death felt more real. He did army fitness training in the park, because feeling physically stronger helped him to feel mentally stronger. To comfort himself sometimes he used the memory of holding Aiden in his arms, when he'd felt the weight of him against his body, stroked his soft skin and held his tiny, cold fingers in his big hand. He said, big tears in his eyes, 'I'm grateful I stroked the top of his head.' Aiden had been real; he had been born. Henry was frightened of losing that memory of him, frightened of a future when he'd forget.

Additionally difficult for Henry was that most of his male friends didn't acknowledge how painful the loss was for him; they would ask about Mimi but assumed it was less painful for him. The quiet anger he felt towards some very close friends who had only occasionally texted meant he couldn't imagine continuing with the friendships. Henry could talk to a cousin and his brother-in-law about his sadness, and the trauma of having seen Aiden being born dead, but it was a no-go area with everyone else. 'Men can cry and can be emotional when their sports team loses, and I just don't get why they can't over things that really matter.'

There was a sense of isolation emerging between Henry and Mimi, which they recognized on a long walk taken over a weekend. They talked a lot, having decided they wanted to manage their grieving process like a project. They sat down and worked out a plan of their future together – what they wanted, how to get there, how to keep communicating with each other. Building this structure helped to bring them together and gave their confidence a boost.

Coming to see me as a couple was an important part of sharing their loss, and helped them to avoid falling into the widening gaps between their pre-existing fault lines. It enabled them really to hear what was going on internally within each of them, for it is sometimes easier to listen with a third person present. As with most couples, each worried about making the other 'miserable' with their misery. Getting the right balance between being open enough to make an emotional connection and far too close to the point of codependency is difficult to effect as a couple. On the whole, Henry and Mimi managed the dance pretty well. Sometimes they surprised each other, hearing things they hadn't known about, but the dynamic that always came through was their sense of being in it together as a team. They now did bootcamp together, meditated together. It was undoubtedly the foundation of their healing.

After a year there was still a rollercoaster of different things to manage. They both felt homesick, wanting the comfort of familiar surroundings, family and old friends. Not knowing whether they should go home or stay left Henry feeling lost, without his usual energy for fighting.

Mimi had decided on the 'I'll fake it till I make it' approach, forcing herself out more, going to classes and volunteering. Acknowledging how badly she felt released her a bit: 'It's like unravelling a thread that's been very tightly knotted.' It was almost as if she had flipped a switch that allowed the preferred version of herself to emerge. The 'faking it' was most noticeable to me upon arrival and leaving: her voice would rise a few notes, and she'd put on a sort of sing-song happy voice that I found irritating. But when I understood better that she did it for Henry, that she wanted to be okay for him even if she couldn't do it for herself, it made sense. There was an invisible see-saw between them: at their best they could pull each other up, while at their worst they pulled each other down. There were competing and conflicting trains of thought which could ambush them both; life and death, hope and despair, power and powerlessness – that sat uncomfortably in them side by side; but it was only through voicing them that they could understand in which direction they were being pulled.

They felt stuck. They had agreed they would put Aiden's ashes in an urn and write him a letter on the anniversary of his death, but three months later they hadn't ordered the urn or written him a letter. Mimi acknowledged she couldn't move forward. But it was more than that. She recognized that, because she didn't have actual memories, it was harder to let go of the few things she did have; his clothes, his bassinet, her breast pump, all imbued with Aiden. 'Memory is all we have, and memories from before are hard to let go of.' Henry said they felt like they'd been in a 'fog', and we all agreed they needed to do physical things, make physical changes, to move out of it. The flat they were renting was the most evocative place for his memory, but it was also a 'ghost flat' – they had never hung a picture or done anything to make it their own.

We began to understand together the complexity of what they were going through. They needed to allow Aiden to 'have his time', to respect the time required by the natural process of grieving, but there was a point where this could become complicated grief and tip into depression. Because the psychological feeling was not to abandon Aiden, but to hold on to him as best they could, it was hard to let themselves make decisions, for that felt like 'forgetting him'. We agreed the fear of forgetting Aiden was great, but that they knew it was an impossibility. They recognized they had to make decisions that would lead to change, which would then free them to move between having happy moments in the present and memories of Aiden in the past.

The following week, I heard they'd had the courage to move forward with their new decisions. Mimi had ordered beautiful containers for Aiden's things, which she was going to embroider with his initials. They were going to move flat, which may not have been the best practical option, because there was the possibility that they would be returning to the States in six months' time. But it would be a shift towards the positive, a fresh environment and, most importantly, it would enable them to get a puppy. Geographically moving away from a problem rarely works, because it travels with you, but this felt different to me, more like a turning point, a step in the direction of hope and slowly rebuilding their trust in life.

In the last year of our time together a recurring dilemma was whether they should try for another baby. Henry wanted to push the boundaries: life seemed so ephemeral to him that he just wanted to 'go for it. It's not that I'm not scared at the thought of trying again.' Mimi was fierce in her uncertainty. The decision felt aeons away, and she chose to block it out. Henry blocked it out too at times: 'When I see people with children, or women with "Baby on board" badges on the tube, I can't even look in their direction, it's too painful.' Mimi found herself wandering into baby clothes shops and flitting through the rails, and then experiencing a surge of terror and running out. And she felt 'abnormally irritated with pregnant women'. They had both armoured themselves against the pain of imagining a new baby, and yet we all knew it was what they wanted most.

Paradoxically, allowing themselves not to put too much pressure on themselves to make a decision worked. In the end, they did decide to try again. This was by no means simple and pain free, because the fear of trying again, of entering the gateway that led to the dream of having a child, also meant entering the gateway that might lead to their child dying and possible childlessness. Once you know through your own experience that your child can die, it can never be ruled out as something that may happen in the future.

Now comes the waiting game, another whole month of hope that builds until it is dashed by the onset of Mimi's period. I fervently hope it won't take too long.

Our work continues.

Phil and Annette

I remember clearly where I was standing, when I received an urgent message to call a good friend of mine. He was very distressed: his best friend's four-year-old daughter, Amber, had just drowned in a swimming pool. I rang her father, Phil, who was on the way to the mortuary to see Amber. With him in the car were his wife, Annette, a 45-year-old French set designer, and their two other children, Beatrice and Henri, aged seven and ten. It was a bad signal and his voice choked as he told me where they were headed. I was impressed that they'd instinctively wanted to take their other children to see her, somehow knowing that to involve them was the right thing; they would need to see Amber's body, for them really to believe that she'd died.

Like everyone who embarks on this sort of conversation for the first time, I'd like a sentence that would magically make everything better, but there isn't one. So I said the only thing I could say: 'I am terribly sorry to hear that your daughter, Amber, has died; I'm sorry that such a devastating thing has happened to you. How can I help?' They both said they wanted guidance, and we agreed to speak at a later time.

I was apprehensive when we next spoke, as I needed to find a way to talk to them about things no one should even have to think about. I told them that it was important to give themselves time to plan the funeral, which was likely to be the last event they would ever plan for Amber. If they took their time, they could think about what they wanted, make decisions and have the time to change their minds, which could later protect them from having regrets. They would need to consider carefully how best to include Beatrice and Henri. What Amber would wear, and what would they like to put in the coffin with her – messages from her siblings, from them, her teddy bear, etc. – were all things they would need plenty of time to discuss.

As I spoke with them, I began to work out what they were like. Phil was more openly emotional. He cried big, heaving sobs that seemed to break through his whole body whenever he said Amber's name. Annette was more contained in her sadness: although certainly in profound pain, it went deeply within her (unlike Phil's, which erupted out of him), and this seemed to me her natural way of being – there was nothing forced or brittle about her manner. Annette's priority was to ensure that her other children were okay, wanting to be positive and to 'keep going'. I was struck by how their instinctive coping mechanisms seemed the reverse of the norm: men are usually more focused on restoring life to normal, and women are more likely to cry overtly, directing their energy on to their loss, angry with their partner as he pushes to carry on.

Following the funeral, we booked Skype sessions, because they lived in Paris. Annette was strikingly beautiful, with brown twinkly eyes and dark hair and that innate Parisian elegance we Brits can never emulate. Phil had a gentle face, sad brown eyes and thick black hair. Wiry and fit, he epitomized the 'greyhound built for speed' appearance. He looked like he had been running miles every day to burn the pain out of his body. He was a teacher, and I could imagine him having a quiet presence that would hold the attention of the class, as well as a spark that would ignite their curiosity.

Phil and Annette were both suffering from post-traumatic stress disorder, which was causing sharp, intrusive memories, flashbacks and a repetitive replaying of Amber's drowning in their minds. A way of understanding a traumatic death is to think of it as 'grief with the volume turned up'. They seemed to be holding the trauma in their bodies, though I would have been able to get a better handle on that if they'd been in the room with me. After we discussed how virtual counselling might work, we moved on to the subject of trauma, and I explained that they wouldn't be able to process their grieving until they'd addressed this. There are different approaches to trauma work, but I go with the view that it is like lots of small pieces of paper that are scrunched up in a bin: our work in therapy is to minutely examine each piece of paper and to put the feelings and facts back together, in order to construct a clear, integrated story. Repeatedly relating bits of the event over and over allows the trauma to be dislodged from the 'fight/flight/freeze' part of the brain and moved to the rational, thinking part, where it can be stored alongside all of our 'normal' memories.

This was painstaking work and could only be done inch by inch, as they learned how to regulate their system through slowing down and breathing, working with their body. When they were able to speak at greater length, they told me their tragic story.

They'd been on holiday in Spain with another family. It was towards the end of a happy day, and everyone was around the pool – four adults and six children. They were clearing up the usual kit after a summer's day: towels, swimsuits, buckets and spades, chatting while being busy. They hadn't noticed Amber silently stepping into the pool. She usually sat on the top step, and maybe this time had slipped or taken a step too far. Drowning is horrifyingly quick and silent. By the time they'd noticed, she was floating head down in the pool. Terror hit them as Annette screamed and Phil jumped in to save her. He desperately tried to resuscitate her while Annette rang for an ambulance. Because they were in a villa up in the hills, it took the paramedics twenty minutes to arrive. They were too late: it takes only two minutes to lose consciousness and four to six minutes to die.

The central trigger for their trauma was seeing Amber floating in the water, pulling her out of the pool, trying and failing to resuscitate her, and then carrying her body to the ambulance. Each time they saw those images it was like a muffled scream breaking out in their bodies. I would do breathing exercises with them, to calm them, and could feel the intensity of it in my body for a long time afterwards.

How could something as ridiculously normal as a child stepping into a pool end so catastrophically tragically? The random cruelty of life. It was just wrong, completely wrong, and it could easily have been any of us in their place. It could certainly have been me: I remember screaming when I spotted our two-year-old son toddling straight to the pond, having escaped through a gate without my knowledge. A few more minutes and his fate would have been very different. There will never be an explanation that makes sense to me.

Early on, Phil and Annette made the very conscious decision that they were not going to let the guilt swallow them up, despite the enormity of it. They strongly believed they owed it to Henri and Beatrice to be okay; they needed to ensure the children had happy times. Phil expressed the conflict with which he was wrestling: 'I feel guilty when I'm okay, and when I feel sad I feel as if I'm showing her that I'm missing her, though the pain of being unhappy makes everything bleak. I'm groping around trying to find a way forward.' Annette kept busy, and seemed to want to actively move them all on. She clearly felt the same depth of sadness as Phil, but her inclination wasn't to talk much about it. She said, 'I just get on with things. I think about her all through my day, and it doesn't get any easier. My eyes have dried up from crying, it's exhausting.'

Their grief ran beneath every minute of their day, although on the face of it they could still have nice times. Knowing they would never see what Amber would be like in ten years' time dragged them down. Phil felt his relationship with time had altered: he simply divided his life into the time before and after Amber had died. The future no longer really existed for him, and any sense he'd once had of linear time was gone.

For Phil, the question wasn't whether he could bear the sadness, but rather how he could bear it. He knew that externally he could put on a show, but that the internal side would be 'untouched by that – it still feels overwhelmingly sad. In as much as there are many facets of me, all those facets are affected by it, and it turns into a bloody big hole. For short periods, the hole isn't the centre of everything; but then it returns when I realize "That's another thing done without Amber." It's mainly about endurance: a bit like climbing Mount Everest with one leg – bloody tough.' As he spoke, I was aware of how robust he must be to endure so much pain. I didn't want to diminish the level of his suffering, but it felt important to acknowledge the role played by his strength as a protective factor.

Annette left her job. It was too difficult to keep working

at something that she said now felt 'pointless'. Although she knew that financially she would need to find a job in the future, for now her only interest was her family. She focused all her highly creative talent on them: going out to places that were fun, painting with the children, cooking with them – weaving new happy experiences into their memories. This didn't blunt her great sense of loss; instead, the loss forged in her the determination to look forward. Phil was unable to return to school for his first term because of the trauma. His memory was unreliable and diminished his ability to hold the children's attention. Watching children going about their lives, while Amber was robbed of hers, was too painful for him. In the second term he took a few classes, and over time he returned to teaching a full timetable.

I was interested in them as a couple and wanted to understand how they were with each other. There was a lightness in their relationship, which, I realized, was in fact deep trust. They dared to love each other fully; they weren't holding anything back. They didn't seem complicated; they might get cross with each other, but the emotions weren't tangled, and they could make up after a fight without finding themselves knee-deep in resentment. Annette spoke much less than Phil, yet it felt balanced between them; in some way, he spoke for them both. When we talked about how different they were in their grief, Phil summed it up matter-of-factly: 'It's something that you go off and do on your own. It's quite lonely. We all share in the family grief, but the grief I feel as an individual doesn't happen at the same time as theirs, and isn't the same as anyone else's. We're each wired differently, and one of us might feel the same thing with a different intensity at a different time. But in the end you have to deal with it yourself.' I inwardly smiled at his accuracy and thought how wonderful it would be if only everyone understood this so clearly.

I would listen and help them to clarify what they were feeling, while supporting their efforts to keep their physical systems balanced – traumatic memories could quickly hurl them into a state of heightened alert, as if they were in danger. I could feel the depth of their pain; one sentence of Phil's has stayed with me ever since: 'The silence is deafening.' I was particularly touched, unfair as it is, by seeing a man able to express his sadness easily, and I knew his ability to weather the pain would ultimately help him to heal. My understanding was that both Phil and Annette had been well-loved children: although there had been difficult events, such as the divorces of both sets of parents, this hadn't created fault lines in either of them. The strength of the secure and predictable love they'd been given growing up had built robust foundations and enabled them to withstand the searing wound of Amber's death.

Every session we would spend time talking about Henri and Beatrice, who had been working through their trauma with a school counsellor. There were times when they would rag about and be happy, and others when the sadness burst through. Beatrice would go into Amber's room, sit on her bed, smell her clothes and cry out furiously, 'I want Amber.' She missed her playmate, her sister, dreadfully. She went to sleep hugging Amber's teddies, and squeezed her eyes tightly to see her in her heart. At other times she would bend her head in the direction of her heart, as if Amber resided there, and whisper to her, telling her stories, her news. She wrote little memories on scraps of paper and drew pictures that she left dotted about the house; occasionally she wrote 'Hello' in the memorial book from Amber's funeral, which was now in their living room. Henri slept with Amber's blanket wrapped around his teddy, which he talked to before falling asleep.

As summer approached, the question of whether the children would want to go swimming needed to be addressed. Phil brought it up with the family while they were having tea, not wanting to make it dramatic, asking them how they felt about going into a pool. Both Beatrice and Henri were surprisingly pragmatic, wanting to swim and saying it didn't frighten them at all. For Phil and Annette, however, it was a different story: the knowledge that their children could potentially die was now unavoidable, and they had little confidence that they could keep their children safe. It would take them a long time to feel a sense of safety and security in their lives again.

Phil and Annette started going out with close friends with whom they felt comfortable. Leaving their home felt scary at first, but gradually they were able to do more. Stepping outside the protection of home meant that they might not be able to cope either with small things going wrong, such as the parking, or, more importantly, with other people's questions. It was difficult to deal with those who hadn't heard about Amber's accident when they asked, in a light casual way, 'How are you all?' Annette said, 'I was in the supermarket and bumped into someone I don't know well, and she asked me. I knew she didn't want the answer I had to give her, she wanted a smile and a "fine". I hated that I knew I was about to throw a bomb at her – which it was. She was very upset.'

The worst question a stranger could ask them was: 'How many children do you have?' They don't expect the answer to be 'I've had three children and one died.' For Phil and Annette there was a weighing up of 'least worst' options.

Should they deny Amber her existence by saying two children? Would it be untruthful to say three children but miss out the 'dead' word? Would they be able to deal with the fallout from the other person's shock if they were indeed to use the 'dead' word? Such fallout can be exhausting, and people have told me how tough it is to be the one saying 'It's okay, don't worry' when they, after all, are the ones who have experienced the death of their child. We agreed together that they shouldn't set themselves rules: it would depend on how they felt at the time, where they were and who asked the question.

At one session Annette said, 'I found pictures Phil had taken of Amber after she died; he'd put them in a special place, and I decided to look at them, and she seemed much more dead than how I remembered her, she looked very dead . . . ha . . . I found that it's hard and just so, so unbelievably sad. I woke up at five this morning, when I couldn't get back to sleep I imagined that she would come in the door, the little figure that used to go "Phewor", power open the door, jump on the bed, climb in over us . . . I miss her so much . . . When I put on a jacket this week that I haven't worn for ages, inside I found a piece of Playmobil that she'd picked up, it had been in her hand, and I remember she'd given it to me . . .' I could feel with Annette that the piece of Playmobil was like holding her in time, as if she were in her pocket – and yet she wasn't there.

I ended the session wondering out loud what it was they got from me, and learned I was the one person they didn't have to protect from how badly they felt, and with whom they could explore the same questions over and over. Also I'd been with them since the very beginning, which represented something significant; for I had witnessed them evolve to the point where they could once again trust in themselves.

On the face of it, Henri had accepted Amber's death in a somewhat mechanistic way, saying, 'There's nothing I can do about it.' He was happy at school with his friends and working well. But this was by no means the whole picture; Amber was with him still, and he was fiercely loyal to her: one day, when a friend's father said, 'There are two children in your family,' Henri had become furiously cross and through burning tears said, 'NO, there are three of us.' When they'd talked together as a family about what to do on Amber's birthday, he'd had the most ideas: he'd wanted a cake with candles, and to send a balloon with a note up to her in the sky. I felt how profoundly unfair it was that both children had to face these unanswerable questions of death when they were so young – yet instinctively they were doing the right things to support themselves.

One day Phil went to stay with Amber's godfather, and he saw for the first time a photograph of her on a chair in the garden. The chair was still there, but she wasn't, and he couldn't stop looking for her. Phil didn't know what to believe: he didn't want to think there was simply nothing after death, but he didn't feel her around him, or an enduring connection to her. People kept saying to him 'You always have her memory', but he said, 'I find that false and soulless. One thing about memories, you realize how few you have, and how limited they can be. If I rely on photos and not on memory, it's less rich. Then there are the memories of the accident: I have to separate those out, but I can't always control them. I like thinking about her, but I always end up with the same idea: she's not here.' He felt she was slipping through his fingers. I told them that memories, when actively searched

for, become less available, like struggling to remember a title
or a name; but if they were to stop looking so hard, the fragments could combine into a complete picture of clear and
replete memories.

Annette didn't have the same sense of constantly searching
for Amber, because she had no trouble recalling her more
recent memories. She said: 'I remember brushing her hair,
and how her hair smelled. I can see Amber running in from
gymnastics, bursting through the door, alive . . . There was
one day I wish I'd recorded: she was entertaining the other
two by telling endless jokes, laughing so much at her own
jokes, pulling faces . . . She was a child who spoke with her
whole body – when I looked at her from behind, I could tell
when she was smiling.' Remembering was a form of healing
for her; it enabled her to make progress. Yet fewer and fewer
people brought up Amber's name, and she had fewer and
fewer opportunities to remember her. It forced her to rely on
being busy and getting on with things as a way of coping.

'Getting on' she was most certainly doing: nine months
after Amber's death, Annette was pregnant. They both had
tearful, happy smiles when they told me the news. This
wasn't in any way an attempt to replace Amber. Friends had
infuriated her by their simplistic view that now she was
pregnant 'all was well'. Having hope while at the same time
grieving for Amber were two processes that ran in parallel
with one another; one didn't cancel out the other. Annette
had had three successful pregnancies, and she was optimistic
this one would be successful too. It gave them all some light
to look towards on their bleakest days.

The anniversary of Amber's death was coming up. An
anniversary is a marker of time, and there is an intensity to
it. The build-up to this one was hard, particularly for Phil,

who wasn't sleeping. As the day approached, his distress levels rose, as he relived the horror of what had happened. The actual anniversary occurred over the Easter holidays, and they decided to spend a few days with each grandparent, which would take them from France to England. The children wanted to be with all their family – their aunts, uncles and cousins as well. They instinctively knew that love was the best balm for loss and that being open to it would help them bear their grief. They wanted to go to the tree that had been planted for Amber when she'd been born, and where some of her ashes had been scattered, in order to feel close to her. Phil felt closer to Amber there as well. Towards the end of our session, he tipped back his head, closed his eyes and spoke up towards the ceiling: 'If I could get to Heaven and say only a few words, they would be about *love*, is she *safe*, is she *happy* and how much I *miss her*.'

Phil worried that as a family they weren't talking enough about Amber, and, although he wanted to speak more about Amber, the rest of the family didn't. As parents, he felt, they should be providing a model for their children about how to grieve. He was constantly negotiating the dilemma of how to live and be in the present, while still holding on to Amber and all the pain that entailed. He had an endless sense of missing her, and hoped talking about her would both keep her spirit alive and give them all a better shot at being better adjusted. I thought he was right.

Annette surprised and touched him with the news that she was going to film Amber's school friends talking about their memories of her. And the following week they would be unveiling a mosaic bench that encircled a tree in the playground at the children's school, organized by some of the other parents; the mosaic depicted images drawn by Henri,

Beatrice and Amber's best friends. Phil hugged Annette in a tight, sweary, loving hug.

A few months later, we realized enough had been done in the way of therapy. They had found a way of living their lives without losing sight of Amber. It was a bitter-sweet ending for all of us: positive in the sense that they no longer needed my support but sad in that we would now be saying goodbye. It had been an intensely intimate relationship, with Amber at its centre.

Reflections

My work with these couples is a small window into their world at the most intensely painful time in each of their lives. There is almost nothing more traumatic than the death of a child. It tears up the rule book of life: we never expect to have to bury our own children; they should be the ones to bury us. These couples were shattered and disorientated: they felt as if they had been thrown into an alien world, which was frightening and confusing, and for which they had no map or compass. The death of a child leaves a fathomless hole, and, of all the losses people suffer, it takes the longest to rebuild their lives afterwards.

Families grieving the death of their son or daughter are grieving a person who was a central part of them, embodied in their being, sometimes giving them their purpose in life and their identity. They are grieving their absence in their everyday life as well as the future that they assumed they would someday see. They are forced to reconfigure their present lives as well as their idea of the future without their child in it.

The couples whose stories I have told here valued their relationships enough to do the psychological work necessary to help them through their suffering. I would urge couples, if they feel they need to see a therapist following the death of their child, to do so together. It is a loss that shakes the relationship and the family system to the core, and it is hard to recover from such a loss without the participation of both parents in counselling. As many parents have said, having a child die 'makes you a member of a club that no one wants to be a member of', and leaves many families with a sense that they are now outsiders. In addition many feel that they have somehow been singled out to have this terrible thing happen to them; in the past, when many more children died, it was still devastating, but there was a kind of consolation in the high numbers. An important step in recovery can be meeting up with other people who have had this experience by becoming part of a support group.

Often the intense grief of grandparents is not recognized. They not only grieve the death of their grandchild, but witness the suffering of their devastated child, while being powerless to change what has happened. Grandparents may play a pivotal role in holding the family together when a child dies, if they have a good enough relationship with their bereaved child. But if the relationship has difficulties, it is possible that this will exacerbate them.

Risks for bereaved parents

Mothers and fathers are at increased risk both of psychiatric disorders and of chronic health conditions following the death of a child, particularly in the first year, when bereaved parents are 70 per cent more likely to be hospitalized for a first psychiatric admission, compared with parents who have not lost a child. I cannot stress enough the importance of getting help when attempting to cope with a loss of this magnitude. Those parents who don't face their grief don't seem very different from other bereaved parents in their first year; but in subsequent years, even decades later, they may suffer more socially, emotionally and physically than other bereaved parents.

The difference between men and women

Mothers tend to be preoccupied with the loss of their child for longer than men. They have higher levels of anxiety, intrusive thoughts, and disrupted sleep. Research shows that men are often unwilling to talk about the death of a child and avoid seeking professional support; this may be because they feel they have to be strong for their wife, or because of the influence of social conditioning.

This does not mean men feel less pain than women but rather that they instinctively manage their pain differently. One of the unintended consequences of this is that men don't get as much care and attention from those around them. It is assumed that because they look as if they are coping that they are, with the result that men often feel their grief as fathers is discounted by others.

Research on the couple's relationship

If couples can find ways of communicating with each other, they can become closer through the loss. They are the only two people in the world that truly know what this experience of their child dying feels like. However, research shows that couples who already have difficulties in their relationship and who don't seek support are more likely to separate following the death of a child.

A key element for recovery is encouraging all aspects of

social support; good friends who stay close and connected beyond the time of the crisis are essential to couples who have been bereaved. Over time, they can help families to re-enter the flow of life – changed, but with less of a sense of being an 'outsider'.

Guilt

Guilt is very intense for bereaved parents. More than in any other bereavement, they tend to hold themselves responsible for the death of their child, regardless of the cause of death. This is heightened when it is a sudden death. Families often go over and over in their minds the circumstances of the death, wanting to go back in time and change any decision that might have brought about a different outcome.

Saying 'You aren't guilty' doesn't work with such couples – any more than telling someone not to worry – for it is a wish-fulfilment that they cannot deliver on. Instead, the guilt needs to be examined in minute detail and brought out into the open. Only then can its force be diminished. This process often helps to clarify the mismatch between what they are saying to themselves in their hearts and what is actually the case in reality. Two voices silently battling become clearer. Logically they might know that the actual cause of death was an accident or natural causes, but the voice coming from their hearts is telling them that this was 100 per cent their fault. Inchoate, unspoken conflict is often at the heart of their unbearable tension, and when it is made clearer some of that tension is diffused.

False assumptions

People who are fortunate enough not to have had a baby or child die often look for ways to soften the blow of the loss for others. Most of us will look for a positive and make the wrong assumption that a baby's dying is less painful than a child's, because the parents didn't know the baby. The pain of a child's loss cannot be measured by their age, but by the love and hope that were invested in them.

Another positive that people look for is the thought that having other children will lessen the pain of the child's death. Research does show that having other children can help, as being forced to carry on for their living children gives parents a sense of purpose in life. This is, however, a simplistic view that mustn't be taken too far. At times the pain bereaved parents feel for the death of their child may overwhelm the love they feel for their existing children.

Hope

Hope is the alchemy that can turn a life around, a vital element that enabled people like Phil and Annette to rebuild their trust in life. But the full impact on families will depend not only on all that happened before and at the time of the death, but also on its ultimate consequences. This means that hope needs to deliver some good luck as well. I have worked with couples who experience further difficult events, such as losing a job, failing to get pregnant or the death of another family member. An additional psychological battering on top of their child's death may tip them into despair.

Accommodation

Accommodation is a therapeutic term used to describe intense loss, its impact, and how we have to change internally to make allowances for this new reality. There is a very good image that represents this. The space or hole that represents the loss is black, bottomless and all-consuming at the beginning, but over time – sometimes a long time – the bereaved person rebuilds their life and, while the hole doesn't diminish in size, their life expands to surround it.

Rando, T. (1993)

Post-traumatic growth

Research has been carried out in the US and the UK that reveals positive change and psychological growth can be achieved after a traumatic event. This does not in any way reduce the severity of the trauma from the event, or imply that it was a good thing. For some people, surviving life-changing events can have unexpected consequences. These people found that they felt more resilient, as if they had grown, and had a greater sense of their robustness in the face of adversity – along the lines of 'If I can survive that, I can survive anything.' It also changed their perception of what mattered in life: for most, this meant placing less value on money and status, and more on relationships and the meaning of life. As a result, those people's relationships tended to deepen and were more satisfying, and they gained a sense of being wiser and more compassionate. Having truly suffered so much, they found that their ability to empathize and sympathize increased, and some experienced spiritual or religious growth as well.

I have noticed such growth with some of my clients, and it is certainly very encouraging. It is further evidence of what never ceases to surprise me: that as human beings we are eminently adaptable, and that those who adapt most are ultimately the ones who thrive.

Statistics relating to child deaths

If we are at the lucky end of a statistical percentage, the numbers don't mean very much. It's when we're at the other end that they become important. Sometimes they give us an idea of just how bad our luck may be, while in others they let us know that we're not the only ones in the world to have suffered such a fate, though it may feel that way at the time.

The number of baby and child deaths over a year has remained stable in the last decade.

- The statistics show one in four pregnancies ends in miscarriage.
- There are about 3,500 stillbirths a year.
- On average 5,000 neonatal and infant deaths occur in a year.
- 7,000 child deaths occur in a year, which is ten child deaths per 100,000 in England and Wales.
- The time of highest risk for children to die is just before birth or in the newborn period. Two thirds of baby deaths occur in the neonatal period, which is the first twenty-eight days of life. After the first year of life, the number of deaths drops dramatically, and rises again only for those aged fourteen to twenty-one having accidents.

Facing your own death

Let me not die while I am still alive

– Hebrew prayer

Jean

Jean was forty-eight years old, small and thin. She looked as if she had stepped out of the 1970s, with a colourful ethnic shirt that hung loosely over hippy silk flared trousers. A headscarf wrapped around her long red wavy hair served as a hairband. She had a peaceful presence, which ran counter to her terrible story. She had recently been given a fatal diagnosis of lung cancer, and a prognosis that she could live six months to a year.

Grief starts at the point of diagnosis, when we can no longer assume, as most of us do, that we are going to continue to live for the foreseeable future. It shatters the blissful ignorance that death happens to other people but not to ourselves.

Jean had a double grief: tragically, her brother had died in a car crash five years before. When she told me this I imagined the terrible anguish of her mother, who would have to cope with the death of two children. Jean was married, with a seventeen-year-old son, James. She had a functioning but not deeply connected relationship with her husband, Simon; they had come together through their love of music. She recognized that he was kind and extremely intelligent but emotionally distant and she was concerned that he might not be able to meet all of James's needs when she died.

She wanted to be able to talk to me about her illness and imminent death, and what this would mean for James. No one in her family would listen: whenever she brought up the subject they would avoid it, and talk instead about the future: 'How is your treatment going?' 'Isn't modern medicine incredible?' They closed down any possibility of discussing her worries. Her death did feel real to me; being only five years older than Jean, I was struck that I was sitting opposite someone of my own generation who would probably be dead within the next six months. My mortality felt fragile.

Jean talked a lot about her brother's death, crying often as she told his story. The suddenness of the phone call that Sunday evening, her regret that she never saw his body – the police had advised against it: it all culminated in a shock that had stayed in her body for a long time.

Jean was extraordinarily calm about facing her own death. I was surprised by this, because it was far from what I imagine I'd feel in her situation, and yet it was authentic. At this point I couldn't fully work out how she came to be so accepting of her own mortality. I had tentatively asked once, and she had changed the subject, clearly not wishing to talk about it. I noted it, and guessed the subject would return.

Much more upsetting for Jean was leaving her son, James. This was her focus, so I made it mine. She now regretted that she hadn't been fully 'awake' to the need to mother James when she'd been physically well enough to do so. What preoccupied her was how he would be looked after when she was no longer present. She never used the 'dead' word, nor did I, which was a relief, because I found it very hard to imagine saying the actual *d* word to her face; perhaps I was picking up feelings she herself was projecting. It gave me some insight into the difficulty others must have had in discussing her death with her: if I found it hard, they would find it even harder. Jean would use phrases such as 'not being here' or 'when I'm gone'. I kept my responses as close as possible to what she said, because I didn't want to disrupt her very delicate way of being by using my own words or thoughts. I strongly disagree with medics and therapists who insist that their patients need to be forced to face reality when they're in denial. My belief is that it isn't our job to march around in hobnail boots in someone else's consciousness, breaking down their important defence mechanisms, as if we can be absolutely certain about what's best for them. Such an approach would most probably have alienated her and she wouldn't have returned, or it would have heightened her defences to the point where no therapy would have been possible.

Jean hadn't given up on life. She absolutely wanted to live for as long as possible, even participating in a trial of a new cancer treatment. As I understood it, her acceptance of her own death came from the fact that her predominant emotions were invested in those she loved, and whom she would be leaving behind, and I continued to be struck by her selflessness as a mother.

One of the most painful discussions we had was about how to convey her fatal diagnosis to James. Having to tell him that she wasn't going to get better felt harder than it had been getting the fatal diagnosis itself. She naturally wanted to protect him from this knowledge, particularly as he was finding being a teenager quite tricky. He was at the mercy of adolescent hormones cascading through his body: she bought him the wrong brand of trainers, he hated doing his homework, and he was often angry in an indeterminate way his mother couldn't entirely understand. Jean suspected he was angry that she hadn't been well, and that she wasn't the mother he would have chosen for himself. 'He wants a healthy mother who can do things,' she told me. Over the past few years she'd had weeks of very strong chemo, then some months of remission, and finally the fatal diagnosis. It meant she was often ill, though she tried to rest while James was at school to enable her to be with him when he got home.

I told her that my overarching view was that, as his mother, she knew best, and that any information I gave her had to be filtered through that particular lens. I also told her that research showed that children fare better if they are told the truth, the same truth as adults, and that what parents think of as protection is experienced by children as exclusion. Following the death, they can be very angry that everyone else knew and they didn't. I was worried that if James wasn't told, and he continued to be angry and difficult with her, he would have many regrets later on, and be furious that he wasn't given the opportunity to be loving, or the opportunity to say 'goodbye' until it was too late. As I told her this Jean didn't cry; instead she wrote some notes in her little book, as she did during every session. She nodded her head and swallowed, and I could see that she had taken a big emotional hit. But somehow she accepted what I'd said and resolved to tell him that weekend. I could feel tears in my eyes at her quiet dignity.

James cried and shouted when Jean and her husband told him. He didn't want it to be true; and he couldn't quite believe it because his experience had always been that after she got ill she got better. He also wanted information, such as how long she would live. They told him the truth as they knew it then: that there was no cure and the medication she was taking now was to stop her being in pain, not to make her better, and that she didn't know when she was going to die. They hoped she had a year at least, maybe more. He cuddled her more than he had for a long time. He remained shaken all weekend and moved between anger and sadness, retreating to his computer to hide from the news he didn't want to have to face.

Jean said she had noticed that lately James was turning more towards his dad, almost like an instinctive survival mechanism, moving in the direction of life and away from death. This is common, and I was in two minds as to whether to tell her: it might help her to understand James's behaviour but it might also considerably worsen her existing pain. In the end, I opted for honesty. I'm not sure whether this helped to ease her hurt; in retrospect, I don't think anything could have done that. She was dying and leaving her much beloved son. Every part of her must have hurt.

As the weeks passed, Jean's health deteriorated. I found it distressing to see her so ill, and acknowledged that I could see how much more difficult it was for her to breathe or to climb the stairs. She treated this lightly, with no self-pity. I was very moved by her, while at the same time finding myself quite nervous – coming so close to her mortality once again put me in touch with my own.

Clearly Jean was well loved and had a good set of friends: 'My friends come to see me. It's very touching, but tiring too.' We agreed a strategy that would enable her to say 'no' to some visitors that didn't make her seem rude, in an effort to protect her very precious remaining time. She set her email to deliver an out-of-office message, and her relief at not having to look at her inbox surprised us both. Courtesy was important to her. Everyone she did see knew she was dying, but again no one mentioned it to her or asked what was on her mind. It was as if talking about her death would in some way hasten it. This wasn't her view: she still wanted to be able to talk about her death in practical terms and was profoundly frustrated by the 'brick wall of denial, that they can't seem to get past'. We discussed what she could do to change this, and agreed that she should organize a number of suppers with her surviving sibling, James's godparents and her husband. She felt it was too distressing to involve her mother, who was in her late seventies and distraught that her second child was dying.

At those suppers Jean stepped out of her usual quiet self and set her agenda. She had written her concerns in her notebook and she listed them all now: who would sort out James's school uniform, who would take him on holiday, who would help him decide which GCSEs he should take, which university he should go to, which girlfriend he should see, etc. She was going to write a birthday card for every year until he was twenty-one, and she wanted to ensure they were given to him. She hated the idea of James being alone with only his loving but autistic father for company for weeks at a time. Over these suppers, plans were made and agreements reached; everyone knew exactly what they would be responsible for. Jean felt hugely relieved, as she had now done her best to mother James into the future in the only way that she could; she couldn't have control over her own death, but she could have some influence over her son's future life.

I suggested that perhaps he could connect to her physically in some way, by rubbing cream on her hands or bringing her a cup of tea, thereby creating those memories of being kind to her and looking after her. She told me he would come to her room when she was in bed and draw pictures while lying beside her – which sounded perfect. I knew every memory he had of her would become more and more precious as time went on; when he started to worry that he might forget her, those drawings would take him directly to the memory of them together. Photographs of them together could also be a touchstone for him: I suggested she take lots of them as a whole family, and of just the two of them.

Our last appointment was by telephone. Jean had been in hospital the previous week and undergone surgery. She was home now, but had been told 'It is more likely that you have days or weeks to live rather than months.' I felt the shock of it catch me in my throat. I said how sorry I was to hear that, and just couldn't imagine how hard it must have been for her. I remembered the words of a doctor with whom I had worked at a hospice: 'However clear the diagnosis of a terminal illness, you can never be prepared for death.'

My words felt desperately inadequate, but they were all I had, and I think my tone conveyed more than my words could. She now had to decide whether to withhold the knowledge of how imminent her death was from James or to have as nice a time as possible with him in these last days of her life. She didn't want them to be marred, but she also knew he would be angry with her for not telling him everything.

After talking about James, Jean cried and told me for the first time that she was frightened. I wanted to switch the focus from James to her, to concentrate on supporting her in her fear. Though it went against all my instincts, I had to respect her wishes when she told me she wanted to use our time to think about her son. In the end, Jean settled on a compromise: she would spend the next week with him, making it a special time for them together, and that afterwards she would tell him that she did not have long to live. She was ridiculously grateful to me for speaking to her, and I felt angry at the cruelty of the world.

She was too ill for further appointments with me. The tone of her lovely email told me she knew we wouldn't speak again. I heard two weeks later from a friend of hers that she had died. Of course I'd known it was going to happen, but it was still a shock. Experience with my clients has taught me that knowing and experiencing are worlds apart. I felt shaken and hoped it had been peaceful and painless. But I'd never know. I went to my local church and lit a candle for her. I find myself wondering about her still.

Barbara

Barbara, who had been diagnosed with kidney cancer seventeen years ago, agreed to meet me at her home to talk about living with a life-threatening diagnosis. I knew very little about her, except that she was extremely quick to respond to my email. When I had to ring her from my car because I was lost, I was surprised by how weak her voice sounded: her words seemed to be struggling to emerge from what sounded like a cavernous chest.

Barbara was waiting for me outside her cottage, kindly waving. She was accompanied by two excited, tail-wagging, barking dogs and my first thought was: oh, God, please don't let me run over those dogs. I didn't, and she welcomed me in, with tea and carrot cake.

Barbara was delicate and frail, and she walked slowly. Over seventy-five, she was beautiful, not with a faded beauty, with a beauty that came alight when she spoke and particularly when she smiled. Her thick grey hair and skin had clearly spent its life outside, but was pale now. She had a twinkle in her eye when she was animated that drew me in.

I didn't fully understand her wry laugh when I said I was interested in how she had managed to live with cancer for so long, until she told me, 'This week has been a very bad one. I've been on a drug trial for the last eighteen months that I fought to get on. It's meant to attack my immune system, a going-forward drug. Anyway, it hasn't worked. They told me the cancer has come back in a big way: I've got it in my stomach as well. It's grown to the size of a tangerine, which is very quick growth, not very good. I've only got months . . .' As she said those devastating words, tears broke through. She didn't want to cry: 'I've been so strong up to now, but I feel weak today, I've had a lot of pain, and I'm tired too.' She put her hand to her mouth, wanting to push back the tears.

I felt a blast of pain from her words and was aware that she had said to me, a total stranger, the most intense words, other than 'I love you', anyone could say to someone else. I knew my response needed to be simple and compassionate, not dramatic. I was struck by the understatement 'not very good'. She was fighting to hold herself together; she didn't like crying, and I didn't want her to feel overexposed with me. I said how sorry I was, how shocking such news must be. I wanted her to know that I'd taken on board the enormity of what she'd said, and how much I felt for her; I needed to keep my voice level and contained yet empathetic.

Barbara smiled, fighting through her sadness. 'I've been dealing with this the last couple of days. You've come at the right time to see someone who has to face up to dying.' That beautiful smile again, ironic this time. Her response showed me she was operating at different levels: knowing the truth about her life expectancy in a pragmatic way and yet also not wishing to know. She was an organized person, a 'perfectionist', she said, and wanted 'to get everything in order. There's always so much to be done. I couldn't see the solicitor this morning because I was crying too much. Maybe I can see him tomorrow.'

To explore further how she felt about her life expectancy I asked whether she wanted to talk to her consultant, imagining she was torn between aggressive treatment, which had horrible side-effects but might buy her more time, and no treatment at all, which might mean she would feel well but live a shorter life. I wondered how could she decide between quality of life and quantity of life, the costs versus the benefits of each. But her instinct was to do battle with the cancer. 'I don't want to hear the bad news. I don't want an appointment with him, if all he has is bad news. I've proved them wrong so many times, and I can do it again.' She fought back tears as she said, 'I don't want to die. I thought I had a year to live, so this is a shock.' I realized how easy it was for me to talk airily about the idea of these choices when they weren't actually my own, when they weren't about my life, my death. For Barbara, and probably for many people, no amount of thinking could override the biological drive to survive.

Yet, underlying her pragmatic response was a much more vulnerable one: fear of facing the unknown. 'I'm petrified I'm going to lose all my faculties. My voice is going – I saw a speech therapist and she basically told me there is nothing she can do . . . I only have the summer and I want it to be relaxed. I want to have as good a time as possible, but I'm scared.' At this point we talked about what she needed, what she wanted in place to support her.

Barbara lived alone but wasn't lonely; she was happy in her own skin. She had fought a hard battle following the death six years earlier of her much loved husband, Paddy, 'a bad grief' she had suffered alone. Although she had found a way of continuing to live, she felt that the pain of that loss was connected to her cancer coming back: the grief had triggered it. Her care for her husband had overshadowed her care for herself, and she had neglected to monitor her own cancer until it was too late.

I could see Barbara was someone who didn't want to make

a fuss, who was polite and thoughtful about others; but the price of that courtesy was that nobody knew what she actually needed. She needed friends to keep her company, to tell her their news, to be around, but she felt everyone was busy; she couldn't disturb them and said tellingly, 'I don't ring them; I expect them to ring me – but then they say I don't want to bother you when you're ill.' I suggested firmly that now was the time to put herself first. She picked up her phone and found a list of priorities she'd written a few weeks before:

- Me
- Pip and Buster (the dogs)
- Friends
- Home
- Horses
- Chickens

I laughed with her at the fact that at least she knew she had to put herself first. Her dogs were her closest companions: they sat on the sofa with her, slept in her room, forced her out for walks, always loved her, were always pleased to see her, were her greatest and most accessible comfort. She'd also loved horses her whole life; their presence, their smell, grounded her. Watching racing calmed her too.

I asked her about her love of gardens and horses, and learned a little more of her story. When she spoke about the past, her voice was lighter, like a youthful version of herself. 'When I was eleven years old I put my foot down: I wanted to ride. My first pony was Patch, a skewbald Shetland. He was my first love, a funny tough little horse who taught me to ride; I lived in his stable. My father was a farmer on a small holding in Lincolnshire; he worked hard and we children helped him all the time, delivering the lambs, milking, feeding the cattle. I sat on his lap on the tractor for hours at a time: I can conjure in my memory the smell of his pipe, which he puffed on as I sat there, chewing the end, I loved it . . .' It struck me as she was speaking that feelings don't age; Barbara's skin, bones, hair, every cell of her being was that of an oldish woman, but when she spoke of her childhood she was six again, sixteen – the feelings brought by the memories were untouched by time.

From there she had worked as a groom at a local estate, which unexpectedly introduced her to a beautiful garden and set her life in a new direction; she told me, 'My love of gardening has given me enduring happiness.' She trained as a landscape gardener, and built up a successful practice over forty years, although she continued to enjoy horses and riding throughout her life.

Barbara had never been loved until she was in her late forties. 'No one ever said "I love you" to me, until I met Paddy. I don't know if it was me, or what it was, but all the relationships I had, and there weren't that many, just never took off – until I met Paddy, my Paddy.' When she met him, he was divorced with one teenage son, with whom it had taken time to develop a good relationship. 'He's better with me now we don't have Paddy to compete over, and he's pretty good – he comes and sees me now and again.' I was wondering whether not having children was a big loss for her when she volunteered, 'I'd have liked children, but it wasn't to be. I had my horses and dogs.'

There was an interesting contradiction between the image she projected and the strength she really had. That sweet, non-assertive politeness, which was very much old school English, meant that she viewed herself as subordinate to her husband; yet this belied the steel in her, which had enabled her to fight against the odds and won years of life for both of them. She'd had a close friend who had also been diagnosed with kidney cancer at the same time, and she had died within the year. Barbara felt this was because her friend had been angry and resentful, always saying, 'Why me?' Whereas Barbara had, with equanimity, said, 'Why not me?'

Barbara's experience with the medical system had been very varied. The lack of information provided and the lack of communication between specialities were incredibly frustrating, and she felt that they'd missed her stomach cancer: she'd been complaining of pain for months. She finally found a consultant whom she could trust and said to him, 'You're my God now,' because she had to have someone in whom she could invest all her hope. But he was phenomenally busy, as most consultants are, so she didn't get information or responses from him for a long time. On the one hand she knew this was because of the demands made upon him by the system, but on the other she just felt like shouting at him. He shut her up by saying, 'Sorry, I've been dealing with a dying patient.'

A little later, Barbara's voice became weaker: she was clearly very tired. I checked that she was going to let people know that she wanted to see them, and that she wouldn't wait for them to ring her. After we agreed we'd meet again, she thanked me, and we both fell back on the usual courtesies and thank yous, as if we'd had a totally uneventful cup of tea, chatting about the weather. Surreal.

Barbara's response to her fatal diagnosis was similar to grief from a death: the push and pull between what can be faced and what can't, the mixed messages and contradictory feelings. That was why she needed support. The friends in her life who loved her could sit with her and watch racing and reminisce; hopefully they would also be able to talk with her about her impending death, if she brought it up.

I realized that how we are in life is how we are in death, only perhaps more intensely. Maintaining her dignity and strength would provide an important pillar of support for Barbara. My job would be to find a way of allowing her to express that dignity and that strength, as well as her fear of the scary unknown. I hoped that, in retrospect, she wouldn't feel unsettled, having told a stranger so much.

I also thought about how she had welcomed me by waiting outside her cottage, and offered me cake and tea in a proper china teapot on my arrival, something I never do – friends are lucky to get a mug and a biscuit out of me, as I'm always busy doing something else when they arrive. Barbara had given me her full attention, and her willingness to look out for me gave me an insight into her generosity as a person. I wondered if she represented the end of an era for that kind of woman, one for whom the covering of mess and difficulty with niceties and politeness, a smile and a cup of tea, is the norm. She had probably paid a high price for this in her lifetime. I decided to explore these ideas with her; there was something poignant about it that stayed with me.

I received a lovely email from Barbara, saying she'd like to see me again, and I was pleased that I hadn't overwhelmed her. I went to see her a couple of weeks later and was relieved to find that she looked and sounded the same: her health hadn't deteriorated; and of course there was tea and cake. I learned that she had been prescribed a new medication, which she hoped would work. She appeared so optimistic and positive that I wondered whether she would bring up her dying, but I knew it wasn't for me to ask her about it directly.

Barbara had not yet consciously engaged in the internal psychological debate that sooner or later everyone in her position must have: when is 'acceptance of death' the right thing, bringing peace and calm; and when is 'giving up too soon' the wrong thing, with every day still worth the battle. It seemed clear to me that Barbara had fought outstandingly against the disease, but that fighting now would only bring her distress, because she was not going to win the war. I hoped that, over time, I could help her to articulate this. We both knew why I was there, and I gave her many opportunities to raise the subject with me by asking open questions such as 'Do you have any worries?' Her response was: 'I don't know whether I can go to the local flower show. I really want to, but I'm worried I'm not strong enough.' It felt to me as if parallel conversations were continually taking place between us: what she said on the surface and what we both knew she was really saying underneath, but didn't want or maybe even didn't need to voice. It was a double-knowing, although the difficulty she had in enunciating the words – she had to fight for breath to speak – was telling us both how ill she really was.

I was aware that she might find it valuable to take stock of her whole life, and, although I was curious, I wouldn't force her if that wasn't what she wanted to do. Her mode of operating in her life, her coping mechanism, was to be passive, and this in some way dampened the intensity of her feelings, kept them neat. The more pressure she was under, the more she needed it, but I tried gently to tease out what emotions I could to ensure she had a buttress to help her withstand her fear of dying. She was able to tell me loving Paddy, along with her work and love of horses, had given her life meaning. 'When he was ill people worried if it was too much for me. Of course it wasn't; I didn't want to be anywhere else or with anyone else. He didn't like the hospice nurses; he only wanted me to nurse him, and I did.' I could hear her pride and love as she spoke, and was aware that she wasn't going to have the love of someone like that for herself.

There was only one moment when the silent dialogue that had been running beneath our words emerged. She was talking about a holiday she'd had last summer. 'I don't want to travel again: my holiday gave me too much time to think. I prefer being busy here . . . and, well, I probably won't have the option.' It was as if she had fallen into the thought unintentionally. As I reflected back what she'd said, tears slowly came into her eyes. Then she turned away and changed the subject – and immediately came back to it, as if the discussion had been continuous. 'I'm not frightened of dying. I'm frightened of dying alone, of being found dead.' We talked about what plans she could make that would ensure that didn't happen. 'I saw the palliative care nurse last week. I could go to the hospice, but I want to be at home . . .' There were more tears, prompting the dogs to jump into her lap and lick her face. She laughed as she cried, stroking them, repeating their names, soothing them and, in doing so, soothing herself. I was pretty sure the hospice could ensure that she had care at home. We agreed it was something she would check when she next saw the nurse, which was in a few days' time.

When I next tried to make an appointment to see Barbara, she didn't respond, and I feared she had died. I was wondering how I might find out when I received a text from her, and I went to see her.

Barbara looked much, much thinner, and she walked with

a stick. Her breath was so short it was difficult to hear what she said. She told me, 'I've really not been very well at all, had a very high temperature. I'm not sure which way I'm bending at the moment – the Macmillan nurse said she's expecting me to die any second, but I'm not sure . . . I'm a cog that doesn't fit, there's no slot for me to drop into.' As she was speaking, she was trying to put on her socks and was too weak to manage it. I offered to help her, but she was determined to do it herself. Yet she needed my help in the end. It was important for her to be functioning normally, but she was very fragile. She did fit that slot: the problem was that she didn't want to drop into it.

I was moved to hear that she had taken her need to have people that loved her around her on board for herself. She'd decided to have a tea party for her birthday. 'It absolutely finished me off.' She was crying as she told me: 'I got quite emotional at the tea party the other day, knowing people were really saying goodbye [more tears]. I don't think anyone saw. I do feel it's got to that stage now . . .' I was about to respond to that, but before I had the chance she shifted the direction slightly. A friend had said to her: 'It [the party] did what you wanted, lots of smiley faces, no reason not to have smiley faces.' I acknowledged that it had been a celebration of her, and she smiled her attractive smile and proudly read out a text one of her best friends had sent her: 'Last Tuesday was the memorable side of love, so, so special.' I'm not sure I fully understood what the message meant, but Barbara clearly did. The whole event held real significance for her, but was bitter-sweet. She'd recognized the importance of feeling loved and of having the opportunity to say goodbye, yet everyone needed to pretend all was well and normal: she had hidden her sadness, as had her guests, I'm sure. I can't help but wonder what it would have been like had they spoken the truth to each other.

As I was sitting with her, I picked up that, although she wanted to be able to tell me what she was thinking, she didn't want me to engage too deeply with her. She was making very profound statements about facing her own death, yet it felt as if a part of her needed to retreat from them, and she certainly didn't want to process any of the emotions surrounding them. I was a sounding board only for the things on her mind that she wanted to voice. She was both retreating from her life and fighting for it.

We went outside into her small and stunning garden, and I could see her visibly relax as she felt the sun on her face and sat in her favourite place. She closed her eyes and absorbed it into her being. 'Ah, happier now . . . I want to be able to ride again.' I could see that her mind was placing her on her horse, the wind in her hair, where she felt safest and most at home, in nature, as a child, as an adult; it soothed her.

The other thing that relaxed her was the closeness she felt to Johnny, her stepson, and the thought that they'd been reconciled. 'Nice that we've sort of been . . . he really cares for me, which is lovely, which I didn't think he did. I feel loved by him. I thought he never loved me before. I was the stepmother [lots of tears], it was very hard. I was petrified when Paddy died that he'd think I hadn't handled it well, but he said I'd handled it beautifully. He's been really supportive and good . . . We say I love you to each other.' I didn't need to say much, only how important the tears were for her – they were releasing old pain and letting in Johnny's love, happy tears.

If there was a message she'd like to give to other people in her position, it was that you needed to get on top of the pain, which her carers had managed for her, and that 'You'll always want more time.' It felt poignant, and like another acknowledgement that she knew she didn't have very long. For she felt exhausted most of the time.

She could accept that she needed help. 'One puff of something and I'd be dead . . . I just want to sleep. But if nobody is here, it's a bit scary.' She'd had quite a battle with the recent Macmillan nurse and asked her to leave, not liking the intrusion, but she now realized she had to stop trying to be in control and let them nurse her. I could see how hard that was for her: relinquishing her control also felt like relinquishing her life.

She was tired and needed to sleep, but her final words to me, which seemed to come more from her unconscious than from her conscious self, were, 'I've been very lonely – nearly everyone in the world is very lonely . . .' Weeks before she'd been clear that she wasn't lonely. I felt as if she were saying we die alone.

I went to see Barbara one more time. She was fading: able to get out of bed to go to the bathroom, but she couldn't walk any further than that. She slept a lot of the time. The new Macmillan nurse was giving her morphine, trying to get the dose right to stop the pain, but not knock her out all the time. I sat with her while she slept, hearing her rasping fight for life.

When she woke, she smiled, and there was a radiance in her face. I asked her what was on her mind, and she told me: 'I'm dreaming a lot. I'm not sure what is dream and what is thought, but videos of past events and times pop into my head. Memories of times I'd been angry or stressed, "forgotten" memories coming from deep inside – images of my mother, and how Paddy loved me . . .' There were tears as she mentioned his name. 'I'm kind of looking at myself differently, why I'd upset people so much. I couldn't see it before . . .'

After a silence, I thought she was dozing, but she said, as if we'd been talking about it, 'I definitely believe in the spirit, leaving the body – very much believe in the spirit, not the God. What do you think?' I said my belief was that we live on in the memories of people whom we've loved and who love us. I said I thought she would live on in this house, and in Johnny. She said, 'I'm very glad that I stayed here. I would love to have more time to love it; I'd like to have the summer. It's all going far too quickly for me – huge – time is precious . . .' Then she said, 'It must be hard to believe if you haven't seen the spirit . . . I saw Paddy's leave his body.' I kept my response simple, listening and letting her know I heard her, was accompanying her. As she fell into another sleep, I heard her say the word 'journey'. It is an overused word, but she was on both a static journey and one that would lead her to an entirely different plain. We were aware of it and in denial of it.

When I left a few hours later, we hugged briefly and she said, 'Thank you. Will you come back?' I said, yes, of course I would, but I think we both knew it was unlikely. Barbara wasn't the big 'hug you, squeeze you' type. I felt shaky as I sat in the car. It had been tough saying the final goodbye; I'd been the one who was grateful.

I was in fact wrong. Barbara recovered from being so ill and I have been back to see her since. At present a new drug is extending her life, and her life expectancy is an unknown quantity to us all. The one thing we can be certain of in life is that we can never know for sure when we are going to die.

Gordon

Gordon wore a white starched shirt, buttoned neatly up to his chin, with fold-back cuffs and cufflinks; his waistcoat had a fob watch hanging from the pocket. He was well into his eighties and still a dapper dresser. He walked, slowly, in highly polished Oxford brogues and used a stick. He was slight of build and very thin, with alabaster white skin and piercing blue eyes behind his spectacles. He looked on the verge of death. He was restless, with a disturbing presence. He knew I was a therapist and had agreed to speak to me at the hospice he visited; I framed our visits in my mind as befriending, providing companionship and emotional support.

He told me in a soft Scottish accent that he had liver cancer, which was inoperable, the cancer having spread throughout his body. I was acknowledging that diagnosis when he said, 'I feel lost; my wife has died.' I could see his look of desolation as his eyes flickered around the room, seemingly searching for a place where he could tether himself. Gordon spoke to me intermittently while reading the local paper. It was a good rhythm because it allowed him to be in charge of the space between our exchanges, but just the way he turned the pages of the paper showed his disquiet: there was a lot of noisy rustling and a constant annoyed muttering under his breath, as if the pages were deliberately placed to irritate him.

I asked him about his wife. 'She wasn't meant to die,' he said 'I was the ill one – she was younger than me, three years younger, eighty-two years old, and healthy. Bit wobbly on her pins, but six months ago she had a massive heart attack, just died then and there. I was in the living room, and I heard this sort of cry and bang from our bedroom, and went upstairs and there she was, dead on the floor.' Tears burst out with these last words: he was extremely distressed. I responded slowly, breathing between words, so that he would mirror me and relax. I told him how incredibly shocking that must have been. I also had to speak up, for, despite his hearing aid, he found it hard to hear me. His sadness turned to anger – 'Fickin' right it was' – followed by a tirade of rage, not completely comprehensible, hands fisting furiously. I saw that 'love' was tattooed across the fingers of his left hand and 'hate' on his right.

Like many of us, I am instinctively wary of the unpredictability of anger, despite its being such a common response in grief, and I managed to persuade myself that I didn't want to upset him by probing too much. I sat silently for a while considering his anger and then went back to basics, acknowledging how difficult his life must be without her, and how wrong it all felt. He softened a bit – I could see it in his eyes – but he changed the subject: 'I want a cuppa.' I began to realize that his illness, or maybe the combination of the illness and his personality, meant that he couldn't hold on to a train of thought for any length of time. It seemed like he went in and out of different rooms in his mind, constantly moving between them because none of them felt like home.

Reflecting on Gordon led me to reconsider my broader understanding of old age and dying. I had often heard how old age reverses the position of parent and child, with the child parenting their parent. This can be tense and difficult if the relationship is already strained, and a real burden of work for the child. I hadn't fully thought about what that is like for the ageing parent – how frightening it would be to feel one's power and abilities diminish over time, how small things would become magnified in the minds of the old as they fought to hold on to control, which would become ever further from their grasp.

I saw Gordon the following week and wondered how he was getting on at the hospice. 'I like it well enough, but I spend hours waiting, waiting for the consultant, hours for the physio; I don't have hours to spare. I've been here three hours today. I'm getting fed up.' He kicked out his leg in agitation as he replied to me.

As Gordon spoke, I realized he had good reason to be angry: not only was he suffering pain and immobility, but he was bereft of almost everyone he'd been close to in his life. He was, on the one hand, a survivor, but he was also very alone. Being in his mid-eighties he had outlived his wife, his six siblings and most of his friends. 'I don't see anyone except my sons and their children. My wife used to ring people up, but I can't be bothered. I'm a miserable git, and I've had enough.' I heard all his contradictions: he didn't want to waste time when his life expectancy was limited, but, at the same time, he felt miserably alone and wasn't sure he wanted to go on living. He wasn't in any psychological state to be made aware of this: he needed compassionate understanding, a simple reflection of what he was saying at that moment. I had to fight to have a connection with him; I couldn't allow myself to be pushed away by his anger. His ability to alienate people had been adding to his upset. I responded to him as best I could, again keeping it simple, imbuing as much warmth into my voice as I could, and it seemed to calm him.

Over the weeks of our sessions I asked him about his life. I heard fragments, which were like mini-film-clips of the memories in his mind. The stories would be interspersed with a comfortable silence, and sometimes he'd snooze. He had become much calmer, but I wasn't sure if it was because I had become familiar to him or because talking about the past cheered him. 'I was a lad, a tough lad, a Teddy Boy, and I had my fights . . . Where I came from there was a lot of sectarianism, Glasgow Celtic and Glasgow Rangers – you were either a Fenian bastard or an Orange bastard, and there was a lot of fighting between us. You'd see a gang of 'em, you'd verbally abuse them, throw bricks and bottles, get them to come closer and then get 'em. You'd be left with a bit of cardigan or shirt or something. The secret was to be quick enough. The bigger boys got the kickin'; I was small and quick, and could run. And if you thought you were going to be caught, trip 'em up and leg it. Mostly just bruises but, a wee bit of breaking into things, if you fly with the crows you get shot with the crows. There was always somebody there that stopped it. Back in the day, they were old school policemen, they'd kick your arses.' As he spoke he accompanied his words with sprightly hand movements, echoing the punches he'd been able to give in the past.

He told me a sweet story from when he was eighteen years old. He wanted to leave his job as a greenkeeper at a local golf course, which was well paid with a house, in order to start work as a joiner, which was a risky decision. He had asked his father whether he approved or not, and he'd encouraged him: 'Go where your heart wants to take you, Gordon, for you aren't in the habit of using your brain.' There were tears in his eyes and a smile as he remembered the love of his father.

He'd been a good joiner, always in demand and never short of money. His great love was the moorland and racing pigeons, both passions having been embedded in him when he was a child: 'I used to go to my gran's house – they lived in a mining village a few miles away. Behind the village was the moorland. I went on the moor, played on my own for hours, watching the blackcock. My uncle would take me with him when he went poaching partridge – he'd throw a big net over the partridge, just enough for the pot. There were bits and pieces of old mines there, old coal mines, and big mining machines that looked like dinosaurs. I used to sit on these machines and try and make them move, sit in them and play. . .' Then his attention would move to the present and his knowledge that he was dying: 'The moor is the best medicine for me anyway. If I fall to the ground, and the last smell I smell is heather and wet moss, I'm a happy man.'

I wanted to know more about his pigeon-racing, and he smiled proudly as he told me, 'We had a lot of silver in the house – I won so many races.' But his most touching memory was from his childhood, again of his father, who'd been a steelworker. 'We walked up the zigzag steps right to the top of St Margaret Chapel in the belfry, up to the top of the big bell, to get pigeon eggs, what my father called "Divine intervention to get Holy pigeons and their Holy eggs" from the chapel. They raced quicker.' He looked happy as he remembered it, and even more so as he was transported back to that belfry in his mind: 'The big oak beam that held the bells – one day he scraped our names on that old beam, it will still be there, covered in dust.'

I began to build up a poignant picture of the man he had been: eloquent, stylish, proud and tough. The kind of man you'd want on your side in combat: loyal and funny and who'd fight the best he could. His was the sort of masculinity that protects men in battle and that is, by necessity, inflexible in nature. I was aware that the clipped nature of his speech when I'd first met him, combined with the pain he was in, had sent out sharp mini-missiles that had been hard to withstand. It required a lot of commitment to stay with him, not to retreat psychologically. Yet beneath that protection was a man who had loved his wife, Carol, deeply for over fifty years and been well loved by his family. Warmth was at the heart of him; it had simply been disguised by his recent losses and pain.

I wondered about his spiritual life. Did he have faith? What did he believe happened to him after death? He'd been brought up as a Catholic, but wasn't much of a churchgoer: 'I kneel and pray by my bed every night.' The image of Christopher Robin inevitably popped into my head, and suddenly I imagined this old man kneeling and praying through the decades. He prayed every night now for his wife and for himself; it sounded meditative and calming. 'The good Lord giveth and the good Lord taketh away, but the good Lord seems to be doing an awful lot of taking.' He gave me a slightly mischievous look as he said that, as if the priest who'd whacked him on the back of the head as a child would do so now, but couldn't. Gordon lost track after that, and his head dipped into his chest. I couldn't grasp what he believed about Heaven, but it was nevertheless a touching revelation.

A few months later Gordon was more distressed. His left hip was excruciatingly painful and it prevented him from being able to walk. He was now in a wheelchair. He had gone to the local hospital and been attended to by medics whom he called 'idiots' – junior doctors who apparently didn't know a thing, barely examined him and just gave him painkillers. 'You wouldn't do this to a dog . . .' he said, his head down, speaking low and furiously. I knew his fury had as much to do with the manner in which they treated him as with their medical ineffectiveness. It is possible with just a look to validate someone as a human being worthy of respect, or to diminish them as an object barely worthy of notice. I asked him what he needed now – what would help him most? 'To see the feckin' doc . . . it's too much.' The consultant who'd organized the MRI had had 'a bad feel about it'. I didn't doubt his experienced guess would be proved correct.

The consultant was right: it was bone cancer, and Gordon's whole body was being overwhelmed by it. He said, 'I'm out of control with everything, I can't get control of anything.' Every problem that was resolved led to a new problem. Medically they had run out of solutions; the aim now was to keep him comfortable and pain free. The consultant had said to him: 'You have weeks or months to live.' I always think when they say weeks or months they mean weeks, but hedge their bets because you can never know. As I was leaving, I saw a badge hanging on the back of Gordon's wheelchair: 'The art of living is to die young as late as possible.' I smiled: he was always a fighter.

The next time I visited the hospice, Gordon was bedridden on a ward with five other men, all equally ill. His son was with him. Although he looked very fragile, with almost yellow parchment skin, his spirits seemed to have lifted. With those bright blue eyes, he gave me a warm smile and with pride introduced his son, also called Gordon. He told me they had managed to stop the pain with a regular morphine pump, which was a great relief.

It was clear there had been a big shift psychologically. He had stopped fighting for life, and the acceptance of his death had calmed him. His preoccupations now were with his death. 'I wanted to make my own coffin, but I don't have the strength, so I've picked out the best one I can . . . I've chosen my headstone: it's got my name and a blue-check pigeon on it. I'll be buried next to Carol.'

Gordon slept much of the time I was there, but I learned he had taken Communion, a bold decision, for, although he'd prayed all his life, he hadn't taken it since he was a young man. He was making peace with his death, and his Catholic faith soothed him. When he didn't want to talk, he turned away from me and watched Buster Keaton films, downloaded for him by his son.

I wanted to find a way of saying goodbye that acknowledged the unlikelihood of my seeing him again, yet without being dramatic. Trying to find the right words was quite stressful, but I need not have worried: Gordon found the words for both of us. 'Watch yerself,' he said as he gave me a hug. I repeated the same words back to him. Such simplicity but with the hug they said it all.

I left feeling immensely grateful to Gordon. He had taught me a great deal and allowed me to accompany him on his deeply personal process of coming to terms with his own death. That I didn't feel sad was a surprise, and different from much of my other work. Instead I felt relieved. He'd had a long and meaningful life, with much love and many good things, but now he'd had enough and it was time for him to die.

A few weeks later Gordon junior was kind enough to let me know in a short note that his father had died. He'd died peacefully at the hospice with his family around him. He had told his son: 'I found Heaven before I died.' I wanted to know more – I like minutiae, every detail – but I was going to have to settle for that final lovely sentence.

Reflections

Our first breath of life signals the success of birth, and it is our last breath that will signal our death. We all know we will die – it is the only truly predictable fact – yet the incredible power of our minds maintains it as our best kept secret. With Jean, Barbara and Gordon, I was given an insight into the delicate balance they had to find between having hope for life and not being cast down by the prospect of death. They had to find a way to accept that death was coming.

When facing our own deaths, we have to accept the loss of what life means to us as well as face the profound loss for those that love us. Despite this, there can be a good death. When the recognition of dying has been accepted, and the focus is no longer on fighting for life, a death that has grace and tenderness, that is painless and peaceful, in a secure loving environment, can be attained. Those that work with the dying, who have more experience than I, shine a light on the unique intimacy of being with someone at the moment of death: they talk of it as a time of life when we have an opportunity to be enriched by a deep inner journey in which success or validation are no longer sought and we are free to be more fully ourselves. At the same time, it is by no means the only way, nor is it appropriate for all. Some people need to go on fighting and may approach death as if they were going to war – and foot soldiers don't stop the fight before they die. Grace and tenderness are not for everyone.

Jean, Barbara and Gordon were able to talk about their fears and wishes in the face of their death, partly because I was a professional and present for that particular purpose. I can imagine that without an outside person asking questions it might have been harder for them to do this, because of the fear and ignorance surrounding death. How we communicate with each other about our own dying is clearly not working: of the 48 per cent of people who die in hospital, only 2 per cent would choose to do so. Less than a third of those dying have talked to their family about their wishes. Families who haven't had those difficult conversations – which might vary from whether they want to be resuscitated and having a living will that facilitates their decision, to being an organ donor – carry a much greater burden of responsibility. The family member will find it almost impossible to feel confident in the choices they do make. Uncertainty is the most distressing aspect of decision-making, and there is always uncertainty about the medical outcome of any treatment for the dying. Add ignorance as to the wishes of the dying person to this mix, and the potential for bad decisions, regret and guilt is intensified.

The time I spent at the hospice has taught me we should all try to talk, plan and prepare for death long before we are actually faced with the end of our life. It helps us to dig deep inside and to discover why we are scared to death of death; our fear can be diffused if we sit quietly and work out what we believe about life and death, and find a way to talk to the people closest to us – particularly those who are going to survive us – about our wishes, our thoughts, our fears. It is also true that, in spite of multiple conversations, we may still not feel prepared when our death is imminent. The shift, for those that can make it, between fighting for life and accepting death comes through a grieving process that is no different from other grieving processes, and occurs when the person feels the pain of the loss of the future they wished for, and finds a way to accept the limited future they will have.

If we choose to believe something that gives us comfort in life and in the face of death, we are likely to suffer less. If we have chosen to talk to the people around us about our dying, they will suffer less too. Nobody can ever know what the dying person's experience is like, but we do know that being present or absent at the dying of someone we love lives in the minds of the people who love them forever, and a death where everyone is aligned in their feelings and thinking is easier.

I have learned from experience there will always be those who cannot talk about their death and who need their defence mechanisms firmly in place. Acknowledgement of death brings them incapacitating fear, so denial is their only option. Be aware that even those in denial may speak about their fears through metaphor; it is therefore important to pick up the cues if they emerge. Of those who don't speak about death, it is likely that some will suffer more as the time approaches: not only will they experience anguish from losing the fight they have battled to win, but they will also have a greater fear of death. It is possible, however, to be in complete denial and still have a good death.

Most of us have witnessed the miracle of medicine. It saves millions of lives every year, but its success gives us all a false impression of its limits. The trajectory of a life-threatening illness, once it has passed the tipping point, can be stabilized for a time by medical intervention, but it cannot be reversed. Patients and families find that hard to accept, always hoping that there is one more intervention or treatment that can be tried, believing they will be the one in a million who beats the odds. There are very difficult decisions to be made with regard to such procedures, i.e., the risk of death from a treatment such as chemotherapy versus the risk of death from the disease itself. This is where the art of medicine comes in: doctors need to talk to the dying patient and their family in a collaborative way and ensure that these profoundly complex decisions are taken together.

When I work with families where someone they love is facing their own death, my central message, in addition to advising them to talk with each other openly and honestly, is to make sure they don't have any regrets. They should spend time together, peacefully reminiscing or in silence, take photographs, maybe write a journal, put the outside world to one side, keep visitors to the few closest family and friends, and focus on this person whom they love deeply – every minute is precious and will be a source of comfort after they have died.

We all know, if we let ourselves think about it, that we want to die painlessly, peacefully and with dignity; and we don't want to die alone – we want to be with the people who love us, in a place where we feel safe. We don't tend to want to be thrown into a medical system where our individual humanity can get lost in the fight for our life. If we can take on board our impending death, as difficult and complex as it is, we might have the opportunity to shape our own end, which may also mean we are less fearful. We can't control the outcome, but we can ensure we use all the available means of support to make it as tolerable as it can be.

It is worth repeating that a key barrier to talking about end of life is magical thinking – that talking about death will in some way hasten it. Or that talking about dying is giving up – which is why we need to have those conversations before we are on the point of death.

Death anxiety

Our attitude to death will most likely be a reflection of how we have lived. If someone is angry in life, they will be more so as they approach death, and vice versa – this is a time when our personality traits are intensified. Many people have a negative attitude towards death, and the awareness of their own mortality and the sense of an impending threat can result in high levels of death anxiety.

It is suggested that when reflecting on the life they have lived, individuals will either experience a satisfying acceptance or perceive themselves to have led a life devoid of purpose and meaning. Unsurprisingly, those who are satisfied with their life and who perceive themselves to have had a meaningful existence have less anxiety about death than those who believe their life had no purpose.

Death anxiety is often increased after someone has experienced the death of someone they love. This is because such an event can trigger thoughts about their own mortality and increases the amount of time they spend thinking about their own death.

In order to manage death anxiety, many engage in defence behaviours such as attempting to distract themselves from the prominent thoughts of death or denying their own vulnerability to death. It has been suggested that it is these defence mechanisms that have led to the belief that death is something to be feared and should be avoided at all costs.

However, research has demonstrated that individuals who have been through a near-death experience often report that they are no longer afraid of death. I have often found that people whose children have died no longer fear death themselves.

Acceptance of death

Research shows that those who accept death are those who are psychologically prepared for the finality of life, are aware of their own mortality and demonstrate a positive emotional response to it.

Yet it is possible that an individual may accept death in general but simultaneously reject the idea of dying themselves. For example, a study that looked at individuals' perceptions of others' deaths in comparison with their own revealed that participants often gave unrealistic representations of what their own death would be like, but then gave realistic portrayals of the deaths of others.

An individual's attitude towards death can be associated with their physical and psychological well-being. This is supported by research indicating that those who have good levels of physical health often report less death anxiety. Acceptance of death has been shown to have a positive impact on health, vitality and well-being in general.

Effects of religion

Religion plays an important part in people's attitudes towards death. Whatever the religion, it may act as a buffer against the fear of death. Many religions have a strong focus on the afterlife, and foster beliefs that death is not something to be feared. Religious people demonstrate an acceptance of death, because they believe existence continues in a happy afterlife.

Effects of social support

Emotional support is the most important form of social support. For people like Barbara, Jean and Gordon, having close relationships with friends and family who cared for them was the most significant influence on their levels of death anxiety. Social support that helps to increase an individual's self-esteem has been shown to reduce the negative effects of undesirable life stress when death is imminent. Individuals with high self-esteem and a good social support network reported lower levels of death anxiety.

Elderly people living in institutions were found to have high levels of anxiety, particularly those who were physically and mentally frail, with low self-esteem and feelings that their lives had served little purpose.

For once there are no contradictions in the research: those who felt they had low levels of social support demonstrated high levels of death anxiety.

Depression

People often ask me what is the difference between grief and depression. Although they may feel similar, the processes are different. Grief is a reactive response to an external event, and that response generates an entire holistic process of its own. Depression is hard to define, but at its most simple is a constant feeling of negativity or anxiety that can stem from a chemical imbalance in the brain. Even when we're in the middle of the grieving process, we will have moments of pleasure or happiness. With depression, the feelings of emptiness and despair are unremitting. Complicated grief has qualities of depression, including feeling suicidal, and requires professional attention. But in matters of the mind it is never possible to formulate definitive definitions, for research shows 15 per cent of all psychological disorders have unresolved grief as their source.

What helps: the work we need to do to help us grieve and survive successfully

Love and work . . . work and love, that's all there is

— Sigmund Freud

Our uniqueness makes the writing of a definitive, prescriptive list of what may help us with our grief impossible, so the guidelines that follow are general ways to think about what helps us at such a difficult time in our lives. Grief requires the commitment of *regularly* doing things that help us, physically and emotionally. This may seem impossible in the first weeks and months of grief for some, while for others it will be a welcome focus.

I have developed the idea of 'pillars of strength' – the key structures that support us and enable us to rebuild our lives. It requires work to build the pillars – they don't just appear out of the blue – as well as a commitment to keep going. The pillars function as an integrated organic whole; we can't just focus on one pillar and leave the rest. They demand our attention and time, and the result of addressing all of them is that the strength they provide will be increased many times over.

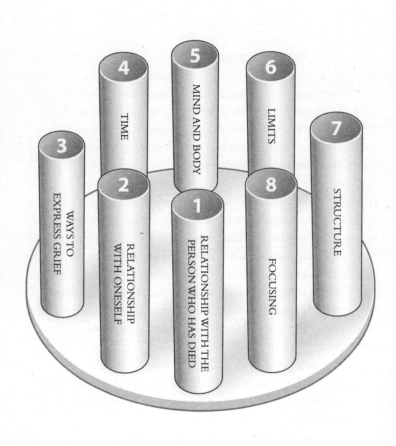

Pillars of strength

1. Relationship with the person who has died

- The biggest indicator of how much pain we are in is the quality of the relationship we had with the person who has died and how much we loved that person. The more important they were in our lives, the more we loved them, the more we will miss them. The contradiction here is that having had a difficult relationship with a significant person in our life who has died can make the grieving process harder, because there are likely to be regrets and no further opportunities to put things right.
- We've seen in the case studies that the relationship with the person who has died continues, although in a radically altered form. They are loved in absence rather than in presence. Some people may need to do this a great deal, others only occasionally or on special days like anniversaries. A central pillar in the support of our system is *finding ways to externalize that relationship*.

  - It may be by wearing something that connects to them, like their watch, a name band or an article of their clothing such as a scarf.

○ Visiting their grave; creating a memory box
  in which you place special objects such as
  their glasses, or cards, or pressed flowers;
  assembling a photograph album; or writing
  to them in a journal or in the form of a letter.
○ Cooking their favourite recipe.
○ Posting an image online you know they'd
  have loved.

There are multiple ways to do this. Finding an external
expression for the continuation of the relationship through
regular rituals is not only important but has been shown to
reduce negative emotions and increase positive ones.

Over time the regularity of these rituals may decrease.

2. Relationship with oneself

• As our relationship with the world and others is
  changed by grief, so does our relationship with
  ourselves change. We need to show ourselves
  self-compassion, to listen to our own needs, to be
  kind and to avoid self-attack in the form of constant
  self-criticism. We need to recognize that feelings are
  not facts: feeling bad, for instance, doesn't make us
  bad. There may be many different conflicting and
  confusing messages going on in our mind, so a
  useful way to clarify what we are thinking is to
  write a journal. Writing down conflicting
  messages – for example, feeling both relieved and
  sad about a death – enables us to see what we are
  telling ourselves, thereby illuminating what is going

on inside. Getting an accurate picture will ensure
we find the right support. It is a well-researched
source of self-support that has been shown to be as
effective as talking therapies.

- We all need defence mechanisms, and it is useful to
be aware of what ours are. In addition, we may need
to work out whether we need to build other
mechanisms in a particular situation. If, for
example, we tend to shut down when we are upset,
it may mean we won't get the support we actually
need. It is best to be aware of this and to tell those
close to us how we are really feeling on the inside.

- Denial in grief is a natural and important part of
self-protection. The acceptance of knowledge is
necessarily incremental in grief because
psychologically we couldn't cope with the full
realization all at once.

- A new loss is likely to bring back the memory of
previous losses. We aren't going mad, nor have we
failed to do the necessary grieving in the past. This
is normal.

3. Ways to express grief

My big shout is that we all need to find ways of expressing
our grief, and it doesn't matter what the way is. As the case
studies illustrate, for some it will be talking to family or
friends, for others it may be writing a journal, and for others
painting, making music or seeing a therapist. There is no
right way to express it. The key is to find a way of connecting to the feelings we have inside, naming them and then

expressing them. If we do this regularly, we can construct a supportive pillar in the management of our pain, which in itself changes over time.

4. Time

It is important to understand that time takes on different hues in grief.

- Allow more time than is often expected to make decisions, both immediate ones such as the funeral (unless there are religious imperatives) and long-term, life ones. We may feel pressurized to take action because the feeling of powerlessness is so strong, but only time can ensure the proper reflection that is necessary if regret is to be avoided.
- Grieving takes longer than anyone wants; we cannot fight it; we can only find ways to support ourselves through it. When we attempt to block it, we lay ourselves open to physical and mental illness. On the positive side, over time the intensity of the pain lessens; we do naturally adjust and re-engage with life.
- Our relationship with time feels changed: the future can look daunting and there can be a longing to return to the past. The best we can do is to keep our outlook short, with attention focused on each day and on each week.

5. Mind and body

A central pillar is our mind and our body, which have been mightily impacted by the death of the person we love. We know from neuroscience that every thought we have has a physiological component that is felt in our body. Mind and body are interconnected to the extent they are called 'mind-body', a single interwoven unit. Neuroscientists talk about it as 'The body remembers the body holds the score', meaning the whole experience is held in our body and unconsciously influences what we think, and the decisions we make. The pain of grief is therefore felt physically in our body and affects our thinking and behaviour; it is often experienced much in the same way as fear, and tips our bodily system into a heightened state of alert. We need to establish a regime that helps to regulate our body, which then helps to support us emotionally. The more *habitual* the action, the more effective it is. The regime should include:

- cardiovascular exercise, which helps to ease the feeling of fear, such as running, walking or any sport
- relaxation/meditation exercise, which helps to manage our anxiety
- eating regularly, without great spikes of sugar, coffee or alcohol, which cause the body to peak, then crash

6. Limits

When we experience a life-changing loss, it is likely to affect our performance at work and our reactions in a social context. An important pillar is to recognize the power to say 'no'. When we find ourselves honestly assessing a situation and realizing it is not right for us, we need the confidence to say 'no'. Paradoxically, this enhances the power of 'yes', for when we have a proper 'no', our 'yes' is infinitely more positive. Friends and family can get very bossy when we are grieving, and very keen for us to get back into the swing of life, but nobody else can know what our limits are; it is up to us to pay attention to them and voice them clearly.

7. Structure

In the chaos of grief we can feel as if our world has tilted off its axis. It can therefore help to build a pillar of structure, although with some flexibility within it, as too much controlling behaviour can be counterproductive.

Develop a structure of good habits:

- Exercise first thing.
- Do some work or chores.
- Take time to remember the person who has died.
- Actively choose to do soothing, calming things, such as buying nice flowers, having a massage, cooking nice food, watching box sets, listening to music, reading (although for some it takes a long time before they can concentrate on reading).
- Have regular times for sleep.

Developing a structure of good habits has a multiplying effect: the more we do them, the better we feel. It takes about six weeks for a good habit to become habitual, until we do it without thinking about it.

8. Focusing

Grief sits in the body. People often talk about it as 'a knot' or as 'a block' in their throat or stomach. Sometimes it feels like their arms, legs or heads are very heavy. Often, when there are no words for these bodily sensations, focusing is a way of finding the words. When I wrote in the case studies about using visualizations with my clients, this is the method I used.

'Focusing' is the technique that helps me to open up and release the bodily intelligence in people, but this can be done on your own. I suggest you direct your attention internally: become aware of a vague sensation in your body and breathe into – 'focus' on – this 'felt sense'. This will give you information that is not in your conscious awareness.

The procedure I ask clients to follow, which you can do for yourself, is:

- Close your eyes.
- Breathe deeply and slowly, in through your nose and out through your mouth, three times.
- Direct your attention internally.
- Move your attention around your body until you find the place where there is the most sensation.
- Breathe into that place.
- Find a word that describes that place – does it have a shape, a colour? Is it hard, soft?
- If the image could speak, what would it say?
- Then follow where the image takes you.

How friends and family can help

Don't walk in front of me. I may not follow. Don't walk behind me . . . I may not lead. Walk beside me . . . just be my friend

– Albert Camus

People need people. We are born for connection. We need people to survive, and to share our life with when we are happy or when we are just getting on. And we need people when we are bereaved. I asked many people who were bereaved what the single most important factor in the rebuilding of their lives was, and every single one of them said my partner, my parent, my friend, my sibling. It may be one close relationship, or it may be many friends and family playing different roles. But the path to rebuilding your trust in life has to be paved with people who care about you. Here is what I've learned, and some of the words of those I asked.

It has always been very clear to me that the friends and family of someone who is bereaved desperately want to help. The difficulty comes when they don't know how. They are likely to be scared of getting things wrong and making them worse, and so do nothing. The attitudes, practices and ideas below will, I hope, give you the confidence you need to overcome any such fear and to move towards the person who is bereaved rather than avoiding them.

There is also an underlying psychological barrier to be

surmounted by friends or acquaintances. When you're in the presence of someone who's in a great deal of pain, that pain is transmitted bodily to those around them; it acts almost like a distress signal. It can trigger a bodily discomfort in others that can feel like fear, though someone may be conscious only of the fact they feel 'funny'. It can be quite a disturbing feeling and many people's instinct is to do something to stop it, to shut it down. This is why the bereaved are often told to 'fix' themselves and to rejoin normal life. Some just want to escape from the source of the discomfort, and their solution is to leg it.

Listening

Be a friend who is prepared to give their time, to listen and to acknowledge the extent of your friend's loss. Listening is the key. Bear witness, and allow your friend to be upset, to be confused and contradictory, or to say nothing at all. Every time they tell their story once more, or are allowed to say how important the person who has died was, the burden of carrying their pain on their own is incrementally a little lighter. People who allow them to talk, talk, talk and tell stories make a difference. Let them know that you are interested to know more. When you can acknowledge how special the person was, you become special to your friend. Different people are comfortable with different amounts of contact: phone or see them every week, day or even every few hours if necessary. Open questions that offer broad answers work better than questions that have a 'yes' or 'no' answer such as 'Are you sad?' Or start the conversation by saying you were thinking about the person who's died, say their name, and then let your friend take the lead and talk about them.

I asked a client, Rebecca, whose mother had died, what she thought friends of the bereaved should be aware of. 'Be open and willing to speak about the death, the person and the loss. When you write or call, don't try to make the loss less. Voice it. Try to find the words for your feelings. If a chasm has been left in your life, say it. If your heart breaks for them, say it, and let them tell you their feelings without trying to tidy them away.'

A bereaved daughter, Katie, described that honesty further: 'I found honesty comforting and easy to deal with. Pretence was complicated and required a degree of emotional and social interpretation that I just didn't have at the time.' Similarly, Antony, a bereaved father, said to me: 'Nor do you need to clothe yourself in a different persona because I'm grieving. Be yourself, for I'm in uncharted territory and need to reach out for something familiar. I needed my friends as stepping stones or beacons.'

Emma, whose father had died, knew clearly what she wanted: 'So often people undervalue what it means just to be there as a friend. They think they need to behave differently in order to fix you. They don't realize that by doing that, they're invading your mental space, and instead of supporting you, they're making you feel self-conscious about the fact that you aren't on good form, that you seem to need fixing – all that does is make you feel like you need to act like everything is okay in order to stop them from trying to help.'

Emma went on to describe her version of the most important tenet of friendship when someone is newly bereaved: 'It's the people who just allow you to go through what you're going through, offering no judgement or opinion on it, but only a hug when you need it, a shoulder to sob on and a comforting presence; making you some soup, sitting with you and watching TV while you just sit and cry quietly; not trying to stop you crying but just holding your hand and giving it a little squeeze now and then – understanding without your having to tell them that you just need to cry and will only stop when you've cried enough and need sleep; and knowing that their quiet presence is making all the difference.'

Rosa, whose mother died, said: 'It sometimes seems to me that we have inside us a basket of memories and sadnesses, and that each time we can tell one of the stories, we let the weight go a little. I remember when my mother died, miles outside London, a colleague with whom I was working – who had never met my mother and whom I hadn't known for that long – took the day off and made the long and tricky journey to be at the funeral. I didn't know she was going to, but now (thirty-six years later) her presence is the thing I remember the most, the thing that touched me the most. It meant that I could talk to her when I got back to London and share my sadness about my mother's passing. It always reminds me that you never quite know what will help people in times of grief, but that you need to try, and you need to try and not be embarrassed.'

Accepting, understanding and encouraging your friend just as they are is invaluable. Penny, whose baby died, said, 'I remember being upset, and saying how surprised I was that I still felt as sad as I did. My husband responded by saying that he thought that I would probably always be sad about it, and that it would always be something to be sad about. Again, the level of understanding helped me to accept what had happened.'

It's not about you

Follow the mourner's lead: they may not want to talk about their grief now, or with you. It is good to say something to acknowledge their loss, but then let them have the control they need (they had none over the death), to choose to talk or not. If they ask you to come and be with them, and want to talk openly to you, go. If they truly do not want you to visit, and do not want to deal with it at that particular time, don't force it upon them. Don't confuse your need to speak or call or be in contact with your friend's need. Some people must have time to focus on the person who has died, time to feel their pain and grieve.

Rebecca gave me an example of how unhelpful even very good friends could be: 'I had a situation where I asked friends and family to sit *shiva* with me [the Jewish mourning tradition] at a certain time and place. These times weren't convenient for two people close to me – they insisted on coming earlier in the day, and to see me at a different location more convenient for them. I really didn't want that to happen, because I was worried about breaking down and being too emotional while I was trying to get my kids sorted with homework and dinner. I explained this, but the two didn't care. They came anyway and spoke about my mother's death, raising all the issues I was temporarily trying to keep contained. Clearly the visit was more about them "ticking the box" of having visited me than about giving me any real comfort.' A summary of this could be 'It's not about you', if you're the friend and you really want to help.

Asking questions is complicated territory, and a lot depends on your motivation in asking those questions. Don't be an ambulance chaser, needing to be in the know. Questions should arise from what your friend is actually saying – an exploratory, sensitive, wanting-to-know-more-about-their-experience sort of question. Not an intrusive session in information-gathering.

Vicky, whose son died many years ago, said what I have heard numerous times in different ways: 'One of the many traumatic things for a grieving person is the upsetting way one has to look after those people who don't know how to handle us. We're already struggling to survive our catastrophe, conserving what little energy we do have, so to have to compensate for their inadequacy would be almost ridiculous if it weren't so painful.' The awkwardness that friends and family feel is very quickly transmitted and picked up, and the social mores of everyone wanting the interaction to be smooth takes over. But, as Vicky clearly shows, it sits as an outraged anger inside the person who is bereaved long after the interaction is over.

Acknowledgement

Death isn't catching, but those who are bereaved might think so, judging by the fear they see in other people's eyes. People are frightened about whether to come forward, about what to say, about saying the wrong thing – so, in the end, they say nothing. All of that comes from a belief that whatever you say should make things better, that you should have enough wisdom to make the pain more bearable. But you can't. Nor do you need to. Being kind enough to dare to acknowledge them and their situation is good enough.

Offering to be there if they need you, suggesting that they

should be the one to ring you, is probably asking too much of your friend at this time. It's better if you take the initiative and make contact, and then follow their lead: they may want to see or speak with you – or not. Often people don't make contact because they feel they don't know the bereaved person well enough. If you are erring one way or the other, better to err on the side of making contact.

There are people in the inner circle of your friend's life, and people a bit further outside. Nothing is always cut and dried – sometimes friendships are formed over the tragedy while others are lost. But when a friend isn't very close, sometimes the bereaved person can give a little signal or make a nudge in the right direction that will get that person onside. I said earlier that the person who is bereaved shouldn't have to be the one to make the effort, but sometimes doing so will bring a friend who really does care closer and allow them to make a contribution to your life.

Some people actively don't want their pain taken away, and there is nothing you can actually do when this is the case. But moving towards them with compassion and kindness helps. Just saying you are sorry when you first see someone and not staring at them awkwardly from across the room is the best route to take.

Katya, a widow whose husband died by suicide twenty years ago, remembers with absolute clarity how friends responded to her at the time: 'After his death, I was never aware of people avoiding me, but I was aware of the enormous kindness, thoughtfulness and love that I was shown. Sometimes, I feel that he was so loved as a person that people still want to reflect that in the way they treat me, even now. I was hugely appreciative of this love and kindness, but, at the same time, and for months after, I felt as though my skin had been peeled off my whole body, I was hurting so much. I couldn't really show this to anyone . . .'

Ellen, whose mother died, told me how judged she had felt by others following the death of her mother, with no simple acknowledgement from others. Yet how different it was when her father died and her friends could acknowledge this and talk about it: 'When I returned to work after my mother died, no one mentioned the reason for my absence of a week. If anything, my office colleagues were rather brusque, establishing a strange and unexpected new formality, a barrier between us. I suspected that not only were they hiding an anxiety that I might suddenly fall apart but that there was a sense of judgement mingled with their pity. My mother had not died of old age in the nice neat way that parents are supposed to, but while she was still young, and horribly and wastefully of the taboo-laden alcoholism. Thirty years ago the shame and criticism implicit in such a death had no hesitation in making itself known. Somehow I felt criticism, even blame, was levelled as much at me as at my mother, and I had rarely felt so lonely. Whatever the circumstances, the death of a parent is like losing a limb. It is a balance-impeding, gravity-threatening, foundations-spinning, knock-for-sixer. You don't know any of that until it happens to you.

'When, many years later, my father also died, the experience was altogether different. We had grown profoundly and mutually rewardingly close during the nine months of his dying. We had discussed love, death, hopes and fears. Nothing had been left unsaid. And when in those first few days afterwards I found the courage to talk to my friends who had gone through the same thing with a parent, the relief in finding common ground, even laughter through the tears, sustained me like nothing else could have done.'

Practical help

Aisa, a bereaved mother, told me that her male friends were good in that they would 'pop by and say "How are you?" Sometimes they would stay with me while I howled. I liked being held by a man, the strength of a man was what I needed.' Vicky, a widow, found her male friends gave her brilliant practical advice, or would come and play football with her son. The male friends really liked being given specific tasks.

But men with other men can be 'hopeless'. Bobby, a widower, said: 'Men are much worse than women at speaking about it. I had a truly terrible dinner with two men friends – they just couldn't do it, I brought up [his wife's] name five times and five times they wouldn't respond.' The five times asked and five times denied has the ring of biblical fury about it. I know the silence is by no means intended to hurt or enrage, and comes from the discomfort of feeling impotent, but if you can find the courage to listen, you will be giving your friend a powerful gift.

Doing practical things is often what really makes a difference. Don't say 'Let me know if I can help'; actually do something helpful. At the beginning of a bereavement, there may be a lot of people around, so bringing food may be the best thing you can do. Taking food around for longer than the initial crisis is rare, and therefore particularly appreciated. Countless people have told me how grateful they were to their friends who made sure they ate or tidied up, who organized their lives because they weren't functioning at all. You can book a massage. You can help to care for your friend's children, who have a long day to get through, with a sad parent who isn't up to much at the end of it.

I have heard many times how a group of friends have created a rota to support a close friend who was dying, or whose husband, parent or child had died. They took it in turns to be there, to walk with them, to bring food. There is something about the collectivity of a team that is particularly supportive and holding. People who are grieving often worry that they are too much of a burden to their friends, but they worry less if they feel responsibility is shared across a group.

Antonia, a widow whose husband had died by suicide, told me: 'There is that feeling of being branded by suicide. I would walk into a room and feel there was a collective shrinking away, as if I were leprous or suicide was contagious. I would imagine the furtive whisper of "She's the one who . . ." and the eager horror. The kindness of people in situations where you cannot hide – sports matches and parents' days, a party – matters hugely. Being scooped up by other families on those particular family days makes the most enormous difference.'

Telling stories, or sending photographs or films, about the person who has died is immensely precious. It is like gold. It can feel like a gift to the bereaved person, as if they've been given something more of the person who has died than what they have now. Danny, a widower, said, 'Being sent films I hadn't had, or photographs, gave me more time with her. Talking to people who had stories to tell me that I didn't know helped to keep her alive, because I wasn't ready to let her go.'

Humour is risky territory because it can go really wrong. But if you know your friend well, sharing something funny with them can be a welcome relief. Laughing and crying are emotions that can be very close to each other, so don't be surprised if laughing with your friend leads to a good cry. But don't worry if that happens. Black humour with the right person, at the right time, can be a welcome break from all the misery. Poppy, whose baby died, said: 'Another friend of mine just tried to make me laugh. She didn't force it on me but sent me stupid videos/photos that were so hysterical you couldn't help but laugh. One was a particularly funny video of some male strippers. You'd have to see it to see the funny side but they were gyrating and flapping their bits in time to a particularly ridiculous song with lyrics along the lines of "You like my sha la la . . . my ding ding dong" but they were all taking themselves terribly seriously. I kept that on my phone for months. Not because I liked looking at willies but because it was just hysterical and always brought a smile to my face!'

I'm sure some would disapprove, but when I'm talking to someone who has had really bad news, I often swear a lot. 'It really is fucking terrible, isn't it?' Or just 'Shit!' I can't quite explain it, but somehow swearing goes straight to the heart of how awful it is without dancing around with adjectives and sympathy, which can be perceived as patronizing. Also swearing gets to the centre of some of the fury people feel.

Honesty

Be honest. Honesty is comforting and easy to deal with. There is a direct cleanness to honesty that cuts through much of the complex messiness of grief, and this can come as an enormous relief to people. Also be honest about what you actually can do rather than covering up because you feel guilty about what you can't. Be specific: say 'I'm going to come round for half an hour' or 'I'll come on Tuesday'; don't say 'I'll come whenever you want, tell me, and I'll be there', and then find you can't deliver on that offer.

Be sensitive

While being honest is important, so is being sensitive. Promiscuous honesty is not a good idea. Jenny, whose son had died very suddenly and tragically, showed me an email whose first line read: 'I've been thinking of you . . .' It then went on to outline in great detail, in the chirpiest tone possible, how all her children were thriving and getting on. Be aware of the bereaved person's feelings when you talk about your own living parent, partner or child, and it is that relation of your friend who has died. Or be aware of showing too openly that your life is trotting along happily, as that can feel like rubbing their nose in your happiness.

Be in it for the long haul

Try to remember to make contact and be supportive after everyone else has gone. Usually three months following the death, people get back to their lives, as they should. But it is by no means over for the person who is bereaved. Sending a text or popping by can be hugely supportive. 'I feel so lonely' is the regular cry of the people I see. Grieving is lonely-making. All that missing, and wanting, and not finding can feel like excruciating loneliness. Warm, caring, human contact helps take the chill out of it. It can't make the pain go away, but being connected and remembered helps your friend to bear it.

One of the things that stops people making contact in the months after the death is that they are worried they will remind their bereaved friend of something they'd rather forget. They may not want to talk to you right at that moment, but be assured they are never going to forget about the person who has died. It will, most likely, be the thing taking up the majority of their head space for far longer than you think.

I spoke to a mother, Elizabeth, whose son had died forty years ago. She had certainly got on with her life and found happiness again. She said: 'It warms me to hear his name. And I like to reminisce, especially on special days like his birthday and the anniversary of his death.' A father, Paul, whose son died many years previously, said something similar: 'For me grief is a way of bringing myself closer to George, so it is not something from which I shy away. It is my grief, but I am no longer afraid of it, as I was in those dark weeks after George died.'

Writing

Letters, cards, texts or emails: it doesn't matter what you write — all are extremely helpful. It is better, however, to say that you don't want a reply, because some people simply can't respond. And it is never too late to send them. It is a welcome surprise to receive a card much later, because it is when everyone else has forgotten and your friend is still grieving.

When you do write, try to make it personal and avoid tired clichés like 'She's had a good innings' or 'Better to have loved and lost', because they are trite and in some way diminish the personal importance of this very loved person who has died. You don't need to go into long explanations of why the person has died or theological explorations about death; just be loving and personal, warm and acknowledging.

Abdul told me he'd received letters that 'talked about my Dad and what they remembered about this and that, what they loved best about him – my favourite parts were any amusing anecdotes of his more eccentric behaviour or personality traits, things that made me smile and cry at the same time, those things that had stuck in their memory and made them like him, remember him.'

Texts are much less demanding than telephone calls because they don't require a response. My cautious note about texts is that if they are your only form of communication they can feel quite distant, so at some point it would be kind to make more direct contact.

When someone is bereaved they don't want to take note of who didn't call, or who said what crass thing. But they do, and it can really tarnish the relationship in the future. If you can see in their eyes they are upset, don't run for the hills. Take a breath, be brave and say, 'I'm sorry. I can see that what I've said has upset you.' That's all it takes.

A bereaved friend's needs may be completely individual. One client, Colleen, whose mother died, said: 'Don't rush to speak of the legacy, the helping, the solution. I found people were so fast to tell me she'll always be there, I'll feel her, she's with me. I didn't feel any of that at first, so hearing it made me feel even worse . . . as if there were something wrong with me, or I was missing something.'

Another client, Jane, of a similar age, whose mother had also died, said almost the opposite: 'I received a letter which struck such a chord in me. "Yet somehow such a period of sadness gives way to a period of joyful reflection, and a celebration of her life. She lives on too in her daughters and grandchildren, the memory of her is etched into you, a sort of spiritual DNA. She may have gone from your lives in an active sense, but yet she is still very much with you, and the generation beyond. The marvellous fact of human existence is to continue her life in those who live on, so that she is not absent, just present differently." I particularly love the "present differently". It is a beautiful letter.'

Try to remember anniversaries and birthdays. It doesn't matter which day it is – whether it's the anniversary of the person who has died or any of the usually happy celebratory days – just send your friend a message, or a text, or a card, or see them. On those special and especially difficult days for your bereaved friend, they are likely to feel raw and in turmoil, as well as with a sense of being on the outside. It can feel to them like the world has moved on, yet their world has stopped, and stopped a year ago exactly. Remembering them when they feel forgotten is a small gesture that can have a large impact.

Your friend's pace of adjustment

Many clients have said to me a version of what Ali said: 'Remember that mourning and healing happen at a deeply personal, unpredictable pace. The most helpful thing you can do for your friend is not to hurry them along if they are taking their time, or judge them if they are quick. Just be there for them, wherever they are at.'

Sharon, whose mother had had a long life, made a similar point, but with the emphasis on the fact grieving is never really over: 'For me, I think what surprised me the most in my own journey was the length of time that it took for me to feel myself again. My expectation, and I think lots of my friends' expectations, were that it was something I should/ would get over quickly . . . it wasn't . . . and it's still something that I need to talk about from time to time. And mum died twelve years ago.'

In response to my asking a bereaved father how friends could help, he showed how life and grief go on: 'In remembering George I need to go to that place that I now keep for birthdays and anniversaries and the occasional one-off. I like it when something about him comes out of the blue; it does me good.'

To some extent anyone reading this book is part of a cohort of people who probably don't need to be reading this chapter. You are more likely to be the kind of person who wants to know how to be as helpful as possible, which automatically makes you helpful. You will have a tendency to be tentative and aware as a friend, sensitive enough to know you can't make assumptions about what your friend will want or need, and that things can change for them from hour to hour, let alone from day to day.

I want to reach those who cross to the other side of the street, those who don't look their bereaved friend or acquaintance in the eye, and do anything rather than mention the name of the person who has died. I'm not sure how to get to them, but, if I could, I would say: acknowledge, listen and simply give them time.

Historical context of death and dying in the UK

British society's attitude to death and dying is by no means fixed and has changed radically through the centuries. In the late middle ages, death was witnessed by many and accompanied by solemn ritual, but from the twentieth century death was very much denied and hidden. Death's victory was medicine's failure, and so it became the ultimate taboo. The key societal changes that brought about the reversal of our rituals surrounding death was the waning of religion, twentieth-century world wars and the success of medicine. Our century is seeing new ways to memorialize the dead, and our attitudes to death are evolving anew.

The Victorians were famously good at death, but couldn't talk about sex; now the reverse is true. Queen Victoria was the leading role model, grieving the death of Prince Albert. She wore her widow's weeds until she died, even to the weddings of both of her daughters. Victorian women adopted similar dress and rituals following the death of their husbands, and family members demonstrated their grief by separating themselves from the community through veils and black cloth. Christianity was still central to the dying; they usually wanted time with their priest to have a private conversation with God. Following the death, funerals played a large part in the mourning rituals, and elaborate memorial headstones were erected.

The First World War saw killing on an industrial scale for the first time in history. The whole nation was overwhelmed by its horror and its death toll of 700,000 military deaths and 17 million killed worldwide. This was rapidly followed by the flu pandemic in 1918 that killed over 200,000 in the UK, and between 50 and 70 million people globally. Shock and grief shook the foundations of all communities. Everybody was grieving someone they loved: a brother, father or son – most of the deaths were men. The rituals carried out by the Victorians, such as sequestering themselves away, were no longer practical or even emotionally possible. Millions of people grieving publicly simply couldn't be psychologically accommodated. The biological imperative to survive took over.

The children of parents who had survived the First World War went on to fight or witness the Second World War. Their belief system was informed by their experience: they didn't see their parents openly mourn, so they learned to suppress their grief and to keep it tightly shut inside. This was the generation who brought about an even greater reduction in the mourning rituals surrounding death and dying, and education about death was withheld from those in every walk of life.

The devastation of two world wars in the twentieth century saw the decline of the Christian faith and the supremacy of medicine. The doctor, rather than the priest, now took the lead, interposing himself between his patient and death. With the development of antibiotics and vaccines, medical intervention prevented many deaths and pushed back against many of the illnesses that had killed people in the past. As a consequence, in this shifting belief system, death was seen not as the will of God but as a failure of the doctor.

The emerging generation of the twenty-first century, who were born four or five decades after the end of the Second World War, feel more secure psychologically. While the nation was under threat and grieving on a vast scale, it was perhaps necessary to shut down emotionally. At present there is no threat of war happening to that degree, so it seems that we and our children now have the 'luxury' to grieve and face death in a different way.

Gradually another shift is taking place in our attitudes towards death and dying. Today those with terminal illnesses are often informed of their impending death. Close friends and family are more likely to discuss it openly. In the last ten years there has been an increasing focus on palliative care and the importance of meeting the individual's needs.

There is a small but growing interest in people talking about death and dying, which, thanks to the internet, has spread quickly around the world. An example is deathcafe. com: there are nearly 3,000 groups in thirty-four countries. Their objective is 'to increase awareness of death with a view to helping people make the most of their [finite] life'. Some of the meetings are small, others much bigger.

Online communication allows the terminally ill, or relations of the dying, to communicate their experience of the dying process digitally. The very sick may not be able to walk or even speak, but they can often still interact online. This could be with their family, or with people around the world, giving daily or even hourly updates on their thoughts and feelings through blogs, tweets and YouTube.

The famous British 'stiff upper lip' is beginning to soften. People who are hiding feelings of grief and not expressing emotions, because of their fear of appearing weak, are now regarded with concern. It is beginning to be recognized that it takes courage for people to show their vulnerability in the face of death and bereavement; it is by no means a sign of weakness – rather, the reverse. This can, of course, cause tension across generations in any family, and there may be anger with parents and grandparents who remain stoically silent and unexpressive.

For young people, social networks have opened up new avenues for expressing grief; online communication in memorializing the dead is becoming increasingly popular. Funerals and gravestones can now be activities on social media; gravestones can have QR codes which, when scanned, upload data about the person who has died. Profile pages of the person who has died provide a place for free expression of grief. For some, seeing young people take selfies of themselves at a funeral may seem bizarre, but it is normal for them to treat funerals like any other event in their lives that needs acknowledgement through the posting of a selfie. Websites such as Facebook can be accessed all over the world, and people can post messages on anniversaries, thus keeping the relationship with the person who has died alive. Social media/networking does seem to be the next step in this evolutionary process. Young people will find contemporary ways to remember their loved ones, and their expression of their loss is heartening. It will be interesting to see how they progress, and whether meaningful change in how people communicate face to face, as well as online, will be created.

History forms the character of a generation. Events influence the experiences and shape the belief systems of those who live at a particular time. It may seem that our rituals and responses to death are established and set practices for us, when in fact our attitudes to death and dying are constantly evolving, whether we want them to or not.

Afterword

I like stories with happy endings, when all the difficulties have been resolved and the key players walk joyously into the sunset. They meet a need that reality can rarely fulfil. This book does not have tidy conclusions, because these stories of life, death and grief are not fiction. They are based on the real experiences of people who are devastated by the death of someone they love. They show clearly that grief has a momentum of its own, and our work is to find ways to express it and to support ourselves through it, while realizing that over time it changes and we are changed by it.

If you have read this far, you will have overcome our reluctance to look at this subject, a reluctance that is quite natural because of our ultimate powerlessness over death, although every single one of us, whoever we are, whatever our story, will be touched by death at some point. You will have seen that when we avoid confronting death, we imbue it with more power to frighten us. As humans, and particularly as humans in the twenty-first century, we seem to be driven to seek perfection, order and the avoidance of all difficulty – of which death and dying is top of the list. Yet in continuing to deny death we are inevitably denying the richness of life. In our heart of hearts we know that the other side of love is loss, and we can't have one without the other. Loss is intrinsic to the human experience, whether it be loss of youth, or health, or the ending of a joyous day, or the finishing of a relationship, or, of course, the death of a loved one. But in order to live truly, to experience life fully, we need to be able to accept that. We sometimes need to be able to sit with pain and to accept discomfort. And at the far end of the spectrum of loss is grief, which is one of the greatest manifestations of psychological pain that we can go through.

You will have seen that I haven't offered neat solutions or quick fixes, which would be more palatable and fit better with our relentless desire to solve everything; but I have shown the extraordinary courage of many different individuals who have found a way to endure the pain of their loss, accepted the support they needed, learned to help themselves and started to live their lives again. I understand it is hard to read about these people suffering, and that this is compounded by not knowing for certain what happened to them in the end. For each of them there were small signals of improvement – like Caitlin's fear receding – and then turning points – like the release that finally allowed Cheryl to feel her loss and cry into her mother's scarf, the decision taken by Phil and Annette to try for a baby, and the powerful images of the supernova experienced by Mussie. Each of these small moments followed by turning points laid down the foundations upon which they built their hopes for the future and enabled them to have the confidence to rebuild their lives. They recognized that an examined death is as important as an examined life. Their futures are now on a secure footing, and they are full of potential, because they have done the hard psychological work of grieving. With luck on their side and renewed hope, they will continue to grow and to engage in life – a different life, but a good life nevertheless.

I don't get to chart their happiness because they can do that very well on their own. I am confident every single one of them feels a profound sense of gratitude for having loved in the way that they did, and in honouring the memory of that person their legacy lives on in them, and each mourner will grow from that experience.

As someone who has been brave enough to read this book, you have, I hope, found these stories inspiring and replaced your fear with confidence . . .

Sources

The place of publication is London unless stated otherwise.

Introduction

Lazare, A. (1979) 'Unresolved Grief', in A. Lazare (ed.), *Outpatient Psychiatry: Diagnosis and Treatment* (Baltimore: Williams and Wilkens)

Zisook, S., Schuter, S., and Schukit, M. (1985) 'Factors in the Persistence of Unresolved Grief among Psychiatric Outpatients', *Psychosomatics*, 26, 497–503

Understanding grief

Klass, D., Silverman, P. R., and Nickman, S. L. (eds.) (1996) *Continuing Bonds: New Understandings of Grief* (Philadelphia, PA: Taylor & Francis)

Parkes, C. M. (2006) *Love and Loss: The Roots of Grief and Its Complications* (Routledge)

Stroebe, M. S., and Schut, H. A. W. (1999) 'The Dual Process Model of Coping with Bereavement: Rationale and Description', *Death Studies*, 23 (3), 197–224

Worden, W. J. (1991; 2nd edition) *Grief Counselling and Grief Therapy* (Routledge)

When a partner dies

Alcohol Concern UK (2016) *Alcohol and Depression Factsheet*

Bennett, K. M., and Vidal-Hall, S. (2000) 'Narratives of Death: A Qualitative Study of Widowhood in Later Life', *Ageing and Society*, 20, 413–28

Berardo, F. M. (1970) 'Survivorship and Social Isolation: The Case of the Aged Widower', *Family Coordinator*, 19, 11–25

Bock, E. W., and Webber, I. L. (1972) 'Suicide Among the Elderly: Isolating Widowhood and Mitigating Alternatives', *Journal of Marriage and Family*, 34, 24–31

Burks, V. K., Lund, D. A., Gregg, C. H., and Bluhm, H. P. (1988) 'Bereavement and Remarriage in Older Adults', *Death Studies*, 12 (1), 51–60

Carey, R. G. (1979) 'Weathering Widowhood: Problems and Adjustment of the Widowed During the First Year', *OMEGA: The Journal of Death and Dying*, 10, 163–74

Carr, D. (2004) 'The Desire to Date and Remarry Among Older Widows and Widowers', *Journal of Marriage and Family*, 66, 1,051–68

—, House, J. S., Wortman, C., Nesse, R., and Kessler, R. C. (2001) 'Psychological Adjustment to Sudden and Anticipated Spousal Loss Among Older Widowed Persons', *Journal of Gerontology*, 56B, 237–348

childbereavement.org.uk – all the information on supporting bereaved children can be found on this website

Cleveland, W. P., and Gianturco, D. T. (1976) 'Remarriage After Widowhood: A Retrospective Method', *Journal of Gerontology*, 31, 99–103

Cramer, D. (1993) 'Living Alone, Marital Status, Gender and Health', *Journal of Community and Applied Social Psychology*, 3 (1), 1–15

Davies, J. (1991) 'A Sudden Bereavement', *Nursing Times*, 87 (33), 34–6

Deeken, A. (2004) 'A Nation in Transition – Bereavement in Japan', *Cruse Bereavement Care*, 23 (3), 35–7

Defares, P. B., Brandjes, M., Nass C., and van den Ploeg, J. D. (1985) 'Coping Styles, Social Support and Sex Differences', in I. Sarason and B. Sarason (eds.), *Social Support: Theory, Research and Applications*, 173–86 (Dordrecht: Martinus Nijhoff)

drinkaware.co.uk (2015) *Alcohol and Mental Health*

Duke, S. (1998) 'An Exploration of Anticipatory Grief: The Lived Experience of People During Their Spouses' Terminal Illness and in Bereavement', *Journal of Advanced Nursing*, 28 (4), 829–39

Fengler, A. P., and Goodrich, R. (1979) 'Wives of Elderly, Disabled Men: The Hidden Patients', *Gerontologist*, 19, 175–83

Ferguson, T., Kutscher, A. H., and Kutscher, L. G. (1981) *The Young Widow: Conflicts and Guidelines* (New York: Arno Press)

Foner, N. (1994) *The Caregiving Dilemma: Work in an American Nursing Home* (Berkeley: University of California Press)

Gerber, I. (1974) 'Anticipatory Bereavement', in B. Schoenberg, A. C. Carr, A. H. Kutscher, D. Peretz and I. K. Goldberg (eds.) *Anticipatory Grief*, 26–31 (New York: Columbia University Press)

Ghazanfareeon Karlsson, S., and Borrell, K. (2002) 'Intimacy and Autonomy, Gender and Ageing: Living Apart Together', *Ageing International*, 27, 11–26

Helsing, K. J., Szklo, M., and Comstock, G. W. (1981) 'Factors Associated with Mortality After Widowhood', *American Journal of Public Health*, 71, 802–9

House, J. S., Uberson, D., and Landis, K. R. (1988) 'Structures and Processes of Social Support', *Annual Review of Sociology*, 14, 293–318

Kubler-Ross, E. (1969) *On Death and Dying* (New York: Collier Books)

Lalande, K. M., and Bonanno, G. A. (2006) 'Culture and Continuing Bonds: A Prospective Comparison of Bereavement in the United States and the People's Republic of China', *Death Studies*, 30 (4), 303–24

Lopata, Z. H. (1973) *Widowhood in an American City* (Cambridge, MA: Schenkman)

Marni, M. M. (1989) 'Sex Differences in Earnings in the United States', *Annual Review of Sociology*, 15, 343–80

Mental Health Report (2016) *The Five Year Forward View for Mental Health. A Report from the Independent Mental Health Task Force to the NHS in England*

Morgan, L. A. (1984) 'Changes in Family Interaction Following Widowhood', *Journal of Marriage and Family*, 46, 323–31

Neria, Y., and Litz, B. (2004) 'Bereavement by Traumatic Means: The Complex Synergy of Trauma and Grief', *Journal of Loss and Trauma*, 9 (1), 73–87

Parkes, C. M., and Weiss, R. S. (1983) *Recovery from Bereavement* (New York: Basic Books)

—, and Prigerson, H. G. (2010) *Bereavement: Studies of Grief in Adult Life* (Penguin)

Perel, E. (2007) *Mating in Captivity* (HarperCollins)

Schneider, D. S., Sledge, P. A., Shuchter, S. R., and Zisook, S. (1996) 'Dating and Remarriage Over the First Two Years of Widowhood', *Annals of Clinical Psychiatry*, 8 (2), 51–7

Schut, H. A. W., Stroebe, M. S., Boelen, P. A., and Zijerveld, A. M. (2006) 'Continuing Relationships with the Deceased: Disentangling Bonds and Grief', *Death Studies*, 30 (8), 757–76

Smith, K. R., and Zick, C. D. (1986) 'The Incidence of Poverty Among the Recently Widowed: Mediating Factors in the Life Course', *Journal of Marriage and Family*, 48, 619–30

Stroebe, M. S., and Schut, H. A. W. (1999) 'The Dual Process Model of Coping with Bereavement: Rationale and Description', *Death Studies*, 23 (3), 197–224

—, and Stroebe, W. (1989) 'Who Participates in Bereavement Research? A Review and Empirical Study', *OMEGA: The Journal of Death and Dying*, 20, 1–29

—, and Stroebe, W. (1983) 'Who Suffers More? Sex Differences in Health Risks of the Widowed', *Psychological Bulletin*, 93, 279–301

Stroebe, W., and Stroebe, M. S. (1987) *Bereavement and Health: The Psychological and Physical Consequences of Partner Loss* (New York: Cambridge University Press)

—, Stroebe, M. S., Abakoumkin, G., and Schut, H. A. W. (1996) 'The Role of Loneliness and Social Support in Adjustment to Loss: A Test of Attachment Versus Stress Theory', *Journal of Personality and Social Psychology*, 70 (6), 1,241–9

Suhail, K., Jamil, N., Oyebode, J. R., and Ajmal, M. A. (2011) 'Continuing Bonds in Bereaved Pakistani Muslims: Effects of Culture and Religion', *Death Studies*, 35 (1), 22–31

Valentine, C. (2009) 'Continuing Bonds After Bereavement: A Cross-Cultural Perspective', *Cruse Bereavement Care*, 28 (2), 6–11

Young, R. M. (1989) *Transitional Phenomena: Production and Consumption* (Free Association Books)

When a parent dies

Bowlby, J. (1979) 'On Knowing What You Are Not Supposed to Know and Feeling What You Are Not Supposed to Feel', *Canadian Journal of Psychiatry*, 24, 403–8

Brown, E. J., Amaya-Jackson, L., Cohen, J., Handel, S., Bocanegra, H. T. D., Zatta, E., Goodman, R. F., and Mannarino, A. (2008) 'Childhood Traumatic Grief: A Multisite Empirical Examination of the Construct and Its Correlates', *Death Studies*, 32 (10), 899–923

Christ, G., Siegel, K., Freund, B., Langosch, D., Henderson, S., Sperber, D., and Weinstein, L. (1993) 'Impact of Parent Terminal Cancer on Latency-Age Children', *American Journal of Orthopsychiatry*, 63, 417–25

Corr, C. A. (1995) 'Children's Understanding of Death: Striving to Understand Death', in K. J. Doka (ed.), *Children Mourning, Mourning Children* (Routledge)

Creed, J., Ruffin, J. E., and Ward, M. (2001) 'A Weekend Camp for Bereaved Siblings', *Cancer Practice*, 9 (4)

Daley, Dennis C., and Salloum, Ihsan M. C. (2001) *Clinicians' Guide to Mental Illness*, 176–82 (McGraw-Hill)

DeSpelder, L., and Strickland, A. (2011) *The Last Dance: Encountering Death and Dying* (Palo Alto, CA: Mayfield)

Dillen, L., Fontaine, J. R., and Verhofstadt-Deneve, L. (2009) 'Confirming the Distinctiveness of Complicated Grief from Depression and Anxiety Among Adolescents', *Death Studies*, 33 (5), 437–61

Dowdney, L. (2000) 'Annotation: Childhood Bereavement Following Parental Death', *Journal of Child Psychology and Psychiatry*, 41, 819–30

drinkaware.co.uk (2015) *Alcohol and Mental Health*

Epidemiologic Catchment Area Study (D. A. Regier, et al.) by National Institute of Health (1990) *Use of Services by Persons with Mental Health and Addictive Disorders*

Fonagy, P., Gergely, G., Jurist, E., and Target, M. (2002) *Affect Regulation, Mentalization, and the Development of the Self* (New York: Other Press)

Fristad, M. A., Jedel, M. A., Weller, R. A., and Weller, E. B. (1993) 'Psychosocial Functioning in Children After the Death of a Parent', *American Journal of Psychiatry*, 150, 511–13

Hayslip, B., Ragow-O'Brien, D., and Guarnaccia, C. A. (1999) 'The Relationship of Cause of Death to Attitudes Toward Funerals and Bereavement Adjustment', *OMEGA: The Journal of Death and Dying*, 38, 297–312

—, Pruett, J. H., and Caballero, D. M. (2015) 'The "How" and "When" of Parental Loss in Adulthood: Effects on Grief and Adjustment', *OMEGA: The Journal of Death and Dying*, 71, 3–18

Horsley, H., and Patterson, T. (2006) 'The Effects of a Parent Guidance Intervention on Communication Among Adolescents Who Have Experienced the Sudden Death of a Sibling', *American Journal of Family Therapy*, 34, 119–37

Jones, A. M., Deane, C., and Keegan, O. (2015) 'The Development of a Framework to Support Bereaved Children and Young People: The Irish Childhood Bereavement Care Pyramid', *Bereavement Care*, 34, 43–51

Kaffman, M., and Elizur, E. (1984) 'Children's Bereavement Reactions Following the Death of the Father', *International Journal of Family Therapy*, 6, 259–83

Kalter, N., Lohnes, K. L., Chasin, J., Cain, A. C., Dunning, S., and Rowan, J. (2003) 'The Adjustment of Parentally Bereaved Children: I. Factors Associated with Short-Term Adjustment', *OMEGA: The Journal of Death and Dying*, 46, 15–34

Kaplow, J. B., Howell, K. H., and Layne, C. M. (2014) 'Do Circumstances of the Death Matter? Identifying Socioenvironmental Risks for Grief-Related Psychopathology in Bereaved Youth', *Journal of Traumatic Stress*, 27 (1), 42–9

—, Layne, C. M., Pynoos, R., Cohen, J., and Lieberman, A. (2012) 'DSM-V Diagnostic Criteria for Bereavement-Related Disorders in Children and Adolescents: Developmental Considerations', *Psychiatry: Interpersonal and Biological Processes*, 75, 243–66

—, Layne, C. M., Saltzman, W. R., Cozza, S. J., and Pynoos, R. S. (2013) 'Using Multidimensional Grief Theory to Explore Effects of Deployment, Reintegration, and Death on Military Youth and Families', *Clinical Child and Family Psychology Review*, 16, 322–40

McLanahan, S. S., and Sorensen, A. B. (1985) 'Life Events and Psychological Well-Being Over the Life Course', in G. H. Elder and J. R. Ithaca, *Life Course Dynamics: Trajectories and Transitions 1968–1980*, 217–38 (NY: Cornell University)

Mahon, M. M. (1994) 'Death of a Sibling: Primary Care Interventions', *Pediatric Nursing*, 20 (3), 293–6

Marks, N., Jun, H., and Song, J. (2007) 'Death of Parents and Adult Psychological Well Being: A Prospective US Study', *Journal of Family Issues*, 28, 1,629–30

Melhem, N., Day, N., Shear, K., Day, R., Reynolds, C., and Brent, D. (2004) 'Traumatic Grief Among Adolescents Exposed to Peer Suicide', *American Journal of Psychiatry*, 161, 1,411–16

Moss, M. S., Resch, N., and Moss, S. Z. (1997) 'The Role of Gender in Middle-Age Children's Responses to Parent Death', *OMEGA: The Journal of Death and Dying*, 35, 43–65

Nickerson, A., Bryant, R., Aderka, I., Hinton, D., and Hofmann, S. (2011) 'The Impacts of Parental Loss and Adverse Parenting on Mental Health: Findings from the National Comorbidity Survey-Replication', *Psychological Trauma: Theory, Research, Practice, and Policy*, 5 (2), 119–27

Pynoos, R. S. (1992) 'Grief and Trauma in Children and Adolescents', *Bereavement Care*, 11, 2–10

Rossi, A. S., and Rossi, P. H. (1990) *Of Human Bonding: Parent–Child Relationships Across the Life Course* (New York: Aldine de Gruyter)

Rynearson, E. K., and Salloum, A. (2011) 'Restorative Retelling: Revising the Narrative of Violent Death', in R. A. Neimeyer, D. L. Harris, H. R. Winokuer and G. F. Thornton (eds.), *Grief and Bereavement in Contemporary Society: Bridging Research and Practice*, 177–88 (New York: Routledge)

Saldinger, A., Cain, A., Kalter, N., and Lohnes, K. (1999) 'Anticipating Parental Death in Families with Young Children', *American Journal of Orthopsychiatry*, 69, 39–48

—, Porterfield, K., and Cain, A. (2004) 'Meeting the Needs of Parentally Bereaved Children: A Framework for Child-Centered Parenting', *Psychiatry: Interpersonal and Biological Processes*, 67, 331–52

Saunders, J. (1996) 'Anticipatory Grief Work with Children', *British Journal of Community Health Nursing*, 1 (2), 103–6

Scharlach, A. E. (1991) 'Factors Associated with Filial Grief Following the Death of an Elderly Parent', *American Journal of Orthopsychiatry*, 61, 307–13

Shapiro, D., Howell, K., and Kaplow, J. (2014) 'Associations Among Mother–Child Communication Quality, Childhood Maladaptive Grief, and Depressive Symptoms', *Death Studies*, 38 (3), 172–8

Stokes, J. A. (2004) *Then, Now and Always* (Cheltenham: Winston's Wish Publications)

Thompson, M. P., Kaslow, N. J., Kingree, J. B., King, M., Bryant, L., Jr, and Rey, M. (1998) 'Psychological Symptomatology Following Parent Death in a Predominantly Minority Sample of Children and Adolescents', *Journal of Clinical Child Psychology*, 27 (4), 434–41

Umberson, D. (1992) 'Relationships Between Adult Children and Their Parents: Psychological Consequences for Both Generations', *Journal of Marriage and Family*, 54, 664–74

—, and Chen, M. D. (1994) 'Effects of a Parent's Death on Adult Children: Relationship Salience and Reaction to Loss', *American Sociological Review*, 59, 152–68

Wheaton, B. (1990) 'Life Transitions, Role Histories, and Mental Health', *American Sociological Review*, 55, 209–23

Worden, J. W., and Silverman, P. R. (1996) 'Parental Death and the Adjustment of School-Age Children', *OMEGA: The Journal of Death and Dying*, 33, 91–102

When a sibling dies

Bank, S., and Kahn, M. D. (1982) 'Intense Sibling Loyalties', in M. E. Lamb and B. Sutton-Smith (eds.), *Sibling Relationships: Their Nature and Significance Across the Lifespan*, 251–266 (Hillsdale, NJ: Lawrence Erlbaum)

Cain, A. C., Fast, I., and Erickson, M. E. (1964) 'Children's Disturbed Reactions to the Death of a Sibling', *American Journal of Orthopsychiatry*, 34, 741–52

Calvin, S., and Smith, I. M. (1986) 'Counseling Adolescents in Death-Related Situations', in C. A. Corr and J. N. McNeil (eds.), *Adolescence and Death*, 97–108 (New York: Springer)

Christ, G. H. (2000) *Healing Children's Grief: Surviving a Parent's Death from Cancer* (Oxford: Oxford University Press on Demand)

Cicirelli, V. G. (1995) *Sibling Relationships across the Lifespan* (New York: Plenum Press)

— (2009) 'Sibling Death and Death Fear in Relation to Depressive Symptomatology in Older Adults', *Journal of Gerontology*, 64b, 24–32

Davies, B. (2002) 'The Grief of Siblings', in N. B. Webb (eds.), *Helping Bereaved Children: A Handbook for Practitioners*, 94–127 (New York: Guilford Press)

Devita-Raeburn, E. (2004) *The Empty Room: Surviving the Loss of a Brother or Sister at Any Age* (New York: Scribner)

Eaves, Y. D., McQuiston, C., and Miles, M. S. (2005) 'Coming to Terms with Adult Sibling Grief: When a Brother Dies from AIDS', *Journal of Hospice and Palliative Nursing*, 7 (3), 139–49

Erikson, E. H. (1964) *Identity: Youth and Crisis* (New York: Norton)

Fanos, J. H., and Nickerson, B. G. (1991) 'Long-Term Effects of Sibling Death During Adolescence', *Journal of Adolescent Research*, 6 (1), 70–82

Fletcher, J., Mallick, M., and Song, J. (2013) 'A Sibling Death in the Family: Common and Consequential', *Demography*, 50, 803–26

Fulmer, R. (1983) 'A Structural Approach to Unresolved Mourning in Single-Parent Family Systems', *Journal of Marital and Family Therapy*, 9, 259–69

Gold, D. T., Woodbury, M. A., and George, L. K. (1990) 'Relationship Classification Using Grade of Membership (GOM) Analysis: A Typology of Sibling Relationships in Later Life', *Journal of Gerontology*, 45, 43–51

Hays, J. C., Gold, D. T., and Pieper, C. F. (1997) 'Sibling Bereavement in Late Life', *OMEGA: The Journal of Death and Dying*, 35, 25–42

Hogan, N., and DeSantis, L. (1994) 'Things That Help and Hinder Adolescent Sibling Bereavement', *Western Journal of Nursing Research*, 16 (2), 132–53

Kellerman, N. P. F. (2000) *Transmission of Holocaust Trauma* (Jerusalem: Yad Vashem)

— (2001) 'Psychopathology in Children of Holocaust Survivors: A Review of the Research Literature', *Israeli Journal of Psychiatry and Related Sciences*, 38 (1), 36–46

Lewis, M., and Volkmar, E. (1990; third edition) *Clinical Aspects of Child and Adolescent Development* (Philadelphia, PA: Lea & Febiger)

McCown, D. E., and Davies, B. (1995) 'Patterns of Grief in Young Children Following the Death of a Sibling', *Death Studies*, 19 (1), 41–53

—, and Pratt, C. (1985) 'Impact of Sibling Death on Children's Behavior', *Death Studies*, 9 (3), 323–35

Moss, S. Z., and Moss, M. (1989) 'The Impact of the Death of an Elderly Sibling', *American Behavioral Scientist*, 33, 94–106

Mufson, T. (1985) 'Issues Surrounding Sibling Death During Adolescence', *Child and Adolescent Social Work*, 2, 204–18

Oltjenbruns, K. A. (2001) 'Developmental Context of Childhood: Grief and Regrief Phenomena', in M. S. Stroebe, R. O. Hansson, W. Stroebe and H. Schut (eds.), *Handbook of Bereavement Research: Consequences, Coping, and Care*, 169–197 (Washington, DC: American Psychological Association)

Packman, W., Horsley, H., Davies, B., and Kramer, R. (2006) 'Sibling Bereavement and Continuing Bonds', *Death Studies*, 30 (9), 817–41

Pretorius, G., Halstead-Cleak, J., and Morgan, B. (2010) 'The Lived Experience of Losing a Sibling through Murder', *Indo-Pacific Journal of Phenomenology*, 10, 1–12

Robinson, L., and Mahon, M. M. (1997) 'Sibling Bereavement: A Concept Analysis', *Death Studies*, 21 (5), 477–99

Robson, P., and Walter, T. (2013) 'Hierarchies of Loss: A Critique of Disenfranchised Grief', *OMEGA: The Journal of Death and Dying*, 66, 97–119

Ross, H. G., and Milgram, J. I. (1982) 'Important Variables in Adult Sibling Relationships: A Qualitative Study', in M. E. Lamb and B. Sutton-Smith (eds.), *Sibling Relationships: Their Nature and Significance across the Lifespan*, 225–49 (Hillsdale, NJ: Lawrence Erlbaum)

Sveen, J., Eilgard, A., Steineck, G., and Kreicbergs, U. C. (2014) 'They Still Grieve: A Nationwide Follow-Up of Young Adults 2–9 Years After Losing a Sibling to Cancer', *Psycho-Oncology*, 23, 658–64

Walker, C. (1988) 'Stress and Coping in Siblings of Childhood Cancer Patients', *Nursing Research*, 37, 206–12

Webb, N. B. (ed.) (2002; second edition) *Helping Bereaved Children: A Handbook for Practitioners* (New York: Guilford Press)

Wright, P. M. (2015) 'Adult Sibling Bereavement: Influences, Consequences, and Interventions', *Illness, Crisis and Loss*, 24 (1), 34–45

Zampitella, C. (2011) 'Adult Surviving Siblings: The Disenfranchised Grievers', *Group*, 35 (4), 333–47

When a child dies

Amick-McMullan, A., Kilpatrick, D. G., Veronen, L. J., and Smith, S. (1989) 'Family Survivors of Homicide Victims: Theoretical Perspectives and an Exploratory Study', *Journal of Traumatic Stress*, 2 (1), 21–35

Badenhorst, W., Riches, S., Turton, P., and Hughes, P. (2006) 'The Psychological Effects of Stillbirth and Neonatal Death on Fathers: Systematic Review', *Journal of Psychosomatic Obstetrics and Gynecology*, 27, 245–56

Bergstraesser, E., Inglin, S., Hornung, R., and Landolt, M. A. (2015) 'Dyadic Coping of Parents After the Death of a Child', *Death Studies*, 39 (3), 128–38

Beutel, M., Willner, H., Deckardt, R., Von Rad, M., and Weiner, H. (1996) 'Similarities and Differences in Couples' Grief Reactions Following a Miscarriage: Results from a Longitudinal Study', *Journal of Psychosomatic Research*, 40, 245–53

Blackmore, E. R., Cote-Arsenault, D., Tang, W., Glover, V., Evans, J., Golding, J., and O'Conner, T. G. (2011) 'Previous Prenatal Loss as a Predictor of Perinatal Depression and Anxiety', *British Journal of Psychiatry*, 198 (5), 373–8

Buchi, S., Morgeli, H., Schnyder, U., Jenewein, J., Glaser, A., Fauchere, J. C., Bucher, H. U., and Sensky, T. (2009) 'Shared or Discordant Grief in Couples 2–6 Years After the Death of Their Premature Baby: Effects on Suffering and Posttraumatic Growth', *Psychosomatics*, 50, 123–30

Calhoun, L. G., Selby, J. W., and Abernathy, C. B. (1984) 'Suicidal Death: Social Reactions to Bereaved Survivors', *Journal of Psychology*, 116, 255–61

Christ, F., Bonanno, G., Malkinson, R., and Rubin, S. (2003) 'Bereavement Experiences After the Death of a Child', in M. Field and R. Berhman (eds.) *When Children Die: Improving Palliative and End-of-Life Care for Children and Their Families*, 553–79 (Washington, DC: National Academy Press)

Clyman, R. I., Green, C., Rowe, J., Mikkelsen, C., and Ataide, L. (1980) 'Issues Concerning Parents After the Death of Their Newborn', *Critical Care Medicine*, 8, 215–18

Cook, J. A. (1984) 'Influence of Gender on the Problems of Parents of Fatally Ill Children', *Journal of Psychosocial Oncology*, 2 (1), 71–91

— (1988) 'Dad's Double Binds', *Journal of Contemporary Ethnography*, 17, 285–308

Cornwell, J., Nurcome, B., and Stevens, L. (1977) 'Family Response to Loss of a Child by Sudden Infancy Death Syndrome', *Medial Journal of Australia*, 1, 656–9

Dyer, K. A. (2005) 'Identifying, Understanding, and Working with Grieving Parents in the NICU: Identifying and Understanding Loss and the Grief Response', *Neonatal Network*, 24, 35–46

Dyregrov, A., and Matthiesen, S. B. (1987) 'Similarities and Differences in Mothers' and Fathers' Grief Following the Death of an Infant', *Scandinavian Journal of Psychology*, 28, 1–15

Dyregrov, K., Nordanger, D., and Dyregrov, A. (2003) 'Predictors of Psychosocial Distress After Suicide, SIDS, and Accidents', *Death Studies*, 27 (2), 143–65

Field, N. P. (2006) 'Continuing Bonds in Adaptation to Bereavement: Introduction', *Death Studies*, 30 (8), 709–14

Forest, G. C. (1983) 'Mourning the Loss of a Newborn Baby', *Bereavement Care*, 2, 4–11

—, Standish, E., and Baum, J. D. (1982) 'Support After Perinatal Death: A Study of Support and Counselling After Perinatal Bereavement', *British Medical Journal*, 285, 1,475–9

Gottman, J., and Silver, N. (1999) *The Seven Principles for Making Marriage Work* (Orion Books)

Hansson, R. O., and Stroebe, M. S. (2006) *Bereavement in Late Life: Coping, Adaptation and Developmental Issues* (Washington, DC: American Psychological Association)

Harmon, R. J., Glicken, A. D., and Siegel, R. E. (1984) 'Neonatal Loss in the Intensive Care Nursery: Effects of Maternal Grieving and a Program for Intervention', *Journal of the American Academy of Child Psychiatry*, 23, 68–71

Helmrath, T. A., and Steintitz, E. M. (1978) 'Death of an Infant: Parental Grieving and the Failure of Social Support', *Journal of Family Practice*, 6, 785–90

Joseph, S. (2013) *What Doesn't Kill Us: A Guide to Overcoming Adversity and Moving Forward* (Piatkus)

Keesee, N. J., Currier, J. M., and Neimeyer, R. A. (2008) 'Predictors of Grief Following the Death of One's Child: The Contribution of Finding Meaning', *Journal of Clinical Psychology*, 64 (10), 1,145–63

Kersting, A., and Wagner, B. (2012) 'Complicated Grief After Perinatal Loss', *Dialogues in Clinical Neuroscience*, 14, 187–94

Klass, D., Silverman, P. R., and Nickman, S. L. (eds.) (1996) *Continuing Bonds: New Understandings of Grief* (Philadelphia, PA: Taylor & Francis)

Kochanek, K. D., Kirmeyer, S. E., Martin, J. A., Strobino, D. M., and Guyer, B. (2012) 'Annual Summary of Vital Statistics: 2009', *Pediatrics*, 129, 338–48

Kreicbergs, U. C., Lannen, P., Onelov, E., and Wolfe, J. (2007) 'Parental Grief After Losing a Child to Cancer: Impact of Professional and Social Support on Long-Term Outcomes', *Journal of Clinical Oncology*, 25, 3,307–12

Lehman, D. R., Wortman, C. B., and Williams, A. F. (1987) 'Long-Term Effects of Losing a Spouse or Child in a Motor Vehicle Crash', *Journal of Personality and Social Psychology*, 52 (1), 218–31

Lohan, J. A., and Murphy, S. A. (2005–6) 'Mental Distress and Family Functioning Among Married Parents Bereaved by a Child's Sudden Death', *OMEGA: The Journal of Death and Dying*, 52, 295–305

Moore, A. (2007) 'Older Poor Parents Who Lost an Adult Child to AIDS in Togo, West Africa: A Qualitative Study', *Omega*, 56 (3), 289–302

Moriarty, H. J., Carroll, R., and Cotroneo, M. (1996) 'Differences in Bereavement Reactions within Couples Following Death of a Child', *Research in Nursing and Health*, 19, 461–9

Murphy, S. A., Braun, T., Tillery, L., Cain, K. C., Johnson, L. C., and Beaton, R. D. (1999) 'PTSD Among Bereaved Parents Following the Violent Deaths of Their 12–28-Year-Old Children: A Longitudinal Prospective Analysis', *Journal of Traumatic Stress*, 12 (2), 273–91

—, Gupta, A. D., Cain, K. C., Johnson, L. C., Lohan, J., Wu, L., and Mekwa, J. (1999) 'Changes in Parents' Mental Distress After the Violent Death of an Adolescent or Young Adult Child: A Longitudinal Prospective Analysis', *Death Studies*, 23 (2), 129–59

Ness, D. E., and Pfeffer, C. R. (1990) 'Sequelae of Bereavement Resulting from Suicide', *American Journal of Psychiatry*, 147, 279–85

Parke, R. D., Dennis, J., Flyr, M. L., Morris, K. L., Leidy, M. S., and Schofield, T. J. (2005; second edition) 'Fathers: Cultural and Ecological Perspectives', in T. Luster and L. Okagaki (eds.), *Parenting: An Ecological Perspective*, 103–44 (Mahwah, NJ: Lawrence Erlbaum)

Peach, M. R., and Klass, D. (1987) 'Special Issues in the Grief of Parents of Murdered Children', *Death Studies*, 11 (2), 81–8

Piaget, J. (1977) 'Developmental Stage Theory', in Howard Gruber (ed.), *The Essential Piaget* (New York: Basic Books)

Rando, T. (1993) *Treatment of Complicated Mourning* (Champaign, IL: Research Press)

Rinear, E. E. (1988) 'Psychosocial Aspects of Parental Response Patterns to the Death of a Child by Homicide', *Journal of Traumatic Stress*, 1, 305–22

Schwab, R. (1998) 'A Child's Death and Divorce: Dispelling Myth', *Death Studies*, 22 (5), 445–68

Shapiro, E. R. (2001) 'Grief in Interpersonal Perspective: Theories and Their Implication', in M. S. Stroebe, W. Stroebe and R. O.

Hansson (eds.), *Handbook of Bereavement: Theory, Research and Intervention*, 301–27 (New York: Cambridge University Press)

Smith, M. E., Nunley, B. L., Kerr, P. L., and Galligan, H. (2011) 'Elders' Experiences of the Death of an Adult Child', *Issues in Mental Health Nursing*, 32, 568–74

Stroebe, M. S., Finkenauer, C., Wijngaards-de Meij, L., Schut, H. A. W., van den Bout, J., and Stroebe, W. (2013) 'Partner-Oriented Self-Regulation Among Bereaved Parents: The Costs of Holding in Grief for the Partner's Sake', *Psychological Science*, 24, 395–402

Sweeting, H. N., and Gilhooly, M. L. M. (1990) 'Anticipatory Grief: A Review', *Social Science and Medicine*, 30, 1,073–80

Wijngaards-de Meij, L., Stroebe, M. S., Schut, H. A. W., Stroebe, W., van den Bout, J., van der Heijden, P., and Dijkstra, I. (2005) 'Couples at Risk Following the Death of Their Child: Predictors of Grief Versus Depression', *Journal of Consulting and Clinical Psychology*, 73 (4), 617–23

—, Stroebe, M. S., Stroebe, W., Schut, H. A. W., van den Bout, J., van der Heijden, P., and Dijkstra, I. (2008) 'The Impact of Circumstances Surrounding the Death of a Child on Parents' Grief', *Death Studies*, 32 (7), 237–52

Wilson, A. L., Fenton, L. J., Stevens, D. C., and Soule, D. J. (1982) 'The Death of a Newborn Twin: An Analysis of Parental Bereavement', *Pediatrics*, 70, 587–91

Facing your own death

Abdel-Khalek, A. M. (1998) 'The Structure and Measurement of Death Obsession', *Personality and Individual Differences*, 24, 159–65

— (2011–12) 'The Death Distress Construct and Scale', *OMEGA: The Journal of Death and Dying*, 64, 171–84

Aday, R. H. (2006) 'Aging Prisoners' Concerns Toward Dying in Prison', *OMEGA: The Journal of Death and Dying*, 52, 199–216

Azaiza, F., Ron, P., Shoman, M., and Gigini, I. (2010) 'Death and Dying Anxiety Among Elderly Arab Muslims in Israel', *Death Studies*, 34 (3), 351–64

Berkman, L. F., Leo-Summers, L., and Horwitz, R. I. (1992) 'Emotional Support and Survival After Myocardial Infarction', *Annals of Internal Medicine*, 117 (12), 1,003–9

Cole, M. A. (1978) 'Sex and Marital Status Differences in Death Anxiety', *OMEGA: The Journal of Death and Dying*, 9, 139–47

Dixson, R., and Kinlaw, B. (1983) 'Belief in the Existence and Nature of Life After Death: A Research Note', *OMEGA: The Journal of Death and Dying*, 13, 287–92

Erickson, E. H. (1959) 'The Identity and the Life-Cycle', *Psychological Issues Monograph*, 1 (1), 50–100

Esnaashari, F., and Kargar, F. R. (2015) 'The Relation Between Death Attitude and Distress: Tolerance, Aggression, and Anger', *OMEGA: The Journal of Death and Dying*, online, 1–19

Evans, J. W., Walters, A. S., and Hatch-Woodruff, M. L. (1999) 'Deathbed Scene Narratives: A Construct and Linguistic Analysis', *Death Studies*, 23 (8), 715–33

Florian, V., and Kravetz, S. (1983) 'Fear of Personal Death: Attribution, Structure, and Relation to Religious Belief', *Journal of Personality and Social Psychology*, 44 (3), 600–607

—, and Mikulincer, M. (1997) 'Fear of Personal Death in Adulthood: The Impact of Early and Recent Losses', *Death Studies*, 21 (1), 1–24

Gesser, G., Wong, P. T. P., and Reker, G. T. (1987–8) 'Death Attitudes Across the Life-Span: The Development and Validation of the Death Attitude Profile (DAP)', *OMEGA: The Journal of Death and Dying*, 18, 113–25

Haisfield-Wolfe, M. E. (1996) 'End-of-Life Care: Evolution of the Nurse's Role', *Oncology Nursing Forum*, 23, 931–5

Hoelter, J. W., and Hoelter, J. A. (1978) 'The Relationship Between Fear of Death and Anxiety', *Journal of Psychology*, 99, 225–6

Kalish, R. A., and Reynolds, D. K. (1981) *Death and Ethnicity: A Psychocultural Study* (Amityville, N Y: Baywood)

Kastenbaum, R. (2000; third edition) *The Psychology of Death* (New York: Springer Publishing Company)

Klenow, D. J., and Bolin, R. C. (1989) 'Belief in Afterlife: A National Survey', *OMEGA: The Journal of Death and Dying*, 21, 63–74

Krause, N. (1987) 'Life Stress, Social Support, and Self-Esteem in an Elderly Population', *Psychology and Aging*, 2 (4), 349–56

Lonetto, R., and Templer, D. I. (1986) *Death Anxiety* (Washington, DC: Hemisphere)

Missler, M., Stroebe, M. S., Guertsen, L., MastenBroek, M., Chmoun, S., and van der Houwen, K. (2011–12) 'Exploring Death Anxiety Among Elderly People: A Literature Review and Empirical Investigation', *OMEGA: The Journal of Death and Dying*, 64, 357–79

Mullins, L. C., and Lopez, M. A. (1982) 'Death Anxiety Among Nursing Home Residents: A Comparison of the Young-Old and Old-Old', *Death Education*, 6, 75–86

Munnichs, J. M. A. (1966) *Old Age and Finitude: A Contribution to Psychogerontology* (Basle, Switzerland: S. Karger)

Neimeyer, R. A. (1998) 'Death Anxiety Research: The State of the Art', *OMEGA: The Journal of Death and Dying*, 36, 97–120

—, and Dingemans, P. (1980) 'Death Orientation in the Suicide Intervention Worker', *OMEGA: The Journal of Death and Dying*, 11, 15–23

—, Dingemans, P., and Epting, F. R. (1977) 'Convergent Validity, Situational Stability, and Meaningfulness of the Threat Index', *OMEGA: The Journal of Death and Dying*, 8, 251–65

—, Wittkowski, J., and Moser, R. P. (2004) 'Psychological Research on Death Attitudes: An Overview and Evaluation', *Death Studies*, 28 (4), 309–40

Nelson, L. D. (1979) 'Structural Conduciveness, Personality Characteristics and Death Anxiety', *OMEGA: The Journal of Death and Dying*, 10, 123–33

NEoLCIN (National End of Life Care Intelligence Network) (2013) National Survey of Bereaved People (VOICES) (Public Health England)

Niemiec, R. M., and Schulenberg, S. E. (2011) 'Understanding Death Attitudes: The Positive Integration of Movies, Positive Psychology, and Meaning Management', *Death Studies*, 35 (5), 387–407

Noyes, R. (1980) 'Attitude Change Following Near-Death Experiences', *Psychiatry*, 43, 234–42

—, Fenwick, P., Holden, J. M., and Christian, S. R. (2009) 'After-Effects of Pleasurable Western Adult Near-Death Experiences', in J. M. Holden, B. Greyson, and D. James (eds.), *The Handbook of Near-Death Experiences: Thirty Years of Investigation*, 41–62 (Santa Barbara, CA: Praeger Publishers)

Pollak, J. M. (1979) 'Correlates of Death Anxiety: A Review of Empirical Studies', *OMEGA: The Journal of Death and Dying*, 10, 97–121

Russac, R. J, Gatliff, C., Reece, M., and Spottswood, D. (2007) 'Death Anxiety Across the Adult Years: An Examination of Age and Gender Effects', *Death Studies*, 31 (6), 549–61

Stillion, J. M. (1985) *Death and the Sexes* (Washington, DC: Hemisphere/McGraw-Hill)

Taylor, L. D. (2012) 'Death and Television: Terror Management Theory and Themes of Law and Justice on Television', *Death Studies*, 36 (4), 340–59

Templer, D. I., Harville, M., Hutton, S., Underwood, R., Tomeo, M., Russell, M., Mitroff, D., and Arikawa, H. (2001–2) 'Death Depression Scale-Revised', *OMEGA: The Journal of Death and Dying*, 44, 105–12

Thorson, J. A. (1991) 'Afterlife Constructs, Death Anxiety, and Life Reviewing: Importance of Religion as a Moderating Variable', *Journal of Psychology and Theology*, 19 (3), 278–84

Tomer, A. (2000) 'Death-Related Attitudes: Conceptual Distinctions', in A. Tomer (ed.), *Death Attitudes and the Older Adult: Theories, Concepts, and Applications*, 87–94 (New York: Brunner-Routledge)

Wong, P. T. P. (1989) 'Successful Aging and Personal Meaning', *Canadian Psychology*, 30, 516–25

—, Reker, G. T., and Gesser, G. (1994) 'Death Attitude Profile-Revised: A Multidimensional Measure of Attitude Toward Death', in R. A. Neimeyer (ed.), *Death Anxiety Handbook: Research, Instrumentation, and Application*, 121–48 (Washington, DC: Taylor & Francis)

—, and Tomer, A. (2011) 'Beyond Terror and Denial: The Positive Psychology of Death Acceptance', *Death Studies*, 35 (2), 99–106

What helps: the work we need to do to help us grieve and survive successfully

actionforhappiness.org

Ben-Shahar, Tal (2011) *Happier: Learn the Secrets to Daily Joy and Lasting Fulfillment* (New York: McGraw-Hill)

Damasio, A. (1999) *The Feeling of What Happens: Body, Emotion and the Making of Consciousness* (Heinemann)

Duhigg, C. (2012) *The Power of Habit* (Random House)

focusing.org The International Focusing Institute

Gendlin, E. T. (1981) *Focusing* (second edition, New Revised instructions) (New York: Bantam Books)

Hone, L. (2016) *Remembering Abi* (blog:i.stuff.co.nz)

Kabat-Zinn, Jon (2012) *Mindfulness for Beginners: Reclaiming the Present Moment – and Your Life* (Louisville, CO: Sounds True)

— (2001) *Full Catastrophe Living: How to Cope with Stress, Pain and Illness Using Mindfulness Meditation* (New York: Doubleday)

Klass, D., Silverman, P. R., and Nickman, S. L. (eds.) (1996) *Continuing Bonds: New Understandings of Grief* (Philadelphia, PA: Taylor & Francis)

Mind.org.uk (2015) *The Mind Guide: Food and Mood*

NICE Guidelines (2009, updated 2016) *Treatment for Mild to Moderate Depression*

Pennebaker, James W. (2004) *Writing to Heal: A Guided Journal for Recovering from Trauma and Emotional Upheaval* (Oakland, CA: New Harbinger Press)

— (1997) *Opening Up: The Healing Power of Expressing Emotion* (NY: Guilford Press)

Schore, A. (2003) *Affect Regulation and the Repair of the Self* (New York: Norton Books)

Tedeschi, R. G., and Calhoun L. G. (2012) *Resilience: The Science of Mastering Life's Greatest Challenges* (Cambridge: Cambridge University Press)

Acknowledgements

All the stories in this book are based on my reflections and what I've learned from clients I have worked with. My understanding of grief has been taught to me through them, and I feel honoured to have known, learned from and been inspired by them. Whenever possible I have consulted past and present clients to ensure they are in agreement with what is being published in order to avoid any distress. An overriding preoccupation while writing has been maintaining the confidentiality and anonymity of my clients – to which end every effort has been made to anonymize people and actual events, while remaining true to the spirit of the work.

This book couldn't exist without those clients who allowed me to chart their grief work. Some let me record and transcribe sessions, others read and commented on my text of our work, and yet others used the case study in our therapy. To every single one of them I am profoundly grateful for their generosity and trust in letting me tell their story of grief.

It is important for me to credit in particular those who are, in my view, the top pioneering grief psychiatrists and psychologists of the last fifty years. They have been the greatest influence on my practice. Their theories of grief, even some of their expressions, have become a part of me and are integrated in different ways throughout the text. These are: Dr Margaret Stroebe and Dr Henk Schut, Dr Colin

Murray Parkes, John Bowlby, Dennis Klass, Phyllis Silverman and Steven Nickman, and Professor William Worden. I believe they have been part of a quiet revolution that has transformed our understanding of grief.

My literary agent, Felicity Rubinstein, first encouraged me to think about writing a book, which I hadn't seriously considered up to that point. Gillian Stern, through her experience, gave me the confidence to find my voice. Venetia Butterfield has been both an intelligent and sensitive editor in drawing the best out of me, and helped to shape the book in its present form. It has been an exceptional gift for me to have this triumvirate of brilliant women to guide me in this new endeavour.

Dr Adrian Tookman, Consultant Physician of Palliative Care, and Lynda Nayler, Clinical Nurse Specialist with Marie Curie Hospice, Hampstead, kindly let me spend time with them at Marie Curie Hampstead. I met and spoke with many of their patients and learned more about palliative care for the older population. Professor Julia Riley, Palliative Care Consultant at the Royal Marsden, also gave me the benefit of her enormous experience in exploring the needs of patients who are dying, as well as giving me helpful comments on the studies.

Professor Tim Bond gave me a great deal of his precious time to guide me through the best ethical practice when publishing case studies. I am indebted to him for the depth of his knowledge and generosity in sharing it with me.

Ann Chalmers and Ann Rowland, from Child Bereavement UK, gave me invaluable constructive feedback. Andrew Reeves, from the British Association of Counselling, gave me excellent counsel that was much appreciated.

I am grateful to Stephanie Wilkinson, who worked hard finding hundreds of excellent research articles on each topic.

I want to thank my extremely talented brother, Hugo Guinness, for giving me his drawing of a dandelion for the book's cover; it is the perfect image, and even more so having been drawn by him.

I am immensely fortunate to have been able to call on this broad list of fantastic people who have told me about their experience of grief, contributed to how friends and family can help, or commented on the book. Geraldine Thomson in particular, Natasha Morgan, Steve Burchell and Kathy Murphy, all psychotherapists and wise colleagues, were extremely supportive and helpful. Friends, both close and more distant, were wonderfully generous with their time, experience and thinking: Rachel Wyndham, Catherine Soames, Juliet Nicolson, Susanna Gross, Clare Asquith, Joanna Weinberg, Tory Gray, DiDi Donovan, Christabel McEwan, David Macmillan, Bettina von Hase, Rosie Boycott, Alexander Dickinson, Linda and David Heathcoat-Amory, Jack Heathcoat-Amory, Patricia Mountbatten, Cathy Drysdale, Catherine O'Brien, Amrita Das, Christine D'Ornano, Dana Hoegh, Fiona Golfar, Hafizah Ismail, Flappy Lane Fox, Tal Fane, Clare Milford Haven, Harry Cotterell, Millie Baring, Dafna Bonas, Peter Laird and Debora Harding. To all of them I am extremely grateful for such a generous act of friendship.

In order to keep the writing flowing, I haven't inserted note references throughout the text, but all the references relating to the case studies, as well as the guidance and research sections, can be found in the 'Sources' section under their part-title or chapter headings. Please accept my apologies if there are any errors or missing references.

The team at Viking Penguin have been terrific: I'd like to thank Isabel Wall, Donna Poppy, Julia Murday and Emma Brown for their help.

I take full responsibility for any errors or omissions.

My beloved husband, Michael, who is part of all I do, has been endlessly patient and encouraging, as well as laughing at me and with me when necessary. Our children, Natasha, Emily, Sophie and Benjamin, have all made insightful suggestions and lovingly supported me while I've been immersed in this project. I am forever thankful to them all.

The website that accompanies this book is: www.griefworks. co.uk. Go there for links to support, information and the forums.

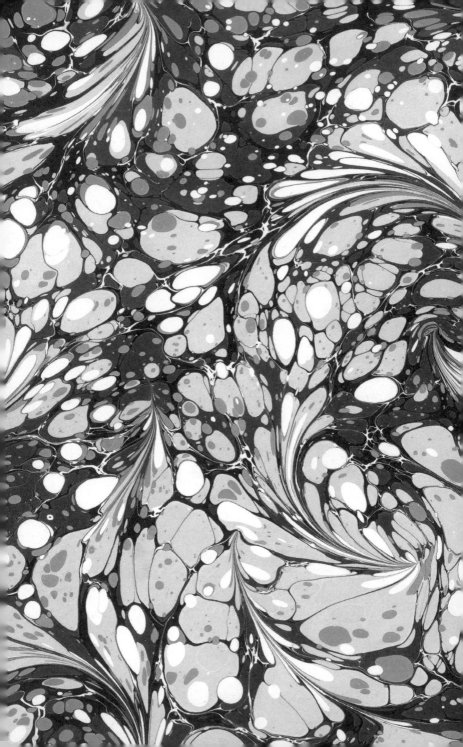